SIBYLS AND SIBYLLINE PROPHECY
IN CLASSICAL ANTIQUITY

CROOM HELM
CLASSICAL STUDIES

SIBYLS AND SIBYLLINE PROPHECY IN CLASSICAL ANTIQUITY

H.W. Parke

Edited by B.C. McGing

ROUTLEDGE
London and New York

First published in 1988 by
Routledge
a division of Routledge, Chapman and Hall
11 New Fetter Lane, London EC4P 4EE

Published in the USA by
Routledge
a division of Routledge, Chapman and Hall, Inc.
29 West 35th Street, New York NY 10001

Printed and bound in Great Britain by
Biddles Ltd, Guildford and King's Lynn

British Library Cataloguing-in-Publication Data

Parke, H.W.
   Sibyls and sibylline prophecy in classical
   antiquity.
   1. Oracles, Greek   2. Oracula sibyllina
   I. Title   II. McGing, Brian C.
   292'.32   BL795.06
   ISBN 0–415–00343–1

Library of Congress Cataloging-in-Publication Data

ISBN 0–415–00343–1

H.W. Parke
1903–1986

Lector, si monumentum requiris,
circumspice.

Contents

Preface   vii

List of Abbreviations   ix

1. The Characteristics of Sibylline Oracles   1
2. The Ancient Scholarly Sources for the Identity of Sibyls   23
3. Archaic Sibyls of Eastern Greece   51
4. Cumae   71
5. The Sibyl in the Classical Period   100
6. The Sibyl in the Hellenistic Period   125
7. The Sibyl in Pagan Rome   136
8. The Sibyl in Christian Literature   152

Appendices:

   I. The *Theologoi*   174
  II. The *Libri Sibyllini*   190
 III. Ecstatic Prophecy in the Near East   216

Bibliography   221

Index   225

Preface

There were in the ancient world at least two major types of oracle: those that provided answers to specific questions put by individual enquirers, as, most famously, at Delphi; and those that offered discursive forecasts, in response to no particular question, for the enlightenment of the world at large. Into this latter category fall such works as the *Oracle of Hystaspes*, the *Bahman Yasht*, the *Oracle of the Potter* and, perhaps best-known representative of the type, the *Sibylline Oracles*. While vagueness and ambiguity were a feature of Delphic and similar oracular responses, a certain degree of precision was necessary, if the answers were to be of any applicable use. The Sibyls, on the other hand, did not labour under the disadvantage of a direct question, and indeed the great strength of Sibylline oracles lay not in their accuracy — even though some of them probably started out life as those most accurate of all prophecies, the ones made after the events they purport to foretell — but in their very vagueness. For in a world without printing and telecommunications, an imprecise original, even if composed for a particular event, could be changed easily enough and reapplied repeatedly down the centuries to subsequent events. The *Bahman Yasht* led a dynamic life in this way right up until the 13th century AD, and the Sibylline oracles too enjoyed a long and fascinating history. The Sibyls themselves, inspired prophetesses of a type well known in antiquity — Cassandra, although not actually described as a Sibyl, was certainly very similar — first appear in Archaic Asia Minor and thereafter take on many guises with great flexibility. Perhaps their greatest success was the de-paganising process they underwent in the Christian era, that eventually saw them triumph in Renaissance Italy, on the ceiling of the Sistine Chapel or the floor of Sienna Cathedral.

It was Herbert Parke's aim in this his last book to trace the origins and development of Sibyls and their prophetic utterances, up to the point when a Byzantine scholar formed the collection we now know as the *Oracula Sibyllina*, probably in the 6th century AD. Since much of the relatively meagre scholarly work devoted to the subject is old or difficult of access, the project was a very attractive one. Before he could carry it through, however, Herbert died early in 1986, and I was asked to prepare the manuscript for publication. Over half of it was already typed when I received it, and I have kept my editorial role to a minimum, apart perhaps from the notes which required more adjustment than the body of the text. I have added the select bibliography and index. Having been a student of Herbert when he was still Professor of Ancient History at Trinity College, Dublin, a sense of *pietas* for a former teacher influenced my decision to take on the task, but more important was the inherent interest of the subject, and the value of ensuring publication of a book written by an acknowledged expert in the field of oracular study. I hope these latter two factors will compensate for whatever faults and shortcomings remain.

Trinity College Dublin   B. McG.

Abbreviations

In the notes, the titles of modern journals have been abbreviated, more or less, as in *l'Année Philologique*; and ancient authors and their works, as in the *Oxford Classical Dictionary*. The following abbreviations are also used:

Diels-Kranz	H. Diels and W. Kranz, *Die Fragmente der Vorsokratiker* (ed. 6 Berlin 1952).
IG	*Inscriptiones Graecae*.
IGR	*Inscriptiones Graecae ad res Romanas pertinentes*, ed. R. Cagnat, J. Toutain, G. Lafaye (Paris 1911–27).
F. Gr. Hist.	F. Jacoby, *Die Fragmente der griechischen Historiker* (Leiden 1926–58).
Parke and Wormell, *DO*	H.W. Parke and D.E.W. Wormell, *The Delphic Oracle* (Oxford 1956).

1

The Characteristics of Sibylline Oracles

It next will be right
To describe each particular batch,
Distinguishing those that have feathers, and bite,
From those that have whiskers, and scratch.

To attempt to describe the content and context of the earliest Greek Sibylline prophecies, and to trace their development down to the point at which the extant Sibylline oracles were produced, presents a peculiarly difficult problem: the actual text of the earliest prophecies is almost entirely lost, and the circumstances of their origin have to be guessed at on the basis of very limited evidence, most of it of much later date. But a hypothesis can be constructed, and the attempt therefore seems worthwhile, even if the results remain largely conjectural. For this purpose, instead of starting with the earliest evidence for the Sibyl, it is better to begin by analysing the developed form of Sibylline prophecy, so as to establish first its underlying characteristics and deduce from them its probable antecedents.

The *Oracula Sibyllina* were assembled in their present form by some Byzantine scholar about the sixth century AD.[1] As extant they consist of twelve books, numbered 1 to 8 and 11 to 14. Books 9 and 10 are lost and Book 7 is very defective. Books 1 and 2 belong together, and Books 11 to 14 appear to have been written at various times to form a sequence. The other books may all have been produced separately. But Book 3 may be only the latter half of a much longer compilation. Also they were composed at widely different dates. For instance the first half of Book 8 refers to the impending fall of Rome which it dates to AD 195, and it must therefore have been circulated towards the end of the second century AD. Book 13 by its references to Roman emperors was written in the late third century AD. At the other extreme, the third book, with allusions to the Ptolemies, contains matter from the period 170–140 BC, although in its present form it may have been put together considerably later, probably during the early Principate. But irrespective of the chief datable references in any book, it may have also embedded in it short passages which look by their form and content as if they might have been written in the classical period or even earlier.

The result is an extraordinary medley, where it is tempting to assign various sections to different periods and contexts on internal evidence, but the judgement involved is often subjective, and the results of dubious validity.

The anonymous editor who assembled the Byzantine corpus makes clear in his preface that he has collected his materials from different sources. Also he stresses the spiritual advantage of studying these Greek writings, which dealt with God and religiously edifying subjects, in complete contrast to pagan literature. So it is to be expected that he did not deliberately include non-Christian matter in his collection. Yet actually it would appear to modern scholars that the original authors of many of the prophecies were not Christians. The bulk of the oracles look as if they took their present form in Egypt or Alexandria in communities of Hellenised Jews; some may derive later from similar circles in Asia Minor. Their frequent emphasis on monotheism and moral purity would satisfy a Christian reader of their proper attitude to the pagan world. Also the occasional interpolation of references to the Incarnation and the Crucifixion served to disguise the non-Christian origin of the bulk of these writings.

Some picture of the mass of material from which the editor of the *Oracula Sibyllina* assembled his corpus is given to us by Lactantius, writing about two hundred years earlier at the beginning of the fourth century. After he has reproduced Varro's list of the ten Sibyls, he continues:

> To all these Sibyls are attributed verses which are extant, except for the Cumaean Sibyl. Her books are kept concealed by the Romans and are not allowed by religious law to be examined by anyone, except the *quindecimviri*. There are indeed single books belonging to single Sibyls. But, because they are entitled with the name Sibyl, people believe they belong to one person, and they are mixed up,

2

and it is impossible to distinguish and assign to each her own work, except for the Erythraean Sibyl who has introduced her own true name into verses and prefaced them by saying she was called Erythraean, though she was born in Babylon. But we shall call them Sibyl without distinction wherever we need to use their evidence.[2]

If, as seems likely, we can take this careful statement of Lactantius literally, he knew nine separate volumes of Sibylline prophecies, which he therefore believed corresponded to the ten Varronian Sibyls excluding the Cumaean. Of these he was sure of the authorship of only one — the Erythraean — because she identified herself in some prefatory verses. But although Lactantius believed the other books each belonged to a different Sibyl, he had decided not to trouble his readers by citing them under conjectural attributions. His practice appears to correspond exactly with this statement. He frequently cites the Erythraean Sibyl, and these quotations correspond to passages in Book 3 of the *Oracula Sibyllina*. Also this is the book which ends by the prophetess describing herself as coming from Babylon and being Erythraean. Her 'true name' probably occurred in what is now a lacuna at this place in our manuscripts. Elsewhere Lactantius cites various prophecies as Sibylline without further designation. The quotations seem to show that, besides Book 3, he also knew, directly or indirectly, Books 4 to 8 inclusive.[3] This suggests that he used six of the nine books which he believed were extant.

Of the surviving *Oracula Sibyllina*, Books 1 and 2 belong together and are not cited by Lactantius, Books 9 and 10 are missing, and Books 11 to 14 again belong together, and are also not represented in his quotations. They had evidently been produced late in the third century and, though possibly in circulation when Lactantius wrote, may not have acquired much authority. Modern scholarship would be in no better position than he in attributing the extant books to the Varronian Sibyls, with one exception: the so-called oracle of the Tiburtine Sibyl, tenth in Varro's list, is represented by a separate manuscript tradition outside the Sibylline corpus. But it appears to have been first concocted after the foundation of Constantinople, and so could not be known to Lactantius.[4]

The evidence of Lactantius, then, illustrates the confused mass of Sibylline prophecy which may still have been in circulation when the editor of the *Oracula Sibyllina* undertook his task.

3

That he had done his work well is proved by the fact that the many passages from the Sibyl earlier quoted or paraphrased by the Christian Fathers can in most instances be referred to places in the extant corpus. In fact only about half a dozen such citations show matter not found in the extant manuscripts.[5] So it could be argued that the *Oracula Sibyllina*, though assembled in the sixth century, give a very fair picture of Sibylline prophecy as accepted into the Christian tradition in the third and fourth centuries. But on that very account they are a distorting mirror for viewing the original pagan material. While the quotations by the Christian Fathers confirm the evidence of the extant manuscripts of the *Oracula Sibyllina*, the quotations in Greek and Roman authors come from a quite different series of earlier Sibylline prophecies. A few of these claim to reproduce the words of the Sibylline books as preserved by the Roman state, and accordingly it is not surprising that they do not appear in our manuscript versions, which are evidently of eastern origin, and do not imply that they have been extracted from the carefully guarded repository on the Capitol and later on the Palatine. But the other quotations in authors such as Dio Chrysostom, Plutarch and Pausanias, who imply that they are citing from current literature, do not occur in the *Oracula Sibyllina*. The only exception is provided by two lines concerning the river Pyramus in Asia Minor, vaguely cited by Strabo as an oracle (*logion*), which do occur in *Oracula Sibyllina*, Book 4, but since Strabo does not even attribute them to the Sibyl, it could be argued that they were simply lines of oracular verse of unknown origin, which were floating in popular tradition until they were picked up and worked into his text by the author of the fourth book. That this could have happened is illustrated by the occurrence also in the *Oracula Sibyllina* of the phrase 'Do not disturb Camarina; for it is better undisturbed.' This hexameter line, often abbreviated to the first clause, was a favourite proverb as a warning against ill-advised interference. But its probable origin was in the first line of a Delphic response given to the people of Camarina in the fifth century BC. From the original Pythian context, it found its way ultimately into Book 3 of the *Oracula Sibyllina*.[6]

So it is impossible to prove any appreciable amount of direct derivation of the *Oracula Sibyllina* from pagan prototypes. But there are a few instances of very plausible parallels in the subjects treated. For instance in several ancient authorities it is stated that the Sibyl in foretelling the Trojan War also foretold that Homer would write about it. In two books of the *Oracula Sibyllina* (3.414ff; 11.163ff) this exact conjunction of subjects occurs. In both instances much of the style and diction used does not look plausibly as if it was composed before the Hellenistic period at the earliest. But this may only indicate that the Jewish and Christian writers of the extant Sibylline oracles chose to borrow the motif from their classical predecessors, while preferring to reproduce it, not in the original words, but in paraphrase. Perhaps the original version was too obviously pagan in sentiment.[7]

Also there are a number of passages in the *Oracula Sibyllina* where the style and subject matter strongly suggest verbal borrowing from a classical original.[8] Lines written in a plausibly epic manner and diction prophesy disasters to cities of Greece and Asia Minor, where it is unlikely that a Jewish writer of late Hellenistic times would be able to maintain the literary illusion, or even have any motive for mentioning these particular cities. Modern scholars have called attention to such apparent examples of borrowing from earlier sources, but the problem is like that of detecting earlier and later strata in the Homeric epics. It would be difficult to arrive at an agreed opinion, and even if the passages were accepted as pre-Hellenistic in origin, this would usually not lead to any sound conclusions about their precise original context and date. At most they provide apparent illustrations of the literary dependence of the authors of the *Oracula Sibyllina* on previous classical tradition.

Therefore the general impression conveyed by the ancient allusions is that pagan authors were not acquainted with Sibylline prophecies in the form in which they have survived; yet they probably had as much other matter available to them, of which their quotations only reproduce a tiny fraction. A certain amount more is probably buried in the text of the *Oracula Sibyllina* themselves, although to sift it out could only be done conjecturally, and much must be completely lost to us — neither quoted by classical authors nor embedded in late Judaeo-Christian pastiche.

However, in spite of the great extent of the loss of early Sibylline material, it is noteworthy that it all, whether early or late, exhibits certain general features which tend to differentiate it from the remainder of Greek oracular texts. This is not surprising if it is recognised that the first authors of the present *Oracula Sibyllina* were Hellenised Jews, who were using their prophetic medium to expound their faith and express their attitude to their pagan neighbours in a literary form which would be familiar and

5

even convincing to Hellenistic readers. To achieve this purpose they had to assume the literary conventions expected of a Sibyl. The matter to be conveyed was sometimes more appropriate to a Hebrew prophet, but the manner had to approximate generally to the style of a pagan prophetess.

The internal references in the third book of the *Oracula Sibyllina* point to the reign of Ptolemy Philometor ('the seventh king') as the time when the Jewish version of Sibylline prophecy was first produced. This period was especially appropriate because of the contemporary growth of Jewish influence both in politics and in literature. Ptolemy Philometor (180–145 BC) introduced large numbers of Jews into Alexandria and allowed them to occupy some of the highest offices in the state. In literature the first steps had already been taken to translate the Hebrew scriptures into Greek, and the work was completed by the mid-second century. Also already before Philometor's reign, Demetrius the Chronographer, a Jew, had attempted to recast the biblical narratives in terms of Greek history, and Ezekiel had written a Greek tragedy on the subject of the Exodus. The Jew, Aristobulus, whom the Christian Fathers classed as a Peripatetic philosopher, dedicated a book to Philometor himself in which he applied to the writings of Moses the method of allegorical interpretation. So it is clear that at this period Jews in Egypt were perfectly capable and willing to make use of the language and literature of their pagan neighbours for the purpose of expressing their own culture. It is appropriate, therefore, that while the *Oracula Sibyllina* are bitterly hostile to idolatry and animal worship, they show no ill-will to the Ptolemies as rulers or to Alexandria as a city; very different from the attitude which they were to assume later towards Rome and its emperors.[9]

What were the stylistic features of pagan Sibylline prophecy, which the Jewish authors had to reproduce? Greek oracles, whether responses delivered at oracle-centres or prophecies circulated in written form, were usually composed in hexameter verse. This convention may have originated at Delphi by the eighth century BC at the latest. In any event, if, as we shall suggest, the Sibylline oracles were first produced in the late seventh century, the hexameter would by then be recognised as the appropriate form for serious and religious utterance. This remained thereafter traditional throughout antiquity. Sibyls never speak in other metres or in prose.[10]

But if the Sibyl's form resembled the Pythia's, her matter was essentially different. While the *prophētai* and *promantides* of the various Greek oracle-centres spoke in response to consultations, the pagan Sibyl's prophecies were discursive pieces of verse addressed to the world in general rather than to any particular enquirer. This statement is in notable contradiction to the account of the most famous of all Sibyls — the Cumaean in Vergil's *Aeneid*. But she stands unique in literature and deserves a separate discussion to investigate her peculiarity.[11] Otherwise the verses attributed to Sibyls and the rare descriptions of them in action all observe the distinction which we have mentioned from all other types of Greek ecstatic divination.

In this respect the Sibylline oracles are in form and content actual prophecies. It has often been pointed out that the *prophētēs* or *promantis* of an Apolline shrine did not set out essentially to foretell the future. In many instances the question put to them was in the form of an alternative, particularly in the traditional formula, 'is it better and more good' that such and such a course of action be followed. The reply was meant to convey divine approval or disapproval, and might be a simple affirmative or negative, but if it was expressed discursively, in prose or in verse, it might picture the consequences of the proposed action, often in ambiguous or obscurely metaphorical phrases. This was in effect a prophecy of contingent happenings in the future, but it was meant primarily to be advice about immediate action. The pagan Sibyl's words on the contrary did not usually offer guidance on controlling the future. They, too, often describe it in superficially obscure and baffling phrases, but treated it as an inevitable fate. In this respect the Sibyls are more like the writers of apocalyptic visions than the Pythia or the Dove Priestesses of Dodona. This was the reason why the Sibyl would commend herself originally to the Jewish imitator as an appropriate model.

Also the Sibyl does not usually start her prophecy from some point in contemporary historic time and continue straight into the future. She begins with some primevally early epoch and leads on in chronological sequence through succeeding ages. For this purpose it had to be assumed by the reader that the Sibyl herself was born in this distant past. The pagan Sibyl foretold the Trojan War and was therefore accepted as preceding it in time. Similarly, in Book 3 of the *Oracula Sibyllina* the Jewish prophetess describes herself as the daughter-in-law of Noah and so can narrate the history of the Tower of Babel and foretell the Exodus.[12]

This placing of the imagined prophetess in the far past had two advantages. First of all, both Greeks and Jews had a conventional respect for the antiquity of tradition. The further back a custom or a principle could be traced, the greater reverence it deserved. So the Sibyl only became more venerable by speaking from the dawn of human history, and since Jewish traditions dated further back than Hellenic, the authors of the *Oracula Sibyllina* exploit this higher antiquity. The second great advantage was that the prophetess who claimed an early origin for herself could also demonstrate her infallibility by foretelling events which the reader could recognise behind a thin cloak of obscurity as part of the known traditions of his nation's past. When Marpessian Sibyl prophesied the disastrous consequences of the birth of Helen, or the Sibyl of Book 3 described in advance the Babylonian captivity, their Greek or Jewish public accepted that these vaticinations both proved the primeval origin of the authoress and at the same time confirmed her foresight.[13]

This literary device of converting comment on the past and present into the form of prophecy spread over a vast period was an invention of the Greeks; in fact the most effective innovation of the original Sibyl. But it would not seem strange to the Jewish writer of the second century BC. Already the age of the Hebrew prophets had receded far into the past. Zephaniah, writing about 500 BC, was accepted as the last who had spoken in the name of the Lord.[14] But the distant forecasts of the prophets could still be expected to apply to the present and future of Israel. So when a writer contemporary with the author of parts of Book 3 of the *Oracula Sibyllina* wished to produce a comment on contemporary events for Semitic readers, he wrote the Book of Daniel in Hebrew, and placed his prophet within a rather shaky historical framework in the courts of the Babylonians and the Medes four centuries before his own date.

The Greeks may have found some difficulty in believing that the authoress of their oracles, current in the present, herself belonged to the primeval past, and it may have been so as to make this a little more plausible that the legend attached itself to the Sibyl that she had attained to some quite extraordinary length of life — usually a thousand years.[15] Thus, being able to prophesy far-off events and then live through the time of the fulfilment of some of them, she could transmit her original oracles to long-subsequent generations. This naïve method of trying to make convincing the fiction of primeval birth by a second fiction

8

of miraculous longevity may perhaps have been felt in a more sophisticated period to be too implausible. Hence the alternative method of achieving the same effect was to frame a story of a primitive manuscript recovered in marvellous circumstances at a later date. This device was applied in practice in the second century BC in an unsuccessful attempt to foist on the Roman people the forged 'philosophy of King Numa', and was used as the fictitious framework for the fabulous account of the Trojan War by Dictys of Crete, who posed as a member of the Greek expedition. The only Sibyl about whom this method was employed was the latest in traditional date, the Sibyl of Tibur. Her statue holding her sacred book was miraculously recovered unharmed from the waters of the Anio. But this can be taken as a Roman device to authenticate a pseudonymous work claiming high antiquity.[16]

However, the picture of the Sibyl with her book was the convention early established by the Greeks. The Pythia prophesied *ex tempore* and her verses were not written down as she uttered them in the Delphic sanctuary. But the Sibylline oracles circulated in book form as did the other prophecies of the period — those of Orpheus, Epimenides, Musaeus and Bacis. This might seem to guarantee them a certain permanence of content, but it was far from being the case. The story of Lasus of Hermione detecting Onomacritus in the act of interpolating Musaeus at the court of Hippias reminds one how early was the practice of faking oracles, and how easily these texts lent themselves to such falsification.[17]

The recognised way for the Sibyl to testify to her primeval birth was for her to assert it herself in her own oracle. This brings us to another point in which she differed from the Pythia. It was ordinarily supposed that when the Pythia prophesied, she was in an ecstasy in which her own personality was completely submerged in that of Apollo. When she spoke in the first person, it was the god himself who spoke. Not merely must references, for instance to 'our temple', be taken in that sense, but also 'mother' is Leto, 'my father' Zeus, and so forth.[18] The Sibylline oracles in this respect are quite different. Though it was usual from the Hellenistic period to suppose that the Sibyl derived her inspiration from Apollo, she does not lose her personality. If she speaks in the first person, it is as the Sibyl herself. In the *Oracula Sibyllina* she can even address God and appeal to him to release her from prophetic ecstasy. So though the inspiration comes from without her and in some sense is imposed on her, she is not submerged by it.[19] She is essentially a clairvoyante rather than a medium. Any other conditions, as we have said, would have made her personal testimony inexplicable.

As the Sibyl in her oracles could express herself in the first person, a conventional practice was developed in these prophecies which is rare in other Greek hexameter verse. The Sibyl tells her name and her paternity as a means of explaining her authority. The earliest Sibyl claimed to be half divine, the daughter of a nymph. The Delphic Sibyl identified herself with Artemis. Pausanias knew an oracle in which the speaker gave her name as Herophile. The Sibyl of Book 3 describes her Babylonian origin.[20] It is quite at variance with the conventions of archaic epic for the author to give a personal statement of this kind. Even Hesiod, when he wished to introduce the *Theogony* by an account telling how he was called to sing it by the Muses, produced a curiously cumbrous statement, partly in the third, partly in the first person. The nearest parallel to the Sibyl's personal revelation is found appropriately in Nicander's two extant hexameter poems. He was an official of Apollo at Claros, as he declares, and, living at one of the traditional sites of Sibylline prophecy, he must have been familiar with the literary technique of the oracles. Also, as Nicander shows, the obvious place to insert such a statement was either at the beginning or the end of the poem.[21] Accordingly we find that the Delphic Sibyl commenced with an explanation of her identity, but the Erythraean Sibyl put her account of herself at the end: at least the Sibyl of Book 3 places there her claim to hail from Babylon and to be erroneously described as Erythraean. The obvious conclusion is that this refutation was put at the point corresponding to the Erythraean Sibyl's original statement.

The Sibyl's oracles, as they were not in answer to particular enquiries, foretold events of general significance involving, not private individuals, but cities and kingdoms: war, famine, pestilence or natural phenomena such as earthquakes, floods, or volcanic eruptions. The limited number of quotations from the pagan Sibyls illustrates this subject matter, and the *Oracula Sibyllina* contain much more of the same kind, which often looks as though it was directly borrowed by the Jewish authors from their gentile predecessors.[22] But besides this, the *Oracula Sibyllina* included other topics which may have been either imitated or original in various degrees.

One element can be excluded from the classical versions. The Jewish Sibyl preaches theology, a panegyric in praise of monotheism with scarifying attacks on the worship of idols and the animal cults of Egypt. One cannot suppose that the pagan predecessors contained anything similar. It was not in the character of Greek polytheism to exalt one deity by decrying others. Also the Jewish Sibyl began with the Creation, paraphrasing Genesis, but could combine this with the Greek version of the *Theogony* reproduced in the terms of Euhemerism. The pagan gods were transformed into human kings, who won deification by their services to humanity. In this form the prophecy could not be earlier than Hellenistic in date.[23] But it may raise the question whether the Jewish author, in imitating his pagan model, was faced with a theogony as a part of the pattern. If the Sibyl had to begin her prophecy with primeval times the natural starting-point for the Greeks was not the creation of man, which was a curiously secondary event in Hellenic mythology, but the birth of the earliest gods. Hesiod had established what was to remain the basic picture, and in the way typical of Greek art this did not preclude imitation, but positively invited it. The composition of a theogony was attributed to all the personages of the archaic period who were regarded as specially prominent as seers and diviners. Orpheus, Musaeus and Epimenides were all credited with such works.[24] So it would be quite possible and appropriate for the Sibyl to have begun with a theogony. However, though the subject is often mentioned in later literature, no such quotations of Sibylline verse occur before the extant *Oracula*. So at most it must be left as a hypothesis based on analogy from the recurrence of the motif there.

Besides starting from the Creation the *Oracula Sibyllina* continued through world history to the Last Judgement. This was a termination not normally accepted as a concept by the classical Greeks. Some philosophers had debated the question whether the cosmos was finite in time, and by the Hellenistic period the Stoics, following on Empedocles, had been prepared to imagine an *ekpyrōsis* in which the universe was consumed in fire. But there was no element of judgement between righteous and wicked in this termination. The Jews had long conceived the picture of a Day of the Lord, when Yahweh would reveal himself in justification of Israel and confutation of the Gentiles. The concept developed from some of the pre-exilic prophets to the Book of Daniel, where, as an apocalyptic vision, it had become closely integrated with contemporary history. It was, at the earliest, in the second century BC that it included some notion of the dead

11

being raised to judgement. Then Jewish and Christian apocalyptic in the next couple of centuries built up this picture which was to become part of Christian thought. The Jewish imitator of the pagan Sibyl would not have found there any convenient model for this motif of final judgement. The nearest he could find was a general tone of scorn for mankind. This was part of that lack of charm which Heraclitus was to stress in his description of the Sibyl, and we find it imitated by Nicolaus of Damascus when he makes her address the Persians: 'Miserable ones, why are you hastening after what is unholy?' This contemptuous attitude can be traced back in Greek literature to Hesiod, where the Muses, when about to confer on him the gift of poetry, begin with the derisory words, 'Shepherds who abide in the fields, ill reproaches, nothing but bellies'. Prophets after this, when speaking a god's message even in their own persons, could treat their human audience as on a lower plane. The most notable example is the line quoted by St Paul: 'Cretans, always liars, evil beasts, workless bellies'. This came from the *Oracles* attributed to Epimenides of Cnossos, and judging by the obvious imitation of Hesiod, it was the first line of an address to his fellow-countrymen in contemptuous scorn at their folly and ignorance, whether uttered by the poet himself or put into the mouth of some divine being. For our purpose it does not matter whether these oracles were pseudonymous or were actually composed by a Cretan seer of that name in the seventh century BC. They were evidently an authentic product of the archaic period and illustrate the features of their type of contemporary literature.[25] The only original lines from the beginning of a Sibyl's prophecy which are quoted are those attributed by Clement of Alexandria to the Delphic Sibyl. In them she identifies herself with Artemis, and directs her vexation not against her audience but against her brother Apollo.[26] But one may conjecture that other oracles may have begun more in the manner of Epimenides. It is from such models that the author of what was originally the beginning of the Third Sibylline Oracle took the pattern for his first line: 'Men mortal and of flesh, who are nought, how do you speedily exalt yourselves with no eye to the end of life?'

This contemptuous attitude was very appropriate to the Jewish preacher condemning idolatry and polytheism in the name of monotheism. But in a simpler emotional way it must have suited the pagan Sibyl. Her subject matter appears to have been mainly a succession of human disasters, but there is no suggestion in our quotations or allusions to the Sibyl that she had any room for the *lacrimae rerum*. Her production was not a tragedy but a horror film. Also, at least judging by the passages in the *Oracula Sibyllina* which appear to be lifted from pagan sources, there was no interlocking pattern or logical structure. A series of forecasts of disasters to fall on different places followed each other without any real connection. The only kind of variation was in the form of expression. Sometimes it would be a plain third-person statement, but more often it was addressed to the place in question by an apostrophe in the vocative.

Some of this material must have looked familiar enough to the Jewish imitator. The Hebrew prophets, as well as addressing the people of Judah or Israel, had also delivered messages of commination against their gentile neighbours. These foretold the disaster and destruction which the wrath of Yahweh would bring upon them, and the form and matter were sometimes strikingly similar to the Sibyl's warnings. The resemblance is no doubt merely coincidental, as prophets such as Isaiah and Zephaniah can neither have known Greek oracles nor influenced them. But it will have made it all the more plausible for the Jewish Sibyllist, while modelling himself on the pagan prototype, to borrow various portions which would serve to reinforce the resemblance. This can be the only reasonable explanation for the passages in several books of the *Oracula Sibyllina* where disasters are foretold for a series of Greek cities, often those in Asia Minor. All the evidence points to the Jews who concocted these particular books being members of some Hebrew community in Alexandria or elsewhere in Egypt. It is quite improbable that they had any particular motive for selecting these Greek cities for specific denunciation. So just as they chose to include a pagan theogony of Euhemeristic form and a forecast of the Trojan War and a mocking reference to Homer, they also borrowed plausible disasters of a particular kind to pad out their religious message.[27]

But the Jewish Sibyllist did not solely deal in doom. It was part of his apocalyptic tradition to believe that after horror and destruction should come a Golden Age for the people of God. Isaiah, centuries previously, had given expression to this glorious hope in words which could never be bettered. The Sibyllist paraphrases him in Greek hexameters.[28] He probably could not have found a corresponding model in the pagan Sibyls. As is well known, the Greeks, while fond of picturing a Golden Age, placed it in the primeval past or in some distant land. Possibly Vergil, when writing the *Fourth Eclogue*, had been influenced indirectly by the Messianic joys foretold by the Hebrew prophets. Some Sibylline version of the Jewish prophecies had guided him to produce his allegorical poem with its strange fusion of eastern and western elements.[29]

The Roman poet was writing at a time when the succession of devastating wars had exhausted much of the Mediterranean region, and war appears to have been the environment in which Sibylline oracles particularly emerged. The Jewish Sibyllist had first produced his oracle under Ptolemy Philometor (180–145 BC), when Egypt was threatened by invasion and Jerusalem had been the object of pagan attack. Our quotations from the earlier Sibyls also are significantly linked with some of the great military turning-points of Greek history — the Peloponnesian War, the battle of Chaeronea, the defeat of the Macedonian monarchy by the Romans.[30] This shows that at the time of major crises such as these there was a revival of Sibylline prophecy; which also suggests that the original creation of the oracles may have been in some such critical period. But this hypothesis can be followed up later. It is sufficient here to note that once the pattern of the Sibylline oracles had been established — a sequence of past and current events described as forecasts — it was easy to adapt the scheme to each successive crisis as it arose. An account of such an event in the form of a forecast could be attached to the end of an existing Sibylline oracle with any convenient adjustments to improve the run of the prophecy. Earlier forecasts could be retained or altered or omitted as convenient.

This kind of process can only be conjectured as at work in the extant *Oracula Sibyllina*, but in case it were regarded as a figment of the imagination, it can be actually demonstrated as happening in other Sibylline prophecies. An oracle of the Tiburtine Sibyl was written in Greek by a Christian in the late fourth century AD, in which he concluded by foretelling the end of the world sixty years after the foundation of Constantinople. This text is only known to us from late Latin translations, but evidently this out-of-date forecast was revived by another Christian living at or near Heliopolis (Baalbek), in the first years of the sixth century. He emended the sixty years to thrice that number, and extended the prophecy in considerable detail over the intervening years, and also inserted specific references to the building and destruction of the great temples at Heliopolis. This version has been lately recovered from a twelfth-century manuscript on Mount Athos.[31]

It illustrates how a Sibylline text could be adapted from one period to another. But also the use of ambiguous and metaphorical language, which was traditional in oracles, had the effect that Sibylline forecasts were sufficiently lacking in specific detail to appear to apply equally well to different periods. For instance a prophecy of an earthquake in Laodicea might naturally suggest the famous event in AD 60. But out of the four prophecies of earthquakes destroying Laodicea, in one example at least it looks as if it referred to an occurrence in the second century BC, not actually recorded in any history.[32] Obviously in a region subject to earthquakes this disaster might have been repeated at an interval of two centuries. But also a Sibylline prophecy originally composed for the earlier occurrence could easily be revived as a forecast of the later. The resemblances of local earthquakes to each other are obvious. But also much of the vaguely colourful verbiage used to describe foreign invasions could be used and re-used with minor changes or fresh interpretations of the obscure language. On the other hand at times it looks as though the author of the oracle wishes to forecast some well-known event from the past, but also to establish his originality by producing a paraphrase in different words of the previous version. So, for instance, we have two different forecasts of the Trojan War.[33] Hence it is often difficult to decide what was the earliest version of a prophecy and where was its original application. Scholars have frequently plumped for one date or another. The correct answer may be that the forecast actually applied to each of several occurrences, and the one for which it was intended in its surviving context is only the latest of various appearances.

This points to a curious dilemma affecting the Sibyl's writing. There was a convention of oblique or ambiguous language as suitable for gods addressing men, and the ambiguity had practical advantages when a diviner wished to hazard a forecast which might later have to be squared with some inconvenient turn of events. But when the diviner wished to produce a simulated prophecy after the event, it was necessary to be sure that the ambiguities were not so opaque or confusing that the ordinary reader could not see the implications of the sayings. The late Sibyllists used a convenient device when wishing to appear to forecast a succession of Roman emperors.[34] They designated each of them by the number which in Greek was expressed by the initial letter of his name. So without precisely naming the individuals they conveyed the impression of foreseeing their identities. This was perhaps a specially Jewish technique as it was to have a long history in the Rabbinical tradition of 'gematria' — cabbalistic interpretation based on the numerical value of letters. But the problem of the amount of ambiguity appropriate to a context was evident at all periods. It could be well illustrated in detail from Aristophanes, who in the *Knights* and the *Birds* mixes quotations from current oracles with concoctions of his own in the oblique style, which was required, but conveyed to the audience obvious meaning to suit his dramatic purpose.[35] Aristophanes could reckon that his hearers, a very large cross-section of the people of Attica, would know certain familiar lines of oracles, and recognise the typical manner of oracular expression. In the fifth century and probably at all times they were evidently not an esoteric literature propagated only inside mystery-cults or religious sects, but circulated widely at a popular level.

Here it is worthwhile to note the one work in Greek literature which owed a considerable debt to the influence of the Sibylline oracles. This is the *Alexandra* of Lycophron, of which the date has been the subject of much controversy. I shall assume that it was written about 273 BC by the tragic poet and scholar attached to the Museum in Alexandria.[36] In form it is a lengthy oracle delivered by Cassandra in prophetic frenzy after Paris had sailed for Greece. The setting is a rocky cave on the acropolis of Ilion, where she had been confined by Priam, and her words are reported verbatim to him by a slave-gaoler, who introduces and concludes the poem by a short prologue and epilogue. The metre throughout is the iambic trimeter, and thus on one side the work is derived from the scenes in Attic tragedy in which Cassandra was introduced as a prophetess. Again the report by the slave as a literary device resembles a messenger's speech. But in another way it deliberately distinguishes itself from tragedy by its complete avoidance of any suggestion of dramatic action. Instead, Cassandra's monologue is essentially a Sibylline oracle transmuted into high literature. Though Cassandra was never described as a Sibyl, she tends to appear together with them when divination is discussed by ancient authors, and Lycophron himself put the comparison into the mouth of the slave, who likens her utterance in a triple metaphor to a Maenad, a Sibyl and the Sphinx.[37] The emphasis here is on frenzied obscurity, and this was the characteristic which struck readers. In the *Suda* it is described as 'the obscure poem'. Lycophron's method was not merely to use the simple metaphors and vague enigmas which are typical of Sibylline utterance. In the manner of contemporary Hellenistic poets he employs rare words and references to little-known legends and revels in these riddling contrivances. Perhaps one may suppose that if challenged, he would have justified this as the correct method to translate Sibylline oracles into high poetry. For he uses all the Sibylline conventions which we have already discussed. For instance, Cassandra speaks in her own person throughout. Also, though her subject is the ill-fated expedition of Paris to Greece and the consequent Trojan War, in the best Sibylline manner she begins with an event in the past — the first sack of Ilion by Heracles. Again, while logically and dramatically it could not be expected that her prophecy would go further than to describe the return of the Greek chieftains as the disastrous vengeance on their triumph, 220 lines at the end of the oracle deal with the Romans as the descendants of the Trojans and the conflict between Europe and Asia. Otherwise, Lycophron again in the manner of a Sibylline prophecy uses the device of a forecast to comment on contemporary events. The victory of Rome in the Pyrrhic War and her subsequent alliance with Ptolemy Philadelphus give the court poet a suitable motif to develop as the climax of his oracular vision. Throughout, the poem is so obscure that it can scarcely rouse emotion in the reader, but its effect has all the grimness and lack of literary charm which Heraclitus and Plutarch felt in the works of Sibylla.[38]

The *Alexandra* was, as we have suggested, the highly mannered product of a court poet at a time of national prosperity, while the sombre utterances of Sibyl emerged as popular literature at times of disaster. This fact, however, showed that they satisfied a popular need and implies that they were themselves a form of folk-literature. This is probably the reason why so little information is preserved about the earliest versions. Our extant poetry from the archaic period was mostly the product of aristocratic society and circulated primarily among the upper classes. But we must imagine the Sibyl's utterances as distributed not so much in literary circles as in the lower strata of society.

If we ask who distributed them, the general answer is the *chrēsmologoi*. These 'tellers of oracles' are familiar figures in Aristophanic comedy, and are mentioned by Herodotus in connection with events from the times of Pisistratus. From these sources we can see that the typical *chrēsmologos* was a professional who had a collection of oracular prophecies, out of which he could extract the appropriate verses for any and every occasion.[39] He did not claim himself to be an original prophet, but attributed his predictions to the authority of Sibylla, Bacis, Musaeus and so forth. It was a recognised belief that past prophecies would one day be fulfilled, and even those which appeared not to have been accomplished might in the future re-emerge to achieve their proper fulfilment. So even alleged responses of the Delphic oracle addressed to past enquirers might be effectively cited again in other contexts. The man who 'collected' and 'told' these oracles was a *chrēsmologos*; for both meanings could be extracted from the title. He based his authority on traditional seers of the past, but, as Aristophanes implies, he was often suspected of actually concocting or doctoring his oracles to suit the requirements of possible clients. No doubt this was true, and accounts for most of the examples which survive. Some are so specific in their detail that it is impossible to suppose that they were not composed *post eventum*, unless one is to believe in an extraordinary degree of second sight. In others the extent of the ambiguity or vagueness of prediction may suggest that they were produced in plausible anticipation of the event with a certain precautionary wording designed to fit any outcome. In one instance it appears that an oracle framed for one set of events was applied by drastic re-interpretation to another.

This form of professional verse-making had a crudely practical end in view rather than a high aesthetic purpose. It is not surprising, then, that at least so far as our limited number of quotations go, the Sibyl's oracles are not notable for their literary quality. The anonymous versifiers who produced them, while hiding behind the mask of the Sibyl, were not great poets, and their inspiration coming originally from the nymphs, lacked the exacting tradition of Apollo and the Muses.[40] But this poverty of style did not preclude a useful function in society. It was not because their grim forecasts contained any element of charm or wish fulfilment, but when a disaster had happened, it was a comfort to feel that this was not simply some arbitrary catastrophe. It had been foreseen and foretold. It was really part of a pattern of happenings. The way of mankind was rough, but not completely dark.

Notes

1. Editions: C. Alexandre (1841–56); A. Rzach (1891); J. Geffcken (1902); A. Kurfess (1951). Discussions: H. Diels, *Sibyllinische Blätter* (1890); J. Geffcken, *Komposition und Entstehungszeit der Oracula Sibyllina* (1902); Rzach, *RE* 2a (1923), cols 2073–183; V. Nikiprowetzky, *La troisième Sibylle* (1970); J.J. Collins, *The Sibylline oracles of Egyptian Judaism* (1974). In the text I use the term '*Oracula Sibyllina*' for the oracles extant in manuscript and fragments attributed to them, and 'Sibylline oracles' for the oracles quoted or referred to in pagan classical authors.

2. Lactant. *Div. Inst.* 1.6.12. He seems to have forgotten that the *Libri Sibyllini* preserved by the *quindecimviri* were not the original 'Cumaean' collection, which had been destroyed in 83 BC.

3. Lactantius cites the Erythraean Sibyl under that title: *Div. Inst.* 1.14.1 (*Or. Sib.* 3.110–50; 199–201); 2.16.1 (*Or. Sib.* 3.228–9); 4.6.4 (*Or. Sib.* 3.775); 4.15.29 (*Or. Sib.* 3.815–18); 7.19.9 (*Or. Sib.* 3.618); 7.20.1 (*Or. Sib.* 3.741–3); 7.24.12 (*Or. Sib.* 3.619–23; 788–94). In one place only, 7.18.7, he cites *Or. Sib.* 3.652–3 simply as *alia* (Sibylla). Besides these passages, which can be located in Book 3, there are fragments 1 and 3 quoted earlier *in extenso* simply as Sibylline by Theophilus of Antioch. The citations from these which Lactantius makes he assigns to the Erythraean Sibyl: *Div. Inst.* 2.12.19 (fr. 3. 6–48); 4.6.4 (fr. 1. 5–6); 1.6.7 (fr. 1. 7; fr. 3. 3–5 and fr. 1. 15–16); 1.8.3 (fr. 3. 1–2). As Theophilus and Lactantius both describe fragment 1 as from the beginning of the prophecy, it is usually supposed that down to the early fourth century this and fragments 2 and 3 formed parts of the opening of *Or. Sib.* 3. In our extant MSS the beginning of this book is defective. Again the only passage where the Sibyl refers to herself as called Erythraean occurs at the end of Book 3 (824), but Lactantius seems to imply (*praelocuta est*) that it occurred at the beginning. Also *Div. Inst.* 5.13.21 is referred by S. Brandt, *Corpus Scriptorum Ecclesiasticorum Latinorum* vol. 19 (1890), 443, to *Or. Sib.* 8.397, but as it is attributed by Lactantius to the Erythraean it should probably be labelled fr. 9 and assigned to the missing beginning of Book 3, which dealt with the insensibility of idols. There are many other books of *Or. Sib.* cited by Lactantius simply as Sibylline.

4. Cf. *infra* pp. 14; 36.

5. *Or. Sib.* fragments 1–8 (Geffcken). These appear to be largely the missing earlier part of Book 3.

6. Strabo 1.3.7; 12.2.4; *Or. Sib.* 4.97. The river Pyramus reappears in *Or. Sib.* 13.57; 133. For further discussion, cf. *infra* p. 133. Camarina, Parke and Wormell, *DO* II, no. 127, and *Or. Sib.* 3.736. Apollo's claim to omniscience (Parke and Wormell, *DO* II, no. 52, 1–2) is plagiarised in *Or. Sib.* 8.361; 373.

7. The Trojan War and Homer, Varro *ap.* Lactant. *Div. Inst.* 1.6; Solinus 2.18; cf. Diod. 4.66.6; Paus. 10.12.2. For a fuller discussion cf. *infra* pp. 109–110.

8. E.g. *Or. Sib.* 3.433ff and 5.306ff.

9. V.A. Tcherikover, *Hellenistic civilization and the Jews* (1959), 347ff; P.M. Fraser, *Ptolemaic Alexandria* (1972), 1.588ff.

10. H.W. Parke, *Hermathena*, 130/131 (1981), 99. *Or. Sib.* 1.146 is a stray pentameter at the end of an interpolation; *Etym. Magn.* 14.7.38, a single iambic line. For hexameters as typical, Tib. 2.5.16; Tertullian, *Nat.* 2.12, and *Suda* H541.

11. Cf. *infra* pp. 79–83; 145–7.

12. *Or. Sib.* 3.97 (Babel); 248 (Exodus); 268 (Babylonian captivity); 823 (Daughter-in-law of Noah).

13. Paus. 10.12.2; *Or. Sib.* 3.266. The two prophetic poems of Marcius, discovered at Rome in 214 BC, were arranged on this principle, evidently in imitation of Sibylline prophecy. The first poem was a *post eventum* forecast of Cannae (216 BC); the second a vague prediction of blessings arising from a celebration of the *Ludi Apollinares*. As Livy neatly expresses it: 'Of the two prophecies of this Marcius, the authority of one, brought to light after the event, was confirmed by what had happened, and this lent credibility to the other, which concerned something still in the future' (25.12.4). The earliest example of a similar technique in Greek literature is in Aeschylus, *Agamemnon*, where Cassandra in ectasy twice mentions the Thyestean feast, before going on to foretell the murder of Agamemnon (1095ff and 1217ff). She cites this instance of second sight as proof of her power of prophecy, but the chorus, though impressed, are not driven to action. Cassandra is in many respects the mythical model of the Sibyl: cf. *infra* pp. 55–8. In Hippocrates, fr. 1, the doctor is advised to win the patients' confidence by describing their past and present symptoms as well as giving his prognosis: see G.E.R. Lloyd, *Magic, reason and experience* (1979), 90.

14. For the end of the prophets, see Joseph. *Ap.* 1.40; August. *De Civ. D.* 18.45.

15. The Sibyl's longevity; the first explicit statement is in Ovid, *Met.* 14.136 where it is indicated that her life was to last for a thousand years. In Phlegon, *F. Gr. Hist.* 257 f 37 v 1. 4, the Sibyl prophesies that she will die in the tenth generation. In the Erythraean inscription (*IGR* IV, no. 1540, l.9) she speaks of having returned to her native land after nine hundred years. Other traces are more vague. In Vergil she is regularly 'the long-lived priestess'. Petronius' folk-tale of her wish to die, and the idea of her shrunk to diminutive size, are embroideries on this theme. I believe that the 'thousand years' occurred in the original version of the Sibylline oracles, and that it was from there that Heraclitus cited the phrase, but others take it differently (cf. *infra* p. 63).

16. For Numa's books see 13.87ff. Pliny, *HN* 13 (Cassius Hemina, fr. 37, Peter); Livy 40.29.3. Dictys, *F. Gr. Hist.* 49 1 2C and 4. Which method Hegesianax of Alexandria used to justify his publication of Cephalo of Gergis (*F. Gr. Hist.* 45 f 1) is not recorded, so the philosophy of Numa might be the first instance of this method. The Tiburtine Sibyl, cf. *infra* pp. 14; 36.

17. Hdt. 7.6.3. For the *Theologoi*, Epimenides, Musaeus and Bacis, see Appendix I.

18. Parke and Wormell, *DO* II, no. 84.9 ('Our temple'); no. 129.2 ('mother'); no. 154.2 ('my father').

19. Cassandra again is the model; in the *Agamemnon* she represents herself as being inspired by Apollo, but though she is subject to

hallucinatory visions, she never loses her own personality and always addresses Apollo, or speaks of him, in the third person, as distinct from herself: see E.R. Dodds, *The Greeks and the irrational* (1951), 83 n. 45. Cassandra was misunderstood by Cicero (*Div.* 1.67): 'It is a god shut up in a human body, not Cassandra, who speaks.' In fifth-century Athens the typical prophet was a medium: Pl. *Ap.* 22 c; *Meno* 99 c; *Ion* 534 c. For the motif that the Sibyl asks for release see e.g. *Or. Sib.* 2.1; 346.

20. Marpessian or Erythraean Sibyl, Paus. 10.12.3; Delphic Sibyl, Clem. Al. *Strom.* 1.21.384 P; Herophile, Paus. 10.12.2; *Or. Sib.* 3.809.

21. Nicander, *Alexipharmaca*, 9 (Claros); 629 (his name); 845–83 (his name in acrostic); and *Theriaca*, 957 (at the end of the concluding address to Hermesianax, to whom he dedicates the work). On the subject of personal statements, generally, see W. Kranz, *Rh. Mus.* 104 (1961), 3–46; 97–124.

22. For the Sibyl's subject matter, Plut. *Mor.* 398C–D, discussed *infra* pp. 114–7.

23. For the beginning with the Creation as in Genesis, *Or. Sib.* 1. I believe that *Or. Sib.* 3 originally began in the same way. Cf. 3.819 on what her father had told her. But the equivalent of Book 1, starting with fragment 1, is missing, lost between the period of Theophilus of Antioch and Lactantius, to whom it was known, and the compilation of the *Oracula Sibyllina*. The quasi-euhemeristic account of the Greek gods, 3.110ff.

24. Orpheus, *Theogony*, Diels–Kranz, IB 12, etc.; and *Oracles*, *id.* 1 A 1, etc. Musaeus, *Theogony*, Diog. Laert. 1.3, etc.; and *Oracles*, Hdt. 7.6; 8.96, etc. Epimenides, *F. Gr. Hist.* 457 fr.1 and 2 (*Oracles*) and f.3–17 (*Theogony*). Theogonies in prose are attributed to Abaris and Aristeas by the *Suda, s.nn.*, but Jacoby regards them as inventions of Lobon, the (?) third-century BC forger (*F. Gr. Hist.* 34 and 35). See Appendix I.

25. Heraclitus, cf. *infra* pp. 63–4; Nic. Dam., *F. Gr. Hist.* 90 f 68.8; Hes. *Th.* 26; Epimenides, *F. Gr. Hist.* 457 f 1 and 2. Cf. Appendix I.

26. Clem. Alex. *Strom.* 1.21.384P. Cf. *infra* pp. 26–7.

27. E.g. Isaiah, 15–17 or Zephaniah, 2. The chief examples of the prophecies of disasters to Asia Minor cities are *Or. Sib.* 3.342ff and 433ff; 4.107; 5.126ff; and 207ff. Stray lines occur elsewhere. It is perhaps significant that *Or. Sib.* 1 and 2, which were most probably written in the third century AD by a Jew resident in Asia Minor, contain no such denunciations of Asian cities. Under the Roman empire there is much less evidence for hostility between Greeks and Jews in Asia Minor than in Egypt, and the author of *Or. Sib.* 1 and 2 may not have wished to provoke it.

28. Golden Age, *Or. Sib.* 2.29ff; 3.619–23, 741–61 and 785–96; 5.381ff. Cf. Isaiah 11: 6–9.

29. For further discussion, see *infra* pp. 145–7.

30. Ptolemy VI Philometor, *Or. Sib.* 3.608 (Collins (*supra* n. 1), 27). Peloponnesian War, Paus. 10.9.11 and *infra* pp. 102–6. Chaeronea, Plut. *Demosth.* 19 and *infra* pp. 119–120. Philip V of Macedon, Appian, *Mac.* 2; Paus. 7.8.9, and *infra* p. 120.

31. P.J. Alexander, *The oracle of Baalbek: the Tiburtine Sibyl in Greek dress* (1967).

32. Prophecies of disaster to Laodicea, *Or. Sib.* 3.470 (earthquake): 4.107 (earthquake with an apparent synchronism with the fall of Corinth and of Carthage); 5.290 (earthquake); 7.22 (not an earthquake but a flood of the river Lycus); 12.280 (earthquake mention after Elagabalus); 14.85 (not an earthquake but a war). For the earthquake of AD 60, Tac. *Ann.* 14.27.

33. Cf. *supra* pp. 4–5 and n. 7.

34. *Or. Sib.* 5.14 (Augustus) and frequently in Books 11–14.

35. For discussion and examples, cf. *infra* pp. 103–4.

36. For the problem of the date of the *Alexandra*, see Ziegler, *RE* 13 (1927), cols 2354, 2381; Josifovic, *RE* Supplementband 11 (1968), cols 925–30; A. Momigliano, *Alien wisdom. The limits of Hellenization* (1975), 15. Fraser (*supra* n. 9), 2.1065 n. 331, does not explain satisfactorily why he believes the *Alexandra* was written in Eretria, not Alexandria. I would have thought its extraordinary erudition could best be explained by the availability of the Museum Library. For a recent discussion, see S. West, *CQ* 33 (1983), 114–35.

37. Cassandra and Sibyls, e.g. Cic. *Div.* 2.112; Cassandra as Sibyl, Lycoph. *Alex.* 1464.

38. The taking of Troy by Heracles, Lycoph. *Alex.* 31–51. The rise of Rome and the conflict of Europe and Asia, *id.* 1226–450. It would not affect my general argument if some part of this section had been interpolated or altered after the original production by Lycophron, *c.* 273 BC.

39. For *chrēsmologoi*, see Parke and Wormell, *DO* II, xv, and J. Fontenrose, *The Delphic oracle* (1978), 145; also M.L. West, *The Orphic poems* (1983), 41.

40. For inspiration derived from nymphs, cf. *infra* p. 58.

2

The Ancient Scholarly Sources
for the Identity of Sibyls

They sought it with thimbles, they sought it with care;
  They pursued it with forks and hope.

Until the latter half of the fourth century BC there is no evidence
for a critical study of the Sibyls. Down till that period Sibylla had
been treated as a personal name, and the extant authors who
mention her work do not imply that there could be more than one
individual of this designation.[1] This may be partly because she
was only introduced by them for specific literary purposes.
Heraclitus used her as an example to add point to one of his
aphorisms in the same way that he named certain poets,
philosophers and politicians.[2] Similarly Aristophanes uses the
name on occasion to raise a laugh when he is satirising the
contemporary oracle-mongers.[3] Euripides went further in providing Sibylla with a mother, Lamia, and a location, Libya.[4] But
both these were the products of his imagination, serving the
purpose of a grotesque and horrific satyr-play. They do not
contribute at all to the historic background of the Sibylline
legend.

However, as the production and circulation of Sibylline
prophecies spread, the figure of the prophetess acquired legendary
associations with various places. The simplest, and probably the
easiest, way of accounting for a local connection was to suggest
that Sibylla had visited the place in the distant past. The
wanderings of contemporary *chrēsmologoi* provided a convenient
analogy. But local patriotism was not content to leave it at that.
Its fabrications appear to have taken two alternative forms. The
locality could claim to be the one and only home of Sibylla and
deny her connection with any other city. As we shall see, the chief

example of this claim is provided by the dispute between Marpessus in the Troad and Erythrae in Ionia, which may have begun already in the fifth century BC. In this instance both places treated Sibylla as the personal name of a prophetess, of whom they each tried to maintain the monopoly. Alternatively, a city might substitute another personal name for Sibylla as that of their local wise woman, and use Sibylla as her professional description. We shall suggest that this was the origin of the name Herophile, often attached to the Erythraean Sibyl but most appropriately personal to the prophetess of Samos.

It was to be expected that some ancient scholar would set out to investigate and record these various traditions. The first was Heraclides of Pontus who, when faced with the multiplicity of local legends, seems to have originated the theory that there had been not one but a number of persons called Sibylla. Heraclides came from a wealthy family belonging to Heraclea on the Black Sea. He emerges as a pupil of Speusippus in the Academy, probably during Plato's absence in Sicily (367–365 BC), and continued in the school until the time of Speusippus' death (338 BC) when he was one of the three candidates for the headship. On his rejection in favour of Xenocrates, he returned to his native Heraclea. The traditions about him suggest a strong personality, whose defection from the Academy aroused bitter feelings which were expressed in the ridiculous tales about his death. He was a complete polymath and a copious writer. Diogenes Laertius lists 47 titles classified under the headings of ethics, physics, grammar, music, rhetoric and history, but does not include the work in which he recorded the Sibyls, though it is well evidenced elsewhere. In later periods Heraclides was mainly read for his dialogues on moral subjects, and his work on the Pythagoreans was the chief source of the romantic view of Pythagoras as a superhuman sage. He enjoyed diversifying his dialogues by introducing picturesque interlocutors, such as a *magus* who had circumnavigated Africa, and miraculous episodes involving oracular responses. This literary interest may have led him to investigate the subject of oracle-centres.[5]

There are four citations by name and title of this work of Heraclides, *Concerning oracle-centres*, and some six more citations by name only without title, which can be ascribed convincingly to the same work because of their content. They indicate that it was a comprehensive survey of the various places where divination was practised not only in Greek sanctuaries, but also elsewhere in the Mediterranean. The book was not confined to Apolline oracles, but included the oracles of Zeus at Dodona and Olympia, of Dionysus in Thrace, and Pluto in Canopus. Heraclides is usually cited, not for the actual oracular responses, but for the legend of the founder or other myths attached to the sanctuaries and for the method of consultation employed there.[6]

It may have been because his approach to the subject of divination was made by recording its local manifestations that Heraclides found himself led to identify Sibylline oracles with particular sites and distinguish between the different prophetesses. Unfortunately our knowledge of his treatment of this branch of the subject depends on a few isolated quotations. So it is impossible to be sure how he covered it. The quotations show that he differentiated the Sibyl of Marpessus (Hellespontine), the Sibyl of Erythrae and the Sibyl who was later called the Delphic. He might have known of other Sibyls, but, if so, our extant authors fail to cite him for them.

Of these three, the reference to the Sibyl of Marpessus comes from Varro through Lactantius. Varro's list will need detailed discussion later. On this Sibyl Heraclides is reported as stating that 'she was the Hellespontine, born in the territory of Troy, at the village of Marpessus near the town of Gergithus. Heraclides of Pontus writes that she lived in the times of Solon and Cyrus.' It looks as though Heraclides already knew a Sibylline oracle containing the lines, which were later to be quoted by Pausanias, in which the Marpessian Sibyl describes her parentage and birthplace. But also Heraclides must have had some other evidence connecting her with Solon and Cyrus. This might suggest Xanthus the Lydian or whatever source lies behind Nicolaus of Damascus' story of the Sibyl appearing and prophesying to Cyrus when Croesus was on the pyre. But if such a narrative was known to Heraclides, how did he decide that this Sibyl was the Marpessian? There is no such indication in Nicolaus. The best conjecture is that Heraclides' text of the Marpessian oracle contained a prophecy or prophecies which could be interpreted as describing Croesus' empire and its fall at the hands of the Persians.[7]

Besides the Hellespontine or Marpessian Sibyl, Heraclides also knew of the Erythraean Sibyl, whom he named Herophile. Our evidence for this comes from Clement of Alexandria, who appends this statement to his more detailed description of the Delphic Sibyl. It is tantalising that he cites no more about the

Erythraean Sibyl, but at least it proves that Heraclides distinguished her from the Marpessian. Therefore he must have written after the Erythraeans had set up their claim, in opposition to the Marpessians, to have possessed the one and only Sibyl. Heraclides, then, must have encountered a second version of the Sibylline oracle, which contained the lines on the prophetess's origin in the modified form which was later known to Pausanias, omitting the reference to Marpessus in favour of Erythrae. Also in this text, as both Heraclides and Pausanias show, she did not simply give her name as Sibylla but called herself Herophile. What the oracle contained as prophecies is here left unmentioned.[8]

Evidently Heraclides, when faced with the rival claims of Marpessus and Erythrae, did not feel compelled to decide for one to the exclusion of the other. Instead he accepted both. In fact this may have been the evidence which led him first to differentiate between Sibyls. But if so, he went further, and from some other source added a third, who prophesied at Delphi. The quotation comes again from Clement, who is comparing unfavourably the antiquity of the Greek wise men and poets with Moses:

> Also the Sibyl was older than Orpheus. More than one story is told about her designation and also about the oracles which are attributed to her: that she was a Phrygian called Artemis, and that she visited Delphi and sang, 'Delphians, servants of far-darting Apollo, I have come to prophesy the mind of Zeus the aegis-holder, as I am wroth with my own brother, Apollo.' And there is another Sibyl also of Erythrae, called Herophile. These were mentioned by Heraclides of Pontus in his *Concerning oracle-centres*.[9]

The Sibyl prophesying at Delphi differs conspicuously from the traditions recalled by Plutarch of a daughter of Poseidon and Lamia or a prophetess brought up by the Muses on Helicon. But again it is the same evidence which was known to Pausanias some five centuries after Heraclides. Pausanias summarised in a sentence the various statements which the prophetess made about herself: 'She calls herself not only Herophile, but also Artemis in her verses, and says she is Apollo's wedded wife and at another time his sister and again his daughter. These poems she composed when she was raving and possessed by the god.' The details of this statement can be discussed more fully in connection with Pausanias' other evidence, but it is clear that he knew the verses quoted by Heraclides as part of an extensive Sibylline oracle. Presumably they formed the beginning, as they start without a connecting particle and in the form of an address to the citizens of Delphi.[10]

Both Heraclides and Pausanias were disturbed by the picture of the Sibyl identifying herself with Artemis, and tried by different methods to explain it away. Heraclides, if Clement reports him correctly, supposed that the speaker was actually a woman from Phrygia, whose personal name was Artemis. Why in addressing the Delphians she should have identified herself with the goddess, Apollo's sister, is not explained. Pausanias instead supposed that the mouthpiece was the Sibyl Herophile, and that the various identities which he mentioned were all assumed by the prophetess at different stages in her ecstatic utterances. So we see two scholars at an interval of five centuries trying to tackle a problem presented by an obscure documentary source. Pausanias elsewhere somewhat ostentatiously mentions the quantity of oracles which he has read. That Heraclides, too, was capable of hunting out documentary evidence is strangely confirmed by the remarkable tradition, preserved by Proclus, that he had been commissioned by Plato to collect copies of Antimachus' poems in Colophon (the poet's native city). His research on the Sibyls had led him to assert for the first time that there had been a number of prophetesses called by this title.[11]

Once the principle had been established that there were various Sibyls with local connections, the field was open for different scholars to produce their individual theses. For instance, Philetas of Ephesus distinguished Bacis, the equivalent on the Greek mainland of the Sibyl, as three persons: the Boeotian, the Athenian and the Messenian, and reproduced the threefold distinction for Sibylla. Only his three were 'the sister of Apollo, as she says in her poetry', secondly the Erythraean and thirdly the Sardian. These look like Heraclides' identifications, as known to us, except that Philetas substitutes Sardis for Marpessus as the locality of his third Sibyl. If she was supposed to have prophesied to Cyrus at Sardis, it might be only a difference of epithet rather than of identity. There is no positive indication of Philetas' date. He is only mentioned three times: in two places in the scholia to Aristophanes and in the *Suda* under Bacis. So he was only remembered for his statements about these diviners in whatever book they occurred. He might have written before Heraclides, but it is much more probable that he was a Hellenistic scholar, following in Heraclides' footsteps.[12]

Apart from lists of Sibyls, the other scholarly products were local histories with notices about the native Sibyl. For instance Apollodorus of Erythrae was cited by Varro as his source for the Erythraean Sibyl. From the phrase which Lactantius uses to describe his statement — *affirmat fuisse civem suam* — we can deduce that, as we might expect, Apollodorus maintained his city's claim to have possessed *the* Sibyl. Also he gave some information about the content of her alleged oracles: 'she prophesied to the Greeks when they were on their way to Ilion, that Troy would fall and that Homer would write falsehoods.' This is the earliest evidence for this subject as mentioned in the Sibylline oracles. If it occurred in this context in the verses attributed to the Erythraean Sibyl, it might obviously have been a reason for dating her to the Heroic Age, and we may see a suggestion of this in the way in which it seems that Heraclides placed her in order between the Delphian Sibyl and the Hellespontine; an order clearly reproduced by Philetas of Ephesus. Apollodorus' own period remains uncertain, except that he must have written before the mid-first century. The claim of Erythrae to possess a local Sibyl is first found in Callisthenes writing about 332 BC. It may be that the emergence of the prophetess Athenais at that time stimulated local ambitions to make a written assertion about the Sibyl as her predecessor; she might previously have only been a subject of folk-tale. In any case Apollodorus' book is most likely to belong to the late fourth century at the earliest, and probably after Heraclides rather than before him.[13]

Another local treatise produced in the Hellenistic period dealt with Cumae and was attributed to one Hyperochus. This was the source which Pausanias cites for the Sibyl of Cumae. The other fragments preserved give a fanciful origin of the name of Rome and a highly conventional picture of the luxury of the early Cumaeans. These suggest that the work was not a genuine local chronicle but a romantic fantasy. In fact it is not certain that it was written in prose: Lloyd-Jones and Parsons treat Hyperochus as a poet. The author's name itself may be a pseudonym with its hint at a Hyperborean origin. The only contribution which Pausanias extracted from him was the personal name, Demo, for this Sibyl. Clearly she had not found her way into the traditions of classical Greece. It was only in the Hellenistic period, after Cumae had already ceased to be an independent Greek city, that the echo of its past reached Hellas, probably through the writings of Lycus of Rhegium and Timaeus. Instead it was by Roman folk-tale and Roman literature that the Sibyl of Cumae won her reputation.[14]

One other Sibyl, who had existed in the archaic period, was lost to the classical age and resurrected by Hellenistic scholar-ship. This was the Sibyl of Samos. Varro cited as his source for her Eratosthenes, the late-third-century BC scholar and librarian of the Museum, who writes that he had discovered her in the ancient annals of the Samians. This clearly implies what our evidence suggests, that the Samian Sibyl had not been recorded by Heraclides or any previous scholar, until Eratosthenes unearthed her in his researches. The Samians had probably been the earliest Greeks to produce a local history. So it is plausible here that Eratosthenes was not referring to documentary sources which he had consulted on Samos, but to the text of some little-read Samian historian which he had discovered in the Museum. If it was an author, Jacoby has shown that he probably had written not earlier than the mid-fifth century BC, and this would be quite consistent with the establishment of Sibylline oracles on Samos at some date in the earlier sixth century. As we shall see, the fact that Varro placed the Samian Sibyl after the Erythraean and before the Cumaean would imply that he found in Eratosthenes some indication that she should be dated before 550 BC. A distant echo of this may be found in the chronological notices of Eusebius and Jerome which offer the alternative dates of 712/11 BC or 666/5 BC for her *floruit*. Eratosthenes had probably mentioned her in his *Chronographiae*.[15]

Hellenistic scholarship was followed by Roman. Varro, the great antiquarian, undertook with countless other tasks to settle the Sibyl's business. His *Antiquitates rerum humanarum et divinarum* was an encyclopaedic survey of institutions, secular and religious, dedicated to Julius Caesar and published in 47 BC. Books 27 to 29 inclusive dealt with priesthoods, and it was probably in them that he mentioned the Sibyls, whom he discussed in connection with the *quindecemviri sacris faciundis*. His notice on the subject is preserved in paraphrase by Lactantius, probably not working direct but through some intermediate source.[16] Varro stated that 'the Sibylline books' by which he seems to have meant in this context all oracles circulating as Sibylline, were not the work of one Sibyl, but were called by the name Sibylline because all female diviners were called 'Sibyllae' by the ancients, either from the name of one Delphic woman, or because they proclaimed the counsel of the gods. For in the Aeolic dialect they used to call the gods not θεούς (theous), but σιούς (sious) and counsel not βουλήν (boulen), but βούλλαν (boullan). But there have been ten Sibyllas.

This is the first occurrence of this derivation and explanation of Sibylla, which was regularly repeated in later authors. Varro himself had a great liking for this kind of etymological method of explaining difficulties. So it may be his own theory. The description of the Greek dialect used, as Aeolic, might suggest that he was following the tradition of the Marpessian Sibyl as the first. But other passages in Varro show a favourite use of Aeolic derivations when dealing with primitive Greek. So it probably is a mere tendency in Varro's etymology.[17] Alternatively, he knew of some author to whom the earliest Sibyl was the Delphic and who claimed that her personal name, Sibylla, became the designation of all subsequent female diviners. Unfortunately, Varro does not name his source for this theory, but from a subsequent indication it may have been the Stoic philosopher, Chrysippus.[18]

However, in recording his list of ten Sibyls, Varro treats us better. As Lactantius explains, 'he has enumerated them under the authors who wrote on the subject of each.' Lactantius does not add, what is obvious, that Varro had arranged his list chronologically from what he reckoned to be the earliest Sibyl down to the latest. The catalogue runs as follows:

(1) 'The first was from the Persians, of whom Nicanor, who wrote the deeds of Alexander of Macedon, made mention.'

(2) 'The second was the Libyan, whom Euripides mentioned in Lamia's prologue.'

(3) 'The third was the Delphian, about whom Chrysippus speaks in the book which he put together on divination.'

(4) 'The fourth was the Cimmerian in Italy, whom Naevius names in his books on the Punic War and Piso in his *Annals*.'

(5) 'The fifth was the Erythraean, of whom Apollodorus of Erythrae asserts that she was his fellow citizen and that she prophesied to the Greeks, when they were on their way to Ilion, that Troy would fall and that Homer would write falsehoods.'

(6) 'The sixth was the Samian, concerning whom Eratosthenes writes that he had discovered her in the ancient annals of the Samians.'

(7) 'The seventh was the Cumaean by name Amalthea, who by others is named Herophile or Demophile. She brought nine books to Tarquinius Priscus.' (Varro proceeds to tell at length the familiar legend of how the Sibyl burnt six of the books, before Tarquinius finally agreed to buy the remaining three.)[19]

(8) 'The eighth was the Hellespontine, born in the territory of Troy at the village of Marpessus near the town of Gergithus, of whom Heraclides of Pontus writes that she lived in the times of Solon and Cyrus.'

(9) 'The ninth was the Phrygian, who prophesied at Ancyra.'

(10) 'The tenth was the Tiburtine, by name Albunea, who is worshipped at Tibur as a goddess by the banks of the river Anio, in whose eddy it is said an image of her was found holding a book, and her lots were removed to the Capitol by the senate.'[20]

It is noteworthy that Varro lists many more Sibyls than his predecessors. He does this by casting his net wider so as to include not only those from Greek sources, but also some for whom he cites only Roman authorities. Also he is prepared to accept all kinds of evidence, not only prose writers but also poets such as Euripides. His sources are authors, not the texts of Sibylline oracles. In fact, unlike Heraclides, he shows no sign of original research in the subject, but merely erudite compilation. The impression left is that he was less concerned with checking the historicity of his specimens than with including as many as possible. Whether he felt there was a special neatness in achieving a total of ten is too difficult to prove.

Because they were cited from scholarly Greek authors writing before Varro's day, we have already had occasion to discuss the third, fifth, sixth and eighth on his list. In spite of the statement that they were recorded with their authors, no author is named for the seventh, ninth and tenth Sibyls: it is not clear whether these omissions were due to Varro himself or produced by oversights on the part of Lactantius or an intermediate source. In the case of the Tiburtine Sibyl perhaps the use of *dicitur* (it is said) implies that Varro had no literary evidence but depended on an orally transmitted legend. As for the Cumaean Sibyl, as we shall see, Varro differed in an important particular from all known versions, and so may have felt he could not name an authority for this prophetess. This leaves unassigned the ninth, the Phrygian Sibyl, which is unfortunate as she seems impossible otherwise to identify in the prophetic tradition.

Varro in extending his list as far as possible added two Sibyls at the beginning who had not been mentioned by previous scholars. The Libyan Sibyl, cited from Euripides, was simply a literary fantasy, and probably achieved her early position in the list from her mythological setting. The Persian Sibyl is a greater problem. Her source is given as Nicanor, the author of a history of Alexander the Great. As this is the only reference to his work, it cannot be determined whether he wrote as a contemporary of the king or as a later storyteller. Again, the name Nicanor is so common, especially among Macedonians, that identification is out of the question. In fact it is not possible, except by conjecture, to go beyond Varro's bare statement. Obviously it is likely that the Persian Sibyl mentioned in a book on this subject was represented by Nicanor as foretelling Alexander's deeds. Varro, as quoted by Lactantius, did not say so, but the Greek writers who built on and paraphrased his list state so specifically. Still, various options are open. Presumably this Sibyl, like all the others, was extant in Greek. Was she represented as warning the Persians of the disaster which would bring an end to the reign of the Achaemenids, thus echoing the sentiments of the many Greeks, mercenaries and others who were in Persian service at the time of Alexander's invasion? Alternatively, did someone on the Macedonian side forge a forecast of Alexander's victories, putting it into the mouth of an alleged Persian prophetess? It is possible even that this Sibylline oracle did not reach its climax in Alexander's victories, but in his tragic death. Just as the Chaldaean priests were credited with having revealed to the king an oracle of Bel warning him against entering Babylon, which he disregarded to his cost, it may have occurred to someone to produce another native prophecy of a Persian Sibyl foretelling Alexander's end.

These, however, can only remain conjectures. The one certain conclusion to be drawn is that Varro found in Nicanor something which he took as evidence that the Persian Sibyl was earlier in date than any of the others. This is not surprising because, as Berosus shows, Mesopotamian traditions claimed to reach back tens of thousands of years. How strictly one should take the ethnic designation 'Persian' is perhaps uncertain.[21]

As the authority for the Delphic Sibyl, Varro cited Chrysippus the Stoic philosopher, not Heraclides, perhaps because to Heraclides she had been actually a Phrygian immigrant, while Chrysippus may have followed one of the traditions which made her native to central Greece. Presumably Chrysippus recorded her in his work on divination. He was the chief protagonist among the Stoics for the view that divination was an authentic science. One of his two books on the subject was devoted to oracular responses. According to Cicero he collected copious examples of the replies of the Pythia together with the evidence confirming them. This suggests that for oracular divinations he concentrated on Delphi and may have included the local Sibyl in the same context. Which tradition he followed is not recorded, but from the order of the Delphic Sibyl in Varro's lists — third after the Persian and Libyan — we can conclude that he dated her in legendary times, perhaps as the predecessor of the Pythia. Probably he ignored the Persian and Libyan Sibyls and made the Delphian the first of her kind. If so, he is also probably the unnamed author from whom Varro reports the derivation of Sibylla from the name of a Delphian woman.[22]

The fourth, Cimmerian, Sibyl was, like the Libyan, a literary fantasy, invented by Naevius so as to provide Aeneas with a prophetess who would on his landing in Italy foretell the future of his descendants in Latium. Naevius was evidently aware that Cumae was not already founded at the time of the Trojan War and so felt the need for a Sibyl preceding the Cumaean. His invention was incorporated into the pattern of prose history by later writers of *Annals*.[23]

Varro told at length the traditional tale how a Sibyl, whom he identifies as the Cumaean, sold the Sibylline books to a Tarquin. The disproportionate treatment was justified because he had introduced the subject of the Sibyls in connection with the *quindecimviri* and so was particularly concerned with the origin of their sacred books. He followed his list by explaining the different sources of the contemporary *Libri Sibyllini*, collected after the originals had been burned with the temple of Juppiter Optimus Maximus in 83 BC. But his failure to cite an authority for the Cumaean Sibyl may be because in this instance Varro differed in one important respect from any of his predecessors. All the versions of the legend not derived from Varro name the king Tarquinius Superbus (534–510 BC) and this was a natural choice, since legend agreed that he was the builder of Juppiter's temple, where the Sibylline books were originally stored. Traditionally at the end of his reign it was so near completion that it was consecrated during the first consulship.

In one respect Varro could justify the substitution of Priscus for Superbus, for according to one tradition Priscus had laid the foundations of the temple of Juppiter Optimus Maximus with the spoils of his Sabine war. So he also could have arranged for the safe deposit of the Sibylline books in their underground chamber.[24] The Varronian dates for Tarquinius Priscus were 616–579 BC, and they would fit with a Sibyl active in the latter part of the seventh century. Why Varro should prefer this dating is not explained in Lactantius, but it may be suggested that it was not because he had any evidence to distinguish between the two kings in favour of Priscus, but simply that he wished to be able to arrange his list of Sibyls in a chronological sequence without overlaps. If for instance the date for the Cumaean Sibyl's activity ended in 600 BC, then the Hellespontine Sibyl who was active in the time of Solon and Cyrus would evidently have flourished around 594/3 to 546/5 BC.[25]

Of the nearest Sibyls in the series, the *floruit* of the Samian Sibyl was at the latest 666/5 BC, which would leave convenient space for the Cumaean Sibyl to follow her. The ninth Sibyl, the Phrygian, is left curiously vague in Varro's list without personal name or authority. So we cannot test whether she would fit conveniently into the latter half of the sixth century BC.

Lactantius, as this shows, did not reproduce in his paraphrase all the contents of Varro's discussion of the Sibyls. For it is impossible to believe that Varro would have substituted Priscus for Superbus in his narrative without offering some comment or explanation. If, as is likely, Lactantius copied his reference from some intermediate source, possibly an anthology of theological literature, the abridgement may already have been made by someone who was not interested in the historical problems of the Sibyls. The Varronian list of the Sibyls had a constant influence on later writers, which is shown by the recurrence of the number ten in this fixed order and the feature of naming the Tarquin as Priscus. In the Latin tradition Isidore reproduces the catalogue with some omissions of details. He abbreviates the story of the Cumaean Sibyl and Tarquinius Priscus, but inserts a reference to Vergil's *Fourth Eclogue*. Also he follows Lactantius in identifying the authoress of the third book of the *Oracula Sibyllina* with Herophile of Erythrae. Although he borrows some details from Solinus, the essential framework remains Varro's list.[26] The canonical figure of ten Sibyls was contradicted by one Latin author, Martianus Capella, who deliberately reverts to the primitive notion of two Sibyls — Marpessian and Erythraean — but adds some unique features of his own.[27]

The Byzantine learned tradition on the Sibyls did not go back to Hellenic sources but based itself on the Christian Fathers, among whom Lactantius, although writing in Latin, won chief influence. The main examples are found in Johannes Lydus, *De Mensibus*, the scholia to Plato's *Phaedrus*, the *Tübingen Theosophy*, and the preface to the extant corpus of the *Oracula Sibyllina*. These all reproduce the list of the ten prophetesses in the same order, but insert minor details: for example, the Samian Sibyl's name is Phyto; the Cimmerian Sibyl was the mother of Evander; Vergil had named the Cumaean Sibyl Deiphobe. Also synchronisms with Deborah and the Judges are added. But the most important alteration is to identify the Persian Sibyl with Sambethe, the Chaldaean or Jewish Sibyl (the authoress of Book 3 of the *Oracula Sibyllina*). This actually contradicts Lactantius, who regarded the authoress of Book 3 as the Erythraean Sibyl and regularly cites her under that designation. But the subject is better discussed later.[28]

So far we have followed over the succeeding centuries the scholarly borrowers from Varro. But much nearer his own date in high literature there occurs in Tibullus, 2.5, a kind of list of the Sibyls, which may be derived directly from the *Antiquitates rerum divinarum*. The poem was written in celebration of the appointment of M. Valerius Messala Messalinus, his patron's elder son, as *quindecemvir sacris faciundis* in 21 or 20 BC. Tibullus expends much of his rather diffuse elegy on the subject of Sibyls, because Messalinus will now be allowed to handle the Sibylline books.

First a Sibyl, otherwise unidentified, foretells the future foundation of Rome to Aeneas as he leaves burning Troy. Then a list of Sibyls is given as an introduction to a paraphrase of the typical contents of their oracles:

> Whatever Amalthea, whatever the Marpessian uttered, what warning Herophile, beloved of Phoebus, gave, and what consecrated prophetic lots the woman of Tibur had carried and borne through the waters of the Anio in the fold of her robe without wetting them.[29]

These could correspond to Varro's no. 7 (the Cumaean, named Amalthea as first preference), no. 8 (the Hellespontine), no. 5 (the Erythraean, usually called Herophile, although Varro as reported by Lactantius does not give her this name, but quotes it as an alternative for the Cumaean) and no. 10 (the Tiburtine). The first three of these could have been borrowed from Varro, but there is nothing to prove it. However, the reference to the Sibyl of Tibur is in quite a different category. The legend about her book being recovered from the Anio undamaged in the arms of a statue does not occur in any other author. As we saw, Varro, according to Lactantius, introduced it with *dicitur* (it is said). It is hard to believe that Tibullus had any other source than the *Antiquitates*, although he gives the story a somewhat different slant. Instead of the statue, it is the Sibyl herself who is described as miraculously bearing her prophetic book through the waters of the Anio. Perhaps this is just Tibullus' introduction of a poetic variation. Varro's version better fits what was obviously the original purpose of the legend — to account by a suitable marvel for the existence of a book of Sibylline prophecies attributed to the local nymph. Her name Albunea appears in Vergil's *Aeneid* as the name of the site of an oracle in the territory of Lavinium. Its derivation from the root of *albus* (white) would suggest a connection with the sulphur-impregnated streams which occur both at Albunea and near Tibur at Albula.[30]

The remaining list of Sibyls to be considered is very different. Heraclides and Varro both incorporated their catalogues in works dealing in a scholarly way with this aspect of the history of religion. Pausanias simply introduced his as a literary digression, so as to diversify the somewhat monotonous catalogue of the chief monuments at Delphi. Similarly, later in his tour, when he reaches the temple, he inserts an immensely long episode on the

Gallic invasion of 279 BC, linking it with the Gallic shields on the metopes. It had, of course, been a traditional device since at least the time of Herodotus to insert the texts of verse oracles so as to give variety to a prose narrative. But Pausanias had a special personal interest in the whole subject of prophetic divination. When we examine his account of the Sibyls, we shall see that he implies that he had done considerable reading on the question. Also casual allusions suggest that he had taken the trouble to visit sites connected with the subject. In the description of the Sibyls themselves he makes it clear that he had travelled to the proper places in the Troad; not merely to Alexandria Troas and the temple of Apollo Smintheus, but also to the out-of-the-way village of Marpessus. In Italy he had been guided round the temple of Apollo at Cumae and had made enquiries on the spot. But his personal commitment to the consultation of oracles is illustrated most dramatically in the fact that according to his own testimony he even went through the lengthy and difficult ritual of consulting Trophonius at Lebadeia, ending in the descent into the cavern.[31]

Therefore Pausanias' evidence on Sibyls needs to be treated as serious and reliable, so far as it goes. In particular it would be quite erroneous to suppose, as was usual in the late nineteenth century, that he is simply reproducing controversial matter from Hellenistic scholars without any private research on the subject. In fact his method is the antithesis of that of Varro and to some extent a return to that of Heraclides: he generally based his study on the reading of books of oracles and drew his conclusions from what he found in their texts or picked up on his explorations.[32]

The first few sentences of his discussion are unfortunately corrupted in our manuscripts. The exact emendations required are uncertain, but the general sense can be recovered without serious doubt. He begins with the Delphic tradition that the woman who sang standing on the rock in the sacred precinct was Herophile by name and was surnamed Sibylla. She was given this epithet from a predecessor, of whom Pausanias says he 'found that she was as ancient as any. The Greeks say that she was the daughter of Zeus and Lamia, the daughter of Poseidon, and they tell that she was the first of women to sing oracles, and the name Sibylla was given her by the Libyans.' So far Pausanias' account partly corresponds with those of previous scholars and partly differs. It is most unlikely that he had even consulted a source in Latin, such as Varro, but he agrees with him in placing the Libyan Sibyl high in antiquity. Varro's first Sibyl, the Persian, perhaps Pausanias had never heard of: for Nicanor must have been a very neglected author, and there is no indication for the independent circulation at this period of oracles attributed to the Persian Sibyl. The Libyan Sibyl appears essentially the same as Euripides' creation; a daughter of Lamia by Zeus and active in Libya. The interesting divergence is that according to Pausanias Sibylla was a Libyan name or title, not a descriptive epithet derived from Aeolic Greek, as in Varro. Even this point might have been made by Euripides, although, if so, it is perhaps strange that no echoes of it occur elsewhere. More likely some Hellenistic scholar commenting on Euripides' fantasy added this conjecture and dated the Libyan Sibyl further back in the mythical period than any other.[33]

Pausanias then returns to the Delphic Sibyl under the name of Herophile, and states that she was younger than the Libyan but evidently born before the Trojan War, for she revealed in her oracle prophetically that Helen would be brought up in Sparta for the ruin of Asia and Europe, and that on her account Ilion would be taken by the Greeks. The presence in the Delphic Sibyl's oracle of matter which would later be borrowed by Homer can be traced back at least to the Hellenistic period. But as the Erythraean Sibyl was also credited with having foretold the Trojan War, it is best regarded as a common theme in Sibylline prophecy.[34] Herophile was frequently used as the name for the Erythraean Sibyl, though not in Varro, where it occurs only as one of the possible names for the Cumaean. But Pausanias indicates that he has taken the name from the Sibyl's own oracle. For after a parenthetical reference to the Delians who attributed to her one of their hymns to Apollo, he adds:

> she calls herself not only Herophile, but also Artemis in her verses, and says she is Apollo's wedded wife and at another time his sister and again his daughter . . . . In another place in her oracles she said that she was of an immortal mother, one of the nymphs on Mount Ida, but of a human father. The verses run thus:

> and I am born betwixt a mortal and a god,
> of an immortal nymph and a father feeding on bread;
> from my mother Ida-born, but my fatherland is red
> Marpessus, consecrated to my mother, and its river is the
> Aidoneus.

38

Pausanias makes it clear that he was somewhat surprised at this extraordinary agglomeration of identities. He offers as an explanation: 'she has composed these verses in frenzy and under the possession of the god.' Otherwise, he seems to accept that she was really named Herophile, and also probably believes in the verses about her parentage and birthplace, which he quotes after his explanation about her derangement.

It would be possible to read Pausanias' account in the sense that he had collected these various personal allusions from a series of stray quotations from the Sibyl which he had encountered in his miscellaneous reading. But in view of the fact that he evidently accepted the theory of a multiplicity of Sibyls, it would be odd if he did not apply that explanation to such conflicting quotations. Instead the most reasonable view is that he had come across a collection of Sibylline oracles passing as the work of a single prophetess but actually a medley from different periods and places. Pausanias accepted the identity of the one authoress, and accounted for the discrepancies by the ravings of a prophetess in a state of divine possession.

Of the personalities involved, the one which Pausanias mentions after Herophile is Artemis, and this can be recognised as the same as the quotation given by Heraclides. The Sibyl in his catalogue, who called on the Delphians, described herself as Artemis and Apollo's own sister. Also the verses starting as an address without a connecting particle look as though they ought to have stood at the beginning of an oracle. Of the other identities the 'wedded wife of Apollo' is the most peculiar. It would flatly contradict the popular legend, which we shall later discuss, that the Sibyl had first promised Apollo her favours in return for the gift of long life, and then had refused them. This is the only place to suggest the Sibyl as actually Apollo's bride. The legend that she was his daughter can be traced elsewhere. The *Suda* baldly records as one of the versions of the Sibyl: 'a daughter of Apollo and Lamia'. She need not be identified with the Libyan Sibyl who was a daughter of Zeus and Lamia, but is to be recognised as the Delphian Sibyl whom Plutarch knew of; she 'arrived (at Delphi) from the Malians and was the daughter of Lamia, whose father was Poseidon.' This Lamia was evidently not the horrific monster of Greek folklore, but the queen who was the eponym of the capital of the Malians.[35]

Pausanias did not follow up the possible identifications of these different Sibylline personalities, but contented himself with having explained them away as due to the prophetess's ecstatic ravings. He goes on to cite with approval the legend attached to the temple of Apollo Smintheus in the Troad. He had been told there that Herophile had become a temple-servant (*neōkoros*) of Apollo, and in response to a dream of queen Hecabe had uttered an oracle which was fulfilled. This legend was evidently invented in Hellenistic times when Alexandria Troas had taken over the control of this region and wished to annex the Sibyl of Marpessus and connect her prophetic activity with their temple. The story that Hecabe, before the birth of Paris, had dreamed that she had been delivered of a firebrand which burned down Ilion, does not occur in Homer but was evidently known by the archaic period, as it is mentioned first in Pindar. Since a prophecy of the Trojan War formed part of the traditional oracle of the Marpessian Sibyl, it was easy as a later development to convert her into a priestess of Apollo consulted on the omen which had foretold that event.[36]

Pausanias was satisfied that his second Sibyl was a native of the Troad. To explain other local Sibyls he used the conventional hypothesis that she had travelled to the various sites with which she was associated. So he states that she spent much of her life on Samos, and also went to Claros, Delos and Delphi. This accounted for the Samian, Colophonian and Delphic Sibyls. Delos is not otherwise credited with a Sibyl: Pausanias probably had inserted it on his own initiative, since he already attributed to her the authorship of the Delian *Hymn to Apollo*. After her travels she died and was buried at the sanctuary of the Sminthian Apollo. Pausanias quotes in full the elegy inscribed on her tomb — a composition of Hellenistic date concocted to support the local claim that she had been a priestess of Apollo there.[37] He ends by noting in a sort of appendix the Erythraeans' case for Herophile, which he recognises as very passionately maintained. He describes in detail how they had explained away and curtailed the verses in which the Sibyl had described her origin from Marpessus, so as to make them support instead a pedigree from Erythrae, but he implies that this is not the authentic version.

The next Sibyl according to Pausanias was from Cumae in Campania, and he cites the local history of Hyperochus for her name, Demo. This is a hypocoristic form of Demophile, one of the three names which Varro gave as variants for the Cumaean Sibyl, but Pausanias shows no signs of having consulted any Latin author. Instead, just as in the Troad, he evidently tried the effect of a personal visit to Campania. The results were rather negative. The Cumaeans had no oracles of this woman to show. But they did exhibit a small water-jug (*hydria*) of stone, which they said contained the bones of the Sibyl. This was probably the same object which was shown a century or more later to the author of the *Cohortatio ad Graecos*, though he described it as a lentil-shaped jar (*phakos*) of bronze containing the Sibyl's remains. One or other of the tourists had failed to preserve a completely accurate note of what was shown by the guides. But the general sense was the same. It may also have been the object which was the foundation of the folk-tale which Petronius produces about the Sibyl hanging in a bottle (*ampula*). The container, however described, was evidently too small to provide room for a normal corpse. Either we are to suppose that, when Pausanias writes of the Sibyl's bones, he pictures them as cremated ashes, or else we must believe, as the folk-tale in Petronius implied, that she had ended by shrinking away until she would fit into a flask. Pausanias may have been told the story, but he had no high opinion of the testimony of the Cumaeans. Elsewhere he mentions that they exhibited in the temple of Apollo pig's tusks which they claimed by a sacred legend were those of the Erymanthian boar, but as he says: 'there is not even a little likelihood in the story.' In the matter of this Sibyl, he probably accepted that she had lived and died in Cumae, but did not wish to commit himself on the details of the local tradition. It is somewhat strange that he does not mention the Sibyl's cave, which had long been identified and was certainly shown by the guides in later days to the author of the *Cohortatio ad Graecos*. It may be simply on grounds of economy of space that Pausanias omits it. He mentions enough to establish the Cumaean Sibyl's name and identity as different from those he had already listed.[38]

His final Sibyl was a prophetess 'brought up in Palestine named Sabbe, whose father was Berosus and her mother Erymanthe. Some say she was a Babylonian, while others call her an Egyptian Sibyl.' The other Sibyls whom Pausanias listed can all be identified in various forms among those counted by Varro. But this Hebrew prophetess appears here for the first time in a catalogue. At least that is the safest assumption to make. Varro had a Persian Sibyl, for whom his authority was Nicanor who wrote a history of Alexander. But except for the fact that these two are the only oriental Sibyls on record, there is no ground for identifying them. Lactantius, who reproduces Varro's lists, does not do so. But, as we have seen, some of the later sources which based themselves on Lactantius insert statements, in approximately the same phrases, that the Persian Sibyl was also the Chaldaean or the Hebrew, that her name was Sambethe and that she was married to one of the sons of Noah. This must be the equivalent of Pausanias' Sabbe, whose name could be taken as another hypocoristic diminutive, standing to Sambethe like Demo to Demophile. Also as Sambethe is accepted as a genuine form of name derived from the Hebrew word, Sabbath, this prophetess was evidently connected with Jewish sources.[39] It is typical of Pausanias that he should disclose an acquaintance with such material. For by a number of references scattered through his work he shows that, not only was he interested in oracles, but also he was personally acquainted with Palestine where he had travelled extensively — which must have been unusual at this period. It is more probable, then, that he had collected this information about the Hebrew Sibyl there or from Jews known to him rather than from a literary source. Modern scholars have plumped for Alexander Polyhistor as Pausanias' authority on the rather feeble ground that he is the only earlier Greek author who shows that he knew Hebrew material in Sibylline oracles. But if, as we shall see, Pausanias might have got his information direct from the text of the prophecy, it would be in accordance with his regular method to have done so. Later the author of the *Cohortatio ad Graecos* knew a Sibyl as the 'daughter of Berosus who wrote the Chaldaean history' and that she set out from Babylon. He believed that she came to Cumae, but frankly admitted that he could not explain how. Probably, as a Christian in the late third century AD, he drew his information directly or indirectly from a version of the third book of the *Oracula Sibyllina* which already had been accepted as a work of prophecy. For it is clear that the Hebrew Sibyl is the only one who can be directly linked with that corpus.[40]

In the epilogue to the third book the Sibyl says:

These things to you when I left the high walls of Babylon in Assyria in frenzied madness sent to Greece as a fire prophesying to all mankind the wraths of God . . . . so that I should prophesy to men divine riddles, and men in Greece shall call me shameless, born of another land, from Erythre, who shall say that I am Sibylla, mad and mendacious, of Circe as mother and Gnostos as father. But whenever all these things have come to pass, then you will call me to mind and no longer will anyone say that I am mad, but the prophetess of mighty God.[41]

It is most tantalising that there is a lacuna towards the end of the first sentence, removing the main verb and also at least the beginning of the next sentence, possibly more. It has long been seen that it is quite likely that the Sibyl had given here her true name and her parentage. This would provide an effective contrast with what follows. Just as Babylon was falsely displaced by Erythre by the Greeks, so Gnostos and Circe and Sibylla (here treated as a name, not a title) require a correct father's and mother's names and a prophetess's name to correspond and give point to the contradiction. It is tempting and not unreasonable to suppose that the missing lines contained the name Sambethe or Sabbe for the prophetess, and Berosus and Erymanthe for the parents. But what might be regarded as an inconsistency must be noted. The prophetess of Book 3 ends by explaining how she had learned earlier events from her parents to whom they had been revealed by God. The rest she herself had received by divine inspiration. The point at which she had passed from tradition and experience to prophecy is indicated by a brief allusion to Noah and the flood, without mentioning the patriarch's name, and ending with a statement that she was his sister-in-law.

The picture of the Hebrew Sibyl sailing in the Ark with Noah was evidently the accepted Jewish invention. It is illustrated again in the statement made by the prophetess in Book 1 of the *Oracula Sibyllina*. The accounts of the Creation and the Flood which form Book 1 are not reproduced, as they should be, before Book 3, which so far as the biblical narrative goes begins with the Tower of Babel. However, the events before that were once described in a book preceding Book 3, as is implied by the Sibyl's concluding words which we have just quoted. But this portion must have been lost before the corpus was put together in the sixth century AD.[42]

If the Hebrew Sibyl was regarded as literally antediluvian in birth, it would be frankly absurd to suppose that her father was the well-known Berosus, author of the Babylonian or Chaldaean History, a work dedicated to Antiochus I. But it is possible that the absurdity did not worry the Jewish author of the third book of the *Oracula Sibyllina*. To him the name may have been just a convenient symbol for a Chaldaean *magus*, and the question of date may have been quite irrelevant. Perhaps one may cite as an analogy that strange piece of humorous parody, Propertius 4.1 where the soothsayer, Horus, asserts: 'The Babylonian Orops, descendant of Archytas, begat me, and my house is derived from Conon as great-grandfather.' This farrago of astronomical ancestry was meant to suggest the kind of absurd claims made by professional diviners. The references to Circe and Gnostos do not correspond to any actual traditions about the Erythraean Sibyl. The nymph, her mother, is nameless in the local inscription, where her father is Theodorus. It looks as though the original Jewish author once more was writing down an arbitrary invention. He knew of Circe as the name of an ancient Greek sorceress, therefore not unsuitable for the Greeks to choose as the mother of a diviner. Gnostos is more mysterious. It is not recognised as a normal proper name. As a common noun it should rather vaguely mean 'kinsman' or 'acquaintance'. More significantly, perhaps, the closely related form *gnōstēs* in the Septuagint would mean 'soothsayer'. In any case, whether these are the explanations or not, the names may be taken as the invention of the Jewish author.[43]

Why did he wish to declare a connection between his work and the Erythraean Sibyl? One explanation may be because of her considerable fame from the late fourth century BC. Of all the local Sibyls she is the most often mentioned, and so as to give his work the authority of pagan prophecy the Hellenising Jew who wrote it chose to associate it, even in this back-handed way, with the Erythraean. But another reason, we may conjecture, was because he had actually cribbed material from her. Varro had recorded, on the evidence of Apollodorus of Erythrae, that his native Sibyl 'had prophesied to the Greeks when they were on their way to Ilion that Troy would fall and that Homer would write falsehoods'. The third book contains a passage dealing with this very subject. The fall of Troy is foretold in an address to the city itself, and is followed by an attack on the mendacity of Homer. He is not named, but in the manner of oracles he is sufficiently indicated by an allusion to his blindness and to the fact that he will call himself a Chian, clearly alluding to the famous ending of the Delian *Hymn to Apollo*. The passage is not likely to have been borrowed word for word from the Erythraean Sibyl, for it is in style and diction rather Hellenistic, while the original Sibylline passage could not have been composed later than in the fourth century. The practice of taking over a theme of prophecy and reproducing it in paraphrase is illustrated again in the case of this very subject by the eleventh book of the *Oracula Sibyllina*, where, because of the connection of Aeneas with Rome, the Trojan War is foretold and Homer described once again, but in different words.[44]

Pausanias, then, as we have suggested, had encountered some version of Book 3 of the *Oracula Sibyllina*, probably in Palestine. This source would have suggested to him to describe this Sibyl with the Hebrew name as brought up there, and her own account stated that she was a Babylonian. Whence he derived the alternative description of her as an Egyptian remains unexplained. Actually much of the content of Book 3 points to some Jewish settlement in Egypt in the second century BC as the most likely place where the core of the oracle was put together. But it is not certain whether Pausanias here had encountered a piece of authentic tradition or just a scholarly guess.[45]

After Pausanias there is no pagan author extant who made a serious attempt to classify the Sibyls. Only Aelian, who was less a scholar than an erudite moralist, makes use of some previous lists. He is illustrating the instances of historic characters of the same name who are liable to be confused, and begins at the lowest point numerically with pairs, such as the two Perianders, proceeding next to threes, such as the Miltiades. Then 'the four Sibyls, the Erythraean, the Samian, the Egyptian, the Sardian: but others say there are a further six, so that there are ten in all among whom are the Cumaean and the Judaean'. The choice of the number four seems unique to Aelian among extant authors. Of them the Erythraean and the Samian present no problems: 'the Egyptian' could be Sambethe, if we accept one of Pausanias' alternative designations, and 'the Sardian' is, as we have seen, the description used by Philetas of Ephesus. But if Aelian borrowed it from him, he did not follow him in limiting the Sibyls to three. The other figure which Aelian recognised was ten, which was no doubt ultimately derived from Varro, but as cited by Aelian shows a discrepancy. Of the two additional Sibyls whom he names, the Cumaean is obvious, but the Judaean raises difficulties. She does not appear in Varro's list, unless we are following the late Byzantine sources who equated her with the Persian. Also, as Aelian has already listed the Egyptian, we are left with two Sibyls from the eastern Mediterranean. Actually, there are in the *Oracula Sibyllina* several books which seem to come from Jewish sources in Egypt, so that by Aelian's date and well before, there could have been another Egyptian Sibyl besides Sambethe. But it is wiser not to attempt a positive solution of the problem on such slight evidence.[46]

The Christian Fathers before Lactantius did not attempt to classify the Sibyls. The Jewish monotheism of the *Oracula Sibyllina* in their earliest forms laid them open to interpretation in Christian terms or even to Christian interpolation. So the idea could gradually develop that the Sibyls had been intended by God as the prophets to the Gentiles parallel to the Old Testament prophets who were God's mouthpiece to the Jews. Hence they are quoted quite often by Christian apologists, but with no attempt to distinguish them or locate them. The one exception before Lactantius is Clement of Alexandria to whom we owe (possibly indirectly) the citation about the Sibyl at Delphi from Heraclides of Pontus. He also used one of Plutarch's Delphic dialogues in a somewhat garbled way on the same subject, and in an extra-ordinary passage in the *Stromateis* he heaps up all the names he can find in Greek literature of prophets and oracle-mongers, male and female. In the middle of this medley he mentions 'the crowd of Sibyls: the Samian, the Colophonian, the Cumaean, the Erythraean, Phyto, Taraxandra, the Macedonian (*Maketis*), the Thessalian, the Thesprotian'. This is a mixture of proper names and local designations most of which have already occurred in our earlier list in one form or another, but several of which are not easily identifiable. They serve to warn us that there was doubtless much more material on the subject of Sibyls in the lost volumes of ancient literature.[47]

Notes

1. This is still a somewhat controversial issue. As we shall see, ancient scholars varied between explaining it as a designation meaning 'prophetess' (Varro *ap*. Lactant. *Div. Inst.* 1.6.3), or as a personal name transferred from an original holder to other seers by analogy (Paus. 10.12.1; Varro *ap*. Lactant. *Div. Inst.* 1.6.3; Appian, *F. Gr. Hist.* 156 f 95). For the view that it was a designation, E. Rohde, *Psyche: Seelencult und Unsterblichkeitsglaube der Griechen* (2nd edn, 1898), 292; E. Bevan, *Sibyls and seers* (1928), 48. M.P. Nilsson, *Geschichte der griechischen Religion* 1 (3rd edn, 1967), 2 (2nd edn, 1961), always speaks of Sibyls in the plural. For Sibylla as originally a proper name, A. Rzach, *RE* 2 (1923), cols 2074–5. There is nothing to show it is not a personal name in Heraclitus, Aristophanes and Euripides, and in Plato, *Theag.* 124D, it cannot be taken otherwise. Plato, *Phaedr.* 244B, should be similarly understood.

The plurals in Arist. *Probl.* 30, Quaest. 1, 954a 3b are best taken as generalising, although it is likely that by the time this was written, legends of at least two Sibyls and two Bacides were current.

2. Heraclitus, *ap.* Plut. *Mor.* 397A. For discussion, see *infra* pp. 63–4.

3. Ar. *Eq.* 61; *Pax* 116; 1095. For discussion, see *infra* pp. 103–4.

4. Euripides, *Fragmenta* p. 403 (Nauck); Snell, *Suppl.* p. 7. For discussion see *infra* pp. 104–5.

5. On Heraclides see F. Wehrli, *Herakleides Pontikos (Die Schule des Aristoteles* vol. 7 (2nd edn, 1969)); H.B. Gottschalk, *Heraclides of Pontus* (1980), who does not deal at any length with this aspect of Heraclides' work. Diog. Laert. 5.86–93.

6. Wehrli (*supra* n. 5), fr. 130–41.

7. Varro *ap.* Lactant. *Div. Inst.* 1.6.9 (Wehrli (*supra* n. 5) fr. 131 a–c); Paus. 10.12.3. cf. *infra* p. 40; Nic. Dam., *F. Gr. Hist.* 90 f. 68.8.

8. Clem. Al. *Strom.* 1.21.384P (Wehrli (*supra* n. 5) fr. 130). Paus. 10.12.1; 7.

9. Clem. Al. *loc. cit.* n. 8.

10. Plut. *Mor.* 398C; Paus. 10.12.2. Cf. *infra* pp. 37–40.

11. Procl. *In Tim.* 1.90 (Diehl).

12. Philetas of Ephesus, Sch. Ar. *Pax* 1071; *Av.* 962; Suda, *s.v..* Bakis; C. Müller, *Fragmenta Historicorum Graecorum* vol. 4 (1851), 474.

13. Apollodorus of Erythrae, *F. Gr. Hist.* 422. I agree with Jacoby that Apollodorus asserted a claim to the one Sibylla for his city, but I do not accept all the arguments in his lengthy commentary. Athenais, Strabo 14.1.54; 17.1.43. Callisthenes, *F. Gr. Hist.* 124 f. 14a.

14. Hyperochus of Cumae, *F. Gr. Hist.* 576; H. Lloyd-Jones and P. Parsons (eds), *Supplementum Hellenisticum* (1983), 498–500. The earliest reference to the Cumaean Sibyl in an extant Greek author is Lycophron (*Alex.* 1277). For further discussion, *infra* pp. 71–2.

15. Eratosthenes, *F. Gr. Hist.* 241 f.26 (Varro *ap.* Lactant. *Div. Inst.* 1.69); *F. Gr. Hist.* 544 f.4. Cf. F. Jacoby, *Atthis: the local chronicles of ancient Athens* (1949), ch. 3, para 4. Euseb. *Chron.* pp. 91.13; 94.12 (Helm).

16. B. Cardauns (ed.), *M. Terentius Varro, Antiquitates rerum divinarum* 2 pts (1976), 1. fr. 56 (Lactant. *Div. Inst.* 1.6). Scholars differ on whether Lactantius copied direct from Varro. S. Brandt, *Wiener Studien* 13 (1891) 255ff was the first to challenge direct knowledge. Cardauns, ibid., 2.165 argues for direct use; R.M. Ogilvie, *The library of Lactantius* (1978), 53, against.

17. As Cardauns (*supra* n. 16) 2.165 points out, Varro thought the Arcadians of Evander's settlement spoke Aeolic, a theory which he may have borrowed from Cato (Joannes Lydus, *De Mag.* 1.5; Peter, *HRR* 1. p. 61 fr. 19). Varro also derived the Latin *bulla* from Aeolic *bolla* (Plut. *Mor.* 288B). Cf. also Varro, *De Ling. Lat.* 21 (Evander), and for Aeolic etymologies, 25.101; 102; 175. It does not affect our argument that σιούς would be better described as Laconian.

18. Cf. *infra* p. 33.

19. For a fuller discussion of this legend see *infra* pp. 76–8.

20. This last clause — 'and her lots were removed to the Capitol by the Senate' — is rather clumsily appended and is found only in two manuscripts, R and S, which are, however, of good authority. There is

evidence elsewhere to suggest that our manuscripts of the *Div. Inst.* represent more than one state of the text. Lactantius appears to have revised it, mostly for theological reasons, but may have cancelled this clause on grounds of style. The reference to the Senate probably derives from Varro, as it implied that this Sibyl was dated after the fall of the kings, and so justified her position last in the series.

21. Nicanor, *F. Gr. Hist.* 146. For explicit mention of Alexander's deeds, Sch. Pl. *Phaedr.* 244B. The Chaldaean priests' warning, Arr. *Anab.* 7.16.5. Berosus, *F. Gr. Hist.* 680 f. 3.13.

22. For Chrysippus' books on divination, Cic. *Div.* 1.6; 1.37; J. von Arnim, *Stoicorum Veterum Fragmenta* vol. 2 (1903), 342–8 esp. nos. 1214–16.

23. Naevius, *Bellum Punicum* fr. 12 (Strezelecki). Piso, fr. 41 (Peter, *HRR*). Serv. *Verg. Aen.* 9.17 (Naevius fr. 13). Auctor *De Orig. Gent. Rom.* 10 (not included by Peter). Cf. *infra* pp. 72–4.

24. Livy 1.8.6.

25. Ancient authorities which tell the legend naming the Tarquin as Superbus, but not specifying the Sibyl: (1) Dion. Hal. 4.62.2 (not citing his source, although he cites Varro on the later history of the Sibylline books). (2) Pliny, *HN* 13.84. (3) Aulus Gellius 1.19. (4) Zonaras 7.11. The identification of the Sibyl as Cumaean occurs only in Varro and later authorities reproducing his list of ten, and in Solinus 2.16 and Tzetzes, *In Lyc.* 1279 (usually printed as Dio Cass. fr. 10.8). But Tzetzes (Dio) and Solinus refer to Tarquinius Superbus, although Solinus inconsistently dates the event to the 50th Olympiad (i.e. 580 BC). Other disagreements between extant accounts are: (1) How many books? Usually nine reduced to three, but three reduced to one in Pliny and Solinus. Tzetzes and Zonaras mention both alternatives. (2) Did the Sibyl burn the books in the king's presence or go away between her offers? Present: Varro, Aulus Gellius, Zonaras(?); absent: Dionysius. Tzetzes in a unique version makes the Sibyl's servant offer the books and burn them after the Sibyl's death. (3) Dionysius and Zonaras make the king consult augurs before his final decision — a feature not found elsewhere. (4) The Sibyl vanishes after the purchase, Varro, Dionysius Aulus Gellius; Solinus refers instead to her grave in Sicily at Lilybaeum, while only Varro and those derived from him name the price (300 philippei).

26. Isidore, *Origines* 8.8.

27. Martianus Capella 2.159 (p. 67.10 Dick). He makes the Erythraean Sibyl come also to Cumae and names her Symmachia, the daughter of Hippotensis.

28. Joannes Lydus, *de Mensibus* 4.47; Sch. Pl. *Phaedr.* 244 B; *Tübingen Theosophy* 121; Prologue to the *Or. Sib.* 29. See also *Chronicon Pascale* 1.201 (Dindorf), which has a list of eleven Sibyls.

29. For the date and family of Tibullus' patron see R. Syme, *History in Ovid* (1978), 118. B. Cardauns, *Hermes* 89 (1961), 357ff, argues that the prophecy to Aeneas takes place at Cumae, i.e. that it was given by the Cumaean Sibyl, while F. Cairns, *Tibullus: a Hellenistic poet at Rome* (1979), 66, maintains that the prophecy was given within sight of burning Troy, i.e. by the Marpessian Sibyl. I prefer the latter. For the list of Sibyls, see Tib. 2.5.67–70. The text of line 68 is disputed. The reading of the best

manuscript (A) is *Heriphile phebo grata quod admonuit*. With corrected spelling of the proper names this presents no difficulty in sense, provided a comma is inserted at the end of the previous line. But Lachmann, following on Huschke, ingeniously changed this to: *Herophile, Phoeto Graia quod admonuit*. I follow A. Kurfess, *Würzb. Jahrb. für Altertumsw.* 3 (1948), 405, in retaining the manuscript reading and punctuating accordingly.

30. Cardauns (*supra* n. 16), 2.166, suggests that both versions were given by Varro, and that Lactantius reproduced one version and Tibullus the other. But this seems to me rather improbable. Albunea as the nymph at or near Tibur, Hor. *Od.* 1.7.12. Albula as the name of the sulphur springs near Tibur (Tivoli), Vitruv. *De Arch.* 8.3.2; Mart. 1.12.2; Stat. *Silv.* 1.3.75 – it is not to be confused with the ancient name of the Tiber (Verg. *Aen.* 8.332). Albunea also appears as the site of an oracle of Faunus in Verg. *Aen.* 7.81. The site, correctly identified with the sulphurous region near Lavinium (Pratica), is fully discussed by B. Twilly, *Vergil's Latium* (1947), 106ff. Nearby were also cults of female fates or prophetesses, as shown by a find of inscriptions (R.E. Palmer, *Roman religion and Roman empire* (1974) 89ff). The extant Tiburtine Sibyl's oracles cannot be traced further back than a Christian author of the late fourth century: see P.J. Alexander, *The oracle of Baalbek: the Tiburtine Sibyl in Greek dress* (1967), 48–66.

31. Digression on the Sibyls, Paus. 10.12.1–11. Digression on the Gallic raid, Paus. 10.19.5–23.14 (cf. 1.4.1–6). Pausanias' reading of oracular texts, 10.12.11. His explorations, 10.12.4 (Marpessus); 10.12.6 (Alexander Troas); 10.12.8 (Cumae — also 8.24.5). For other examples, 9.15.1 (Ammon); 9.39.5–14 (Trophonius). I believe that Pausanias' curiously oblique description of the interior of the temple of Apollo at Delphi is explained by the fact that it was closed at the time of his visit: H.W. Parke, *Hermathena* 49 (1935), 102–5.

32. For the late nineteenth-century view, see, for instance, E. Maass, *De sibyllarum indicibus* (1879), 22ff.

33. For a fuller discussion of the Libyan Sibyl see *infra* pp. 104–5. Maas, loc. cit. n. 32, is needlessly dogmatic in denying that Euripides can have derived the name Sibylla from the Libyans.

34. For the Delphic Sibyl producing verses borrowed by Homer, see Diod. 4.66, where she is identified as Daphne, the daughter of Tiresias dedicated as a spoil from the capture of Thebes by the Epigoni — a curious intrusion from the legend of Manto. Also Bocchus fr. 1 (Peter). Herophile of Erythrae foretelling the Trojan War, Apollodorus of Erythrae, *F. Gr. Hist.* 422 f 1.

35. The Sibyl as Artemis, Heraclides Ponticus *ap.* Clem. Al. *Strom.* 1.21.384P (cf. *supra* pp. 26–7). For an obscure reference to the Cumaean Sibyl as Apollo's sister, Sch. Lycoph. *Alex.* 1279. As Apollo's daughter by Lamia, *Suda*, Σ 355. Plut. *Mor.* 389c. For Lamia, the eponymous queen of the capital of the Malians, see Schwenn, *RE* 12 (1924), col. 546, no. 2–3. Cf. *infra* p. 114.

36. Pind. *Paean.* 8a.17 (Snell).

37. D.L. Page, *Further Greek epigrams* (1981), 489–90.

38. Paus. 10.12.8 (*F. Gr. Hist.* 576 f.2). *Cohortatio ad Graecos* 37.

Petronius, *Sat.* 48.8. The alleged tusks of the Erymanthian boar, Paus. 8.24.4.

39. The equation of the Persian and the Chaldaean Sibyl, cf. *supra* pp. 32–3. For Sambethe as a Jewish name in Ptolemaic Egypt, and Sambas as a common hypocoristic form in the Roman and Byzantine periods, see V.A. Tcherikover *et al.*, *Corpus Papyrorum Judaicarum* III (1964), 43ff, section XIII.

40. Pausanias' references to Palestine, 1.4.7; 4.35.9; 5.5.2; 5.7.4; 6.24.8; 9.19.8. Alexander Polyhistor, *F. Gr. Hist.* 273 c 79b (pp. 110–11). *Cohortatio ad Graecos*, 37: the author knows *Or. Sib.* 3.721–3, and so could have collected the data about the Sibyl from the oracle itself, adding the identification of Berosus as the historian. It was a favourite late legend that the Erythraean Sibyl had come to settle in Cumae — cf. *infra* pp. 78–9.

41. *Or. Sib.* 3.809ff.

42. *Or. Sib.* 1.289–90. For evidence of the book missing before *Or. Sib.* 3, cf. the heading, 'from the second book concerning god'; fr. 1 (Geffcken) introduced by Theophilus, *Ad Autolycum* 2.36, 'Sibylla . . . in the beginning of her prophecy'. Lactantius (*Div. Inst.* 4.6.5) quotes fragment 1.5 as *Sibylla Erythrae in carminis sui principio*. For a retrospective reference to the events before the Flood, *Or. Sib.* 3.820.

43. Berosus, *F. Gr. Hist.* 680. Erymanthe is unexplained. Can it be another of the Jewish author's inventions? I would suggest, however absurd, that he might have derived from ἐρι and μάντις — 'good prophetess'.

44. Apollodorus of Erythrae, *F. Gr. Hist.* 422. *Or. Sib.* 3.414ff (Trojan War); 3.419ff (Homer); 11.127ff (Trojan War); 11.163ff (Homer).

45. One may note the curious fact, unexplained, that in the *Chronicon Pascale* 1.201 (Dindorf), the Erythraean Sibyl is described as flourishing in Egypt in 804 BC.

46. Ael. *VH* 35.

47. Clem. Al. *Strom.* 1.21.384P (Heraclides); 1.15.358P (Plutarch); 1.21.398P (the great medley list). No doubt many scholarly works containing lists of Sibyls are lost; for example, Rufus (second/third century AD), *F. Gr. Hist.* 826 T.2 (Phot. *Bibl.* 161, 103–4), is said in the fourth and fifth books of his *Mousike Historia* to have dealt with Sibyls.

3

Archaic Sibyls of Eastern Greece

As the man they called 'Ho!' told his story of woe
  In an antediluvian tone.

The Sibylline oracles, as we have seen, were discursive poems in
hexameter verse. The speaker was a woman who claimed more
than human insight into the future and, uttering words in her
own person, foretold mostly disasters. Some of these were past
events of Greek legend, such as the Trojan War; others were
historic happenings thinly veiled in obscure and symbolic
phrases. As the earliest extant reference to Sibylla is dated about
500 BC, these oracles are shown to be originally a product of the
archaic period. If one tries to be more precise in defining the
context of their origin, one is driven back on conjecture. The
earliest Sibyls of later scholarship, such as the Persian and the
Libyan, can easily be rejected as fictions. The Delphic does not
seem to be founded on a genuine primitive tradition. Everything
points to Hellenic Asia Minor as the first home of this form of
prophecy. There one encounters rival claims to antiquity which
have been variously assessed by ancient and modern scholars.

The key document in this controversy, as we have seen, was
quoted by Pausanias. It consisted of the four lines of hexameter
verse, taken from her oracle, in which the prophetess describes
her origin: 'and I am born betwixt a mortal and a god, of an
immortal nymph and a father feeding on bread; on my mother's
side Ida-born, but my fatherland is red Marpessus consecrated to
my mother and its river is the Aidoneus.'[1] Marpessus was a
village in the interior of the Troad, reckoned politically as in the
territory of the Gergithes, a native tribe centred on Gergis or
Gergithus. Pausanias, who had evidently travelled in the neigh-

bourhood, probably on purpose to view the site, mentions the reddish soil and the river Aidoneus, which vanished underground and returned again to the surface. This peculiarity must have given the river its name associating it with Hades. John Cook has explored the district and identified the location, which still exhibits these features. Marpessus must always have been an out-of-the-way and unimportant place. Pausanias describes it in his own day as ruinous and having some 60 inhabitants. By his time it was politically part of Ilion, to whose territory Gergis had been assigned by the Romans in 189 BC as an honour for the Troy to which they traced their legendary origin.[2]

The Erythraeans, as Pausanias explains, disposed of this very positive evidence in favour of Marpessus by a series of ingenious re-interpretations and alterations. They said that 'Ida-born' meant 'born on the wooded hills' on the ground that *ida* here was not a proper name but a word for a wooded hill. Philologically this was not in itself objectionable. Also it was easy to change 'red' (*erythre*) into the proper name Erythrae, which was derived from the same root. Then all that was needed was to delete the final line with its mention of Marpessus and the Aidoneus, and the Sibyl was made to say that she was a native of Erythrae.

Some modern scholars have accepted all this argument and believe in the truth of the Erythraean case. But it is much more plausible to treat it all as special pleading and to suppose that the Marpessian version was the original text of the oracle, rather than to take it that the original text had been what the Erythraeans alleged and that it had been expanded by some Marpessian forger into the longer version, as quoted by Pausanias. I believe that the best case can be made out for the birthplace of Sibylline prophecy in the Troad, and that this supposition is supported by various other arguments.

The Troad itself need not appear an improbable region for the production of hexameter verse in the archaic period. It is usually agreed that the *Homeric Hymn to Aphrodite* has signs of a local connection with that neighbourhood. The legends linking the south Troad with the sons of Aeneas are less to be taken as evidence of an authentic connection with the Trojan hero than as a proof that from the archaic period the inhabitants of this region took a lively interest in the epic tradition. So it is possible to believe that in the post-Homeric times someone in the Troad could have composed the earlier Sibylline prophecies.

The unimportance and isolation of Marpessus make it all the

more convincing that some foundation lies behind the legend. Otherwise the choice of this place as the home of the prophetess lacks much motive. Her title also appears to have been originally a personal name, not found elsewhere in Greek but probably Asianic in derivation and belonging to the native language of the Gergithes. So the possibility is at least open that there was an actual person behind the legend — a local wise-woman, whose name was borrowed to provide the pseudonym for some archaic writer of oracles. If one needs to confirm that this was feasible, a curiously close parallel is available from seventeenth-century England in the person of Ursula Shipton, Mother Shipton of Knaresborough. Her name was used to cover prophecies from the period of the Civil Wars. But whether she was an actual individual living in the early sixteenth century in an out-of-the-way village in the north of England, as was alleged, or whether she was a literary figment, is disputed.[3]

The earliest Sibylline oracle might have been composed by someone from elsewhere in Greece, who simply chose to imagine a Sibylla of Marpessus as the pseudonymous author. In fact Marpessus might have been selected as the source, because it was out of the way and therefore not likely to be investigated by the sceptical, while the Gergithes, whom Herodotus described as the remnants of the Teucri, could appropriately be credited with possessing ancient traditions.[4] But this kind of complicated imaginative construction, involving some knowledge of the local features of Marpessus, would be more likely to be the work of some Hellenistic writer rather than one of the archaic period. Yet the rival claims of Marpessus and Erythrae had already been launched before the end of the fourth century as is shown by their appearance in Heraclides. Hence, though the historical existence of Sibylla, as of Mother Shipton, must remain uncertain, the connection of the early oracle with the Troad is reasonably likely, just as Mother Shipton's prophecies certainly originated in the north of England. Once Marpessus had become the source of a tradition of fictitious prophecy, it had an effect on the picture of the prophetess. For, as we shall see, the mythical themes which clustered round her had strong links with the Troad.

It is a commonly expressed view that the Sibyls appropriately originated in Asia Minor, because that continent was the primal home of ecstatic prophecy. Of course it is true that many examples of such a form of divination are found in Asia from records going back to very early periods, but one must also admit that some kind of ecstasy can be traced in any direction in the world. If we are to avoid the pitfalls in any rash application to the Sibyl's origin of a diffusionist explanation, we must consider carefully how far the records of ecstatic prophecy elsewhere correspond to the special characteristics of Sibylline oracles.[5]

Recent evidence from inland Syria in the period 750–650 BC shows Balaam delivering a very Sibylline type of oracle, the chief difference between him and Sibylla being that he received his inspiration in a vision of the night. As this proves the existence of a literary text in Aramaic of a Sibylline character, it would not be impossible to believe that it might have circulated to places reached by Greeks and have been understood by one of them who used Aramaic as a means of communication. The main point against a connection between Sibylla and Balaam is that the Troad as a district is much less likely to have been in contact with the ports of Phoenicia than Euboea or Corinth or even Miletus.

Alternatively, there is evidence for Aeolis having had early contact inland with the powers to the East. Cyme had links with King Midas of Phrygia.[6] But there is unfortunately no evidence surviving for Phrygian or Lydian prophecy. When Herodotus records the Lydian kings' use of divination, the only source which he mentions (apart from Apolline oracle-centres) is the Telmessians of Caria, who were apparently consulted to interpret omens. He assigns one consultation to the end of Croesus' reign and another legendary instance to the reign of Meles, an early Heraclid. Also the acquisition of the kingship of Phrygia by Gordius was attributed to his consultation of the Telmessians. Might one conclude from these examples that the Phrygians and Lydians had no native system of divination, but depended on sending to Caria for the interpretation of omens, just as Romans sent to Etruria for *haruspices*?[7] If they had taken over any practices of divination from their predecessors, the Hittites, there is no evidence that these would have included anything like Sibylline prophecy.

The other direction from which Sibylla might have derived a model was from Assyria. Burkert has lately called attention to the possibility of contact between Hellenic and Assyrian cultures in the seventh century, when the power of Ashurbanipal reached to Cyprus and Cilicia. There is no doubt that features in Assyrian arts and crafts influenced Greece, and even the Greek epic by the title of the *Cypria* admitted some debt to Cyprus. But in themselves cuneiform tablets could not have conveyed meaning to the Greeks. So the existence of one quasi-Sibylline prophecy in the library of Ashurbanipal is not of itself sufficient ground on which to build a theory of the oriental origin of Sibylline prophecy. Burkert argues for wandering diviners and magicians, but even if they are admitted as a possibility, it is hard to believe that their influence would exhibit itself first in the Troad.[8]

In the view of the present writer there are no such striking resemblances between Eastern prophecy and Greek Sibyls as to compel one to believe that there was an inspiration derived from the Orient. Contacts with Aramaic in Phoenicia would probably be more likely than with Akkadian on the fringe of the Assyrian empire. But neither is a necessary hypothesis. The characteristic elements of the Sibylline oracles do not need an external explanation to account for their origin.

The lines giving Sibylla's genealogy do not do anything to fix her date, except in so far as a person of such half-divine origin would usually be assigned to mythical periods. But Pausanias, who quotes the lines, was satisfied that she was born before the Trojan War, because she prophesied such events as the birth of Helen with its disastrous consequences. Elsewhere we hear of Sibylline oracles that went further and actually foretold that Homer would borrow verses from her to adorn his epic, and this was confirmed by the occurrence of such lines in the *Iliad*. We need not, of course, suppose that Homer was actually named by Sibylla. It would be sufficient, and more suitable to oracular style, if she had referred to him by an easily understood periphrasis, such as 'the man of Chios' as used by Semonides of Amorgos as early as the beginning of the sixth century BC.[9]

Ancient scholars treated all this as serious evidence, and believed that Sibylla had lived before the time of the Trojan War at the latest. But now we would not doubt that her pseudo-prophecies must be read in an opposite sense as a proof that these Sibylline oracles were composed after the *Iliad* had begun to circulate freely in Eastern Greece. This is no precise indication of dates, but suggests a period not much before 600 BC as an earliest *terminus post quem*.

Plagiarism from the *Iliad* was not the only link between Sibylla and the epic tradition. Two legendary motifs attached to her appear in the Epic Cycle and the Homeric Hymns, though not in the works of Homer himself. One is the penalty which falls on the maiden who promises Apollo her favours and then withholds them. The other is the error of asking the gods for long life or immortality but not for immortal youth. The first is associated particularly with Cassandra, who in the *Iliad* is the fairest of Priam's daughters but not otherwise remarkable. In the *Odyssey* she has become Agamemnon's share of the booty of Ilion, and is killed together with him by Clytemnestra. In the *Iliou Persis* she is dragged from the sanctuary of Athena's statue by the lesser Ajax (and later accounts add that she was raped by him).[10] These episodes could all be regarded as logically the dramatic consequences of being the most beautiful daughter of the king of a captured city. The theme that she was a prophetess is quite unrelated to the Homeric scene, and seems to turn on her link with her brother, Helenus. He is represented by Homer as outstanding both as a warrior and as a seer; a useful foil to Hector. But Homer, as is his usual practice when describing divination, does not picture him as giving discursive forecasts. Instead he advises on action through an intuitive knowledge of the minds of the gods. His role as a prophet took on more importance in the legends of the fall of Ilion, where he is made the source of revelations about the charms needed to capture the city. Helenus and Cassandra were treated together as prophetic in the *Cypria*. The Proclus summary (an abridgement of a paraphrase) baldly states: 'Thereafter Alexandros (Paris) built ships on the advice of Aphrodite, and Helenus foretold to him about the future, and Aphrodite bade Aeneas sail with him, and Cassandra revealed about the future.' It is teasing to find the brother and sister behaving in this exactly parallel way. The bare summary does not explain why they both are shown producing discursive prophecies of the consequences of Paris' voyage. Did Helenus forecast success — a return with a beautiful bride, and Cassandra disaster — the consequent sack of Ilion?[11]

The only other place where we find the brother and sister linked again in this way is in a legend explaining how they acquired the gift of divination. As children they had been left overnight in the temple of Apollo, and in the morning serpents were found licking their ears. This motif was evidently based on a primitive superstition, found also in the legend of Melampus the prophet, that this action of the serpents conveyed the gift of understanding the speech of birds. It has no function in conferring the power of ecstatic divination and was essentially unconnected with Apollo. But later an effort had been made to drag in the god by placing the scene of the miracle in his temple.[12]

The motif that Apollo had been the frustrated lover of

Cassandra appears first in Aeschylus' *Agamemnon*, where it is worked out in detail in a dialogue between her and the chorus. From the form of the presentation it is generally believed that the legend was expected to be already familiar to the audience, and scholars usually assume a derivation from Stesichorus' treatment of the *Oresteia* in the mid-sixth century. But this may have been an intermediate stage in the transmission of the motif, whose earliest appearance may have been in the *Cypria*. Apart from the tragic irony of the prophetess who foretells disaster but cannot convince her hearers, the motif was useful as providing a satisfying explanation for what was otherwise a curious implausibility: if Cassandra foretold the fall of Troy, why did no one stop Paris from sailing?[13]

The theme of the gift of prophecy combined with the curse of failure to convince the hearers may well have been invented for this context in the Epic cycle, but it would be equally useful if attached to Sibylla, who similarly foretold disasters which were never averted. Yet actually there is no ancient authority for this application. Instead the legend of Apollo, the frustrated lover, is joined with the second motif which we have mentioned — the mistaken prayer for long life, not immortal youth. It appears first in a late narrative in Ovid, who tells in his own vividly sophisticated manner what must have been a long-established legend. The Cumaean Sibyl explains to Aeneas that she is not a goddess, though she has been offered immortality if only she would yield her virginity to Apollo. The god, wooing her, promised her the fulfilment of her wish, and she grasped a handful of sand and asked for as many years as it contained grains. This was granted, but she had forgotten to ask for eternal youth. Although she would have obtained that also, if she had yielded herself to him, she refused, and therefore was fated to grow older and older until she had reached the number of the grains of sand. When she was speaking to Aeneas, she had lived seven hundred years and had still three hundred remaining. By then she would have shrunk to the tiniest scale until there was nothing left but her voice.[14]

The relations of Apollo and the Sibyl in this later narrative are rather confused, but it appears as if the grant of her wish was designed as a payment in advance, and eternal youth would have followed her actual submission to the god. One model at the back of the legend is the story of Tithonus, the brother of Priam, who was carried off by the Dawn Goddess. She asked Zeus to give him immortality, which was granted, but had failed to ask for youth. So when he became utterly feeble, she shut him away in a room from which his voice flowed ceaselessly. This is the version in the *Homeric Hymn to Aphrodite*, which is usually recognised as having some connection with the Troad. Hellanicus made the Dawn Goddess turn Tithonus into a cicada (*tettix*): he was reduced to a twittering voice that went on and on. In Homer the Dawn Goddess rises from Tithonus' bed with no suggestion that he is other than a normal consort.[15]

The two motifs originally linked with Cassandra and Tithonus have become combined in their attachment to Sibylla, and in the process have become somewhat distorted from their original forms. Neither Ovid nor any other author gives a legend to explain how Sibylla received her gift of prophecy, and in this they may correctly represent ancient tradition. When Sibylla claimed to be born of a nymph that was probably in itself sufficient. These primitive spirits of the wild could inspire frenzy, which might take the form of prophecy. Bacis, the counterpart of Sibylla on the Greek mainland, is explicitly described as inspired by the Nymphs. So there was no need to introduce Apollo into the legend of Sibylla as the source of her prophecies. In fact, it was highly appropriate, we shall see, for there to be instead a love-hate relationship between the two.[16]

Sibylla might also have inherited longevity from her mother, whom she describes as immortal. Nymphs were not always reckoned to be immortal, but lived far beyond the human span. However, it was particularly important, as we have seen, for Sibylla to be able to claim a primeval origin, so as to be able to make her prophecies antedate the legendary events which they described. That a thousand years was the traditional version of her lifespan is shown not only by Ovid, but by the earliest reference to her by Heraclitus. When he says that her prophecies reached a thousand years he is not dating her origin conjecturally, but reproducing some claim of antiquity found in her own words.[17]

If, as we have suggested, we can take the end of the seventh century as the earliest probable period for the origin of the Sibylline oracles, it was a time when Apolline divination was well established in Asia Minor. The oracle-centres of Didyma and Claros could trace their origins to pre-Hellenic cults in these sites, and their importance was growing with the development of Miletus and Colophon, their neighbouring Greek city-states. Also the Apolline cult at Delphi, beginning in the eighth century and becoming the most important mainland oracle-centre early in the seventh century, had been recognised by Midas of Phrygia, and by the mid-seventh century was exercising strong influence on Lydia. Hence any new form of prophecy arising in this period would have to explain its relationship to Apollo. The legend of Cassandra provided a convenient model of a prophetess of doom estranged from the god. So it became applied to Sibylla in a conveniently adapted form suggested by the myth of Tithonus.

Besides these links with Homer and the post-Homeric epic, an argument for dating Sibylla to the end of the seventh century can be drawn from one prophecy attributed to one of the Sibyls in a late source. Solinus, probably drawing on some Hellenistic treatise on divination, states that 'long before it happened, Herophile of Erythrae warned that the Lesbians would lose their command of the sea.' The conventional list of the thalassocracies ('those who ruled the sea') was drawn up by some Hellenistic scholar, and according to it the Lesbians held this command about the end of the seventh and the beginning of the sixth century BC. This was the period when Mytilene under the leadership of Pittacus dominated the island and engaged in territorial expansion on the coast of the Troad. It is most improbable that Sibylla actually used the word 'thalassocracy' — which was a concept not earlier than the fifth century in origin. But it is easy to suppose that in some allusive verses she may have foretold that the naval power of Lesbos would collapse. The Hellenistic scholar then paraphrased this prediction in the terms of his own day. One need not suppose that the Sibylline warning was forged *post eventum*, and so belongs to a period in the sixth century when Mytilene's power had declined from its previous pinnacle. To those living in the Troad within possible reach of Lesbian aggression the fall of its naval strength must have been something to wish for and an attractive subject of popular prophecy. Then, when the power of Mytilene dwindled, the forecast could be regarded as fulfilled and on the strength of this success would retain its position in the body of oracles transferred from the Marpessian to the Erythraean Sibyl.[18] For we should note that the claim of Erythrae, supported by doctored lines from the oracles of the Marpessian Sibyl, indicates that the Erythraean Sibyl took over some at least of the prophecies of her predecessor.

For the history of the Sibyls the prophecy about the Lesbian thalassocracy is important as an example unlikely to have been forged. The relations of Mytilene and her neighbours were not of major importance to the later Greek world, but it is exactly appropriate that a passage of this sort should occur originally in the writings of a prophetess of Marpessus in the late seventh century BC. Yet though appropriate as a topic, it would not be sufficient of itself to inspire the invention of Sibylline prophecy. What was the disaster, actual or imagined, which gave the primal impulse to create these oracles? The Cimmerian invasion in the first quarter of the seventh century is rather too early to fit with our estimate, and there is no reference connecting it with Sibylla. The next events of sufficient magnitude are the rise of the Lydian hegemony and its pressure on the Greek colonies of Aeolis and Ionia. Here we have some evidence for a connection.

Heraclides of Pontus, as we saw, stated that the Marpessian Sibyl 'lived in the time of Solon and Cyrus'. From his method it is likely that he based this supposition on some passages in her oracles which could be interpreted as referring to these persons or events connected with them. That there could be some connection drawn between the Sibyl and the fall of Lydia is confirmed by another piece of evidence — Nicolaus of Damascus' account of Croesus on the pyre.

The very detailed section of his *Universal history* which dealt with the Lydian kings was to some extent based on Herodotus, but also drew much native tradition from the lost works of Xanthus the Lydian. As Jacoby has pointed out, Nicolaus sometimes lifted passages from his authorities, but at other times worked up his various sources into set pieces of his own sensational writing. Such a passage is the scene of Croesus on the pyre. The main source is Herodotus, but it is recast so as to include other matter, which, apart from Nicolaus' own fantasies, must be based ultimately on Xanthus:

As Croesus was mounting the pyre, Sibylla was seen to descend from a height so that she herself might observe the happenings. Quickly a murmur passed through the crowd that the singer of oracles had come, and all were in expectation to see if she would be inspired with regard to the situation. After a short pause she shouted vehemently: 'Miserable men, why do you pursue what is impious? Neither Zeus nor Phoebus nor famous Amphiaraus will permit it. But obey the undeceiving oracles of my words, lest you perish by an evil fate for your folly against God.'

Cyrus, when he heard her, bade them distribute the
oracle among the Persians that they might be warned
against their error.

(Nicolaus, unlike Herodotus, represents the decision to burn
Croesus as taken by the Persians against the will of Cyrus.)[19]

This Sibylline oracle cannot have been borrowed by Nicolaus
from Xanthus verbatim, because of the extraordinary reference to
Amphiaraus. This is clearly derived from Herodotus, who had
inserted in his account of the testing of the oracles by Croesus two
references to the fact that, besides the Pythian Apollo, Amphiaraus
too had proved to have an undeceiving oracle-centre and had
therefore been rewarded by the king with a shield and spear of
gold.[20] These insertions create a serious break in the pattern of
the unique infallibility of the Delphic oracle, which Herodotus
otherwise reproduces. He had received his main narrative at
Delphi, where it had been concocted in explanation and
justification of Croesus' gifts to the Pythian Apollo. But he had
also in his travels observed the striking, though lesser, dedication
to Amphiaraus. So he felt compelled to insert it in the scheme of
Delphic responses, even though it was essentially inconsistent
with that context. It is most unlikely that Xanthus or any other
source combined Apollo and Amphiaraus in the same way, and
so it was from Herodotus' narrative that Nicolaus drew the
notion of making them both, with Zeus, defenders of Croesus.
The resulting conjunction is very questionable theology.

Sibylla's actual words must, then, be Nicolaus' invention, but
it is most unlikely that he invented the whole idea of her
participation in these events. It was not the only occurrence of
her name in Nicolaus' history. An earlier extract mentions baldly:
'[Cyrus] sent for Sibylla from Ephesus, the prophetess called
Herophila.' This may have been intended to prepare for her
appearance at Croesus' pyre, but without the full text of
Nicolaus' narrative it is too difficult to work out such details. The
one point which may be made is that evidently Xanthus had
associated Sibylla with Cyrus and Croesus, and the most likely
explanation for this feature is that Sibylline oracles were extant in
his day, the mid-fifth century BC, which could be interpreted as
foretelling the fall of Croesus and the victory of Cyrus.[21]

It is a plausible enough conjunction. Although Herodotus
begins his history with the dramatic assertion that Croesus was
'the first to begin unjust deeds against the Greeks', this

judgement is scarcely sustained by the details of his narrative. It ignores the reports elsewhere of Alyattes' attacks on Greek cities; also Herodotus' general picture of Croesus remains sympathetic. He is hybristic in his pride, but this is drawn in a way to suggest that he was the victim of an exaggerated form of human weakness. In the end he is preserved to act as the sage counsellor to Persian kings.[22] However, this may not have been quite the view of him and his overlordship held by contemporary Aeolians and Ionians. To many of them the Lydian monarchy may simply have been overbearing and tyrannical. Hence it would be quite likely that prophecies which foretold the fall of Lydia might have had popular appeal. They may have been produced originally before the war with Persia, and have forecast the defeat of Alyattes or Croesus in general terms and obscure imagery. After the event they would be doctored to suit the actual course of history, and as the fall of Lydia simply meant the subjection of the Greeks to another and more efficient imperialism, the words of Sibylla may have painted a succession of gloomy pictures. If this was the context for the origin of the Sibylline oracles, it suggests why from the beginning they had a somewhat anti-Apolline colouring. Behind the exaggerations and distortions of Herodotus' Delphic source it is clear that from Gyges to the end of his dynasty the Mermnad kings by their gifts had kept on good terms with the Pythian Apollo, and had received his support. Similarly Croesus at least, if not his predecessors, had been generous to Apollo of Didyma and some of the other sanctuaries of Apollo in Hellas. So whoever produced the Sibylline prophecies foretelling the fall of the Mermnads must have been conscious that this was inconsistent with the general trend of the Apolline oracles.[23]

One may be tempted to ask why, if Sibylla prophesied the fall of Croesus, Herodotus did not quote her in his history. The first explanation that may occur to one is the fact that these oracles were probably circulated at a popular, even vulgar, level in society. But it is somewhat inconsistent with this argument that, as we shall see, Herodotus was quite prepared to make extensive use of the oracles of Bacis, who was the European counterpart of Sibylla.[24] The most likely explanation, then, is that after Herodotus had encountered at Delphi the cycle of legendary oracles which told the story of Croesus and his predecessors, its pattern of *hybris* and *ate* fitted his dramatic purpose so well that the introduction of other prophecies about Croesus and Cyrus would only have confused the picture. They were probably framed on a quite different model of a succession of imperialistic monarchies replacing one another in a depressing decline of human happiness.

This was the Sibyl and her oracles as known to Heraclitus, who in one of his obscure sententious aphorisms, as quoted by Plutarch, said: 'But Sibylla with raving mouth uttering things without laughter and without charm of sight or scent, reaches a thousand years by her voice on account of the god.' This is the earliest reference to Sibylla extant, and it is therefore peculiarly teasing that, as it comes to us through Plutarch, it remains permanently uncertain which exactly are the words in the sentence which belong to Heraclitus and which are Plutarch's paraphrase or amplification. Also, as we have not got the rest of the aphorism, the purpose of Heraclitus in naming Sibylla remains conjectural. Earlier editors of Plutarch were inclined to assign the whole sentence or most of it to Heraclitus, but recent commentators on Heraclitus take the opposite course and cut down the actual quotation to the mere phrase 'Sibylla with raving mouth'. This seems to me to be too extreme a view, leaving us with a quotation scarcely worth an attribution. Also the reference to Sibylla as 'reaching a thousand years' would appear to be part of Heraclitus' quotation as it was certainly part of the Sibylline tradition. Plutarch might have inserted it from his general knowledge of the subject, but it is more likely to belong to Heraclitus' original statement, which he would have derived from some passage in Sibylla's own oracle. There is a later instance of the Sibyl actually referring in an oracle to the thousand years of life conferred on her by the god.[25]

Of the three adjectives which Plutarch applies to describe the Sibylline style, 'without laughter' is the most likely to be original to Heraclitus: but the other two may be Plutarch's embellishments. He had just referred to the fact that the Pythia on duty did not wear purple robes or use scent. So it was especially suitable to pick up these points. Also he has a well-known preference for grouping phrases in threes. Heraclitus may have confined himself to emphasising the grim seriousness of her matter as well as her frenzied manner. But it is dangerous to try to draw conclusions from this quotation, as the process tends to lead to a circular argument in which the later characteristics of the Sibylline traditions are read back into the sixth century. It is not even certain that Heraclitus ended by implying approval of ecstatic prophecy as a form of wisdom.

Yet one thing at least can be deduced from Heraclitus' mention of Sibylla: by about 500 BC her prophecies were sufficiently familiar, so that he could refer to her by name as a well-known example without further explanation. Here it is worthwhile to recall the unexplained statement in Nicolaus of Damascus that Cyrus had fetched the Sibyl from Ephesus to Sardis. This is strange, for one would have expected the place mentioned to be either Marpessus or Erythrae, especially as the Sibyl is given the personal name of Herophile, often associated with the latter. If this goes back to a mid-fifth century BC source in Xanthus, it may show that Sibylla was even more familiar to Heraclitus and his fellow Ephesians than has usually been supposed. There may in his day have been a tradition that she herself had lived in Ephesus. Our sources for the locations of the Sibyls are mostly so much later in date that it would not be impossible for the existence of an Ephesian Sibyl to have been obliterated by subsequent legends.

The essential point is that if it is accepted that the Sibylline oracles were originally produced in Marpessus, an out-of-the-way village in Aeolis, or even somewhere else in the Troad, before they could become a popular phenomenon, they had to obtain a footing in one or more of the large centres of population and communication. Ephesus was just such a place. As we shall see, it was ultimately Erythrae which became the legendary centre of Sibylline oracles, but there is no evidence that it was so at this date, and it would have been a much less important centre than Ephesus for the diffusion of prophecies. That Heraclitus should refer in this way to a prophetess with local connections would not in itself be at all strange. As another of his examples he mentions by name Hermodorus, an Ephesian politician.[26]

There was also another city of Ionia where the legend of the Sibyl can be shown to have developed locally by the time of Heraclitus. This was on Samos. We owe our limited knowledge of the Samian Sibyl to Eratosthenes, the great Hellenistic scholar, who discovered her in the ancient records of the island. He evidently dated her in the archaic period; the late chronographers, who may have been derived from him, offer alternative *floruits* at 712/11 or 666/5 BC. The most that we might deduce from this is that the Samian Sibyl's oracles appeared to foretell events from the beginning or middle of the seventh century.[27]

Only one anecdote, recorded by Valerius Maximus, purports to tell about the Samian Sibyl, but it is obviously unhistoric:

The Samians, when the men of Priene begged for help against the Carians, were filled with haughty pride, and instead of a fleet and an army sent them Sibylla in mockery. But the Prienians welcomed her gladly, for they interpreted it that she had been given them as a defence by divine guidance, and by her true foretelling of their fate found her a leader to victory.

This story is an obvious and rather feeble imitation of the legend of Tyrtaeus, the lame schoolmaster, sent in mockery by the Athenians to help the Spartans during the Messenian revolt, who proved to be their salvation by his poetry. The motive of a response from the Pythia is omitted. The Tyrtaeus legend was a fourth-century BC fiction, and therefore the story as applied to the Samian Sibyl must be even later in date. Hence there is no ground for supposing that this was the actual reference to the Sibyl unearthed by Eratosthenes. The story will not have been invented in this form before the Hellenistic period, and the highly critical Eratosthenes would not have set much value on such a trivial tale. Instead it was concocted on the model of the Tyrtaeus legend by someone writing after the rediscovery of the Samian Sibyl.[28]

So we have no evidence to show what the reference to the local Sibyl in the Samian chronicles contained. All one can note is that Samos early in the sixth century had produced in Asius an epic poet who was capable of ingenious constructions and modifications in Greek myths. So the tradition of hexameter verse was well established on the island.[29] Also the local tyranny culminating in the reign of Polycrates might well provide the material and the impulse for native prophecies. Finally, one may notice what may be a mere coincidence but is curiously appropriate in the context. As we have seen, the earliest name attached to the Sibyl by those who treated it as a title rather than a personal appellation was Herophile. This occurred in the Sibylline verses as later circulated and was apparently used by Xanthus the Lydian in the mid-fifth century for his Ephesian Sibyl. By the late fourth century when the Samian Sibyl had been forgotten, Heraclides of Pontus associated the name with the Sibyl of Erythrae, and this became conventional in later authors, though not used officially in Erythrae. But the connection with Samos was not abandoned. Pausanias recorded that Herophile had spent long on Samos — evidently an attempt by some scholar to preserve the notion of

Herophile as the Erythraean Sibyl and at the same time to compromise with a tradition linking her with Samos. Actually this link with the island is curiously suggested by the evident derivation of the name itself. While Sibylla is un-Hellenic in appearance and has no obvious meaning, Herophile is plainly Greek and can be translated 'beloved of Hera', the goddess most famously worshipped on Samos.[30]

It would be plausible that if a legend of a prophetess had been introduced into Samos, either direct from the Troad or from elsewhere in Asia Minor, her inspiration would be ascribed not to the nymphs, but to the great local goddess, Hera. Apollo was not prominently worshipped on the island, and the only evidence there for an oracle-centre of his is slight and dubious.[31] Admittedly there is no evidence either for any oracular consultation of Hera on Samos, but this may be a mere instance of our lack of documents from archaic periods, for elsewhere the goddess did give responses, as is proved by a casual reference in Strabo, showing that Hera had a primitive oracle-centre on the Greek mainland in the territory of Corinth (now Perachora).[32] Excavation on the site has failed to produce any definite evidence for practices of divination, but has shown that the cult there dated back into the Geometric period. On Samos the cult showed local features, but some traditions traced back its origin to Argos. So one can justifiably draw some analogies between Perachora and Samos, and believe that divination could be one of the primitive functions of Hera.

This hypothesis would explain why a Sibyl in Samos in the sixth century BC, whether a real person or a pseudonym, could have been called Herophile, and then this name have become crystallised in some oracular verses. The Sibylline tradition on Samos had evidently died out not later than the fifth century, and was not rediscovered until the work of Eratosthenes after the middle of the third; but the verses of Herophile continued to circulate in Ionia and, at some date well before the latter part of the fourth century BC, had already been purloined by Erythrae, which thus stepped into the place vacated by Samos.[33]

The mention of Sibylla in the local records of Samos and her association by personal name with the island's patron goddess both suggest that the Samian Sibyl did not merely infiltrate the populace, but was accepted with some degree of official recognition. This supposition is made more plausible when one notes how Polycrates apparently had rather strained relations with

Delphi, and was treated by the oracle with hostility on the one occasion when he tried to create a *rapprochement*.[34] If this story gives a fair picture of the situation, it would have been appropriate for the tyrant to have cultivated an alternative form of prophecy to that of the Pythian Apollo. In fact, can the Samian Sibyl have not merely produced discursive forecasts, but also have been a source of oracular replies? If so, Samos was the first place where the Sibyl took on this additional function which we find her fulfilling at Cumae.[35]

Notes

1. Paus. 10.12.3. The adjective in the second line applied to Sibylla's father is κητοφάγοιο in all MSS — a unique word. Even if κῆτος could be used of tunny or other large edible fish, which is doubtful, it would be highly inappropriate to suggest that an inhabitant of Marpessus was a fisherman or lived on this diet. What is needed is some adjective simply implying 'mortal' in contrast to the nymph as mother. Dindorf's emendation σιτοφάγοιο is the best, though palaeographically hard to justify. It was usual from the late nineteenth century to explain away this passage as a forgery concocted by Demetrius of Scepsis from local patriotism, e.g. E. Maass, *De sibyllarum indicibus* (1879), 22; Sittig, *RE* 8 (1913), cols 1103–4, *s.v.* Herophile. But there is nothing to connect Demetrius with the subject of Sibyls, and clearly this evidence was already known to Heraclides Ponticus. Cf. *supra* p. 25.

2. Marpessus, Paus. 10.12.4. J.M. Cook, *The Troad: an archaeological and topographical study* (1973), 281ff. For the Roman grant, Livy, 38.39.10.

3. For Mother Shipton see W.H. Harrison, *Mother Shipton investigated* (1881); *Dictionary of National Biography*; K. Thomas, *Religion and the decline of magic* (1973), ch. 13.

4. Hdt. 5.122; 7.43.2. How far this is historically true need not concern us here. For Gergis at the beginning of the fourth century BC, cf. *infra* p. 107.

5. See Appendix III.

6. See G.L. Huxley, *GRBS* 2 (1959), 94ff, though I do not find myself in agreement with his assignment of the Delphic Sibyl to this date nor with a direct connection at this period between Cyme and the Cumaean Sibyl. See also L.H. Jeffery, *CAH*, vol. 3.1 (2nd edn, 1982), 832.

7. Hdt. 1.78 (Croesus), where the Telmessians are accurately described as ἐξηγηταί; 1.84.3 (Meles). Nicolaus records two Heraclid kings named Meles, but which was the one intended by Herodotus is not ascertainable. Actually they look like a doublet, for each is associated by Nicolaus with a famine followed by the consultation of an oracle, but no details are given to identify it: Nic. Dam. *F. Gr. Hist.* 90f.16 μαντεία; 45 (μαντεία and χρησμολόγοι). Arr. 2.3 (Gordius). On the Telmessians of Caria, see H.W. Parke, *The oracles of Apollo in Asia Minor* (1985), 184.

8. W. Burkert, in R. Hägg (ed.), *The Greek renaissance of the 8th century B.C.* (1982), 115–19. He makes a good case for the transference of certain cult practices like extispicy and religious concepts. But this is quite a different process from the transfer of literary forms and ideas. M.L. West (ed.), Hesiod, *Theogony* (1966), 16–31, argues persuasively for the succession myth as transferred from the Near East, but in the Minoan–Mycenaean period when relations were very different.

9. Semonides of Amorgos, *Anthologia Lyrica Graeca* (Diehl) fr. 29.1. M.L. West, *Iambi et Elegi Graeci* (1972), 114, places this under Simonides of Ceos, *Dubium*, fr. 8. For alleged borrowings by Homer, cf. *infra* pp. 109–10

10. Hom. *Il.* 13.165; 24.699; *Od.* 11.422. *Iliou Persis*, p. 108 (Allen).

11. For Helenus in the *Iliad* as a diviner, H.W. Parke, *Greek oracles* (1967), 14ff; and prophesying the means to capture Ilion, *Little Iliad*, p. 106 (Allen). Helenus and Cassandra prophesying to Paris, *Cypria*, p. 102 (Allen).

12. Anticlides, *F. Gr. Hist.* 140 f.17 (Sch. Hom. *Il.* 8.44); Eustath. *Il.* 663, 40; Hygin. *Fab.* 93, where it is confused with the more familiar story about Cassandra and the gift of prophecy from Apollo. For Melampus, see H.W. Parke, *The oracles of Zeus* (1967), 166.

13. Aesch. *Ag.* 1202ff. Cf. also A. Nauck, *Tragicorum Graecorum Fragmenta* (2nd edn, 1889), p. 919 no. 414. Pindar, *Pyth.* 11.33, referring to her as a prophetess, may be written before Aeschylus' *Agamemnon*, but does not explain how she received the gift. For later accounts, Apollod. 3.12.5 and Serv. *Verg. Aen.* 2. 247. The earliest evidence of Cassandra as prophetic may be archaeological. Cf. K. Schefold, *Götter- und Heldensagen der spätarchäischen Kunst* (1978), 258 — representations of the rape of Cassandra with a lizard as the symbol of a prophetess.

14. Ovid, *Met.* 14.130ff.

15. *Hom. Hymn*, 5 (Aphrodite) 218ff. Hellanicus, *F. Gr. Hist.* 4 f.140. Dawn leaving Tithonus' bed, Hom. *Il.* 11.1 and *Od.* 5.1.

16. Bacis, Ar. *Pax.* 1070; Paus. 4.27.4; 10.12.11; Appendix I, pp. 181–6.

17. For the longevity of nymphs, *Hom. Hymn*, 5 (Aphrodite) 257; Hes. fr. 304 (Merkelbach and West). For Heraclitus, cf. *infra* p. 63.

18. Solinus 2.18. The Thalassocracy list, A.R. Burn, *The lyric age of Greece* (1960) 58; 218. For possible echoes of the prophecy, *Or. Sib.* 5.121; 316.

19. Heraclides, cf. *supra* pp. 24–7. Nicolaus of Damascus, *F. Gr. Hist.* 90 f. 68, 8. The Sardian Sibyl, cf. Philetas of Ephesus, *supra* pp. 27–8 and Aelian, *supra* pp. 45–6.

20. Hdt. 1.46; 92.

21. Nicolaus, *F. Gr. Hist.* 90 f.67. 2.

22. Hdt. 1.5.3. Contrast Gyges, 1.14.4 and Alyattes, 1.16.2; 17.1. For the Delphic view, see Pind. *Pyth.* 1.94: 'The kindly-hearted goodness of Croesus is not forgotten.'

23. For the Mermnads and Delphi, Parke and Wormell, *DO* I, 126ff. For Croesus and Branchidae, Hdt. 1.92.2; 5.36.3.

24. Cf. *infra* Appendix I, pp. 182–3.

25. Frag. 92 (Diels–Kranz) = Plut. *Mor.* 397B. On how much of the

quotation is original, see M. Marcovich, *Heraclitus* (1967), fr. 75; C.H. Kahn, *The art and thought of Heraclitus* (1979), fr. 24, p. 124ff; G.S. Kirk and J.E. Raven, *The presocratic philosophers* (1957), 212 n.l. For the Erythraean Sibyl referring to her thousand years, Phlegon, *F. Gr. Hist.* 257 f. 37.

26. Frag. 121 (Diels–Kranz). Hermodorus, Münzer, *RE* 8 (1913), col. 860, Hermodorus (3); Strabo 14.2.5; Pliny, *HN* 34.21.

27. Eratosthenes, *F. Gr. Hist.* 241 f.26. Cf. *supra* p. 29.

28. Val. Max. 1.5 ext. 1. Cf. Julius Paris, 1.5 ext. 1. E. Rohde, *Psyche: Seelencult und Unsterblichkeitsglaube der Griechen* (2nd edn, 1898), 314 n. 58, appears to assume that this anecdote comes from Eratosthenes, and therefore discounts his evidence. But this assumption is unfounded. For the legend of Tyrtaeus, probably invented in the fourth century BC, Parke and Wormell, *DO* I, 219.

29. On Asius, see G.L. Huxley, *Greek epic poetry from Eumelos to Panyassis* (1969), 95.

30. Herophile, Nic. Dam. *F. Gr. Hist.* 90 f.67, 2 (source Xanthus the Lydian ? but it might be added by Nicolaus); Heraclides Ponticus, fr. 130 Wehrli (Clem. Al. *Strom.* 1.21.384P); Paus. 10.12.5. If the late chronographic tradition could be derived originally from Eratosthenes, it would be significant that in Eusebius, Armenian version (Helm, 1911), 663 BC and Jerome, p. 91.13 (Helm), 712–711 BC and p. 94.12, 666–663 BC, the Samian Sibyl is called Herophile. Augustine, *De Jud.* 18.23, describes the Samian Sibyl as contemporary with Numa (715–673 BC) — this might be derived through Varro from Eratosthenes. The alternative tradition about her name is first found as an insertion in the lists derived from Lactantius: Joannes Lydus, *De Mens.* 4.47 W; Sch. Pl. *Phaedr.* 244B; the *Suda* 354. There the form is Φύτω which also occurs earlier in Clem. Al. *Strom.* 1.21.398P without being attached to any particular Sibyl. H. Diels, *Sibyllinische Blätter* (1890), 52, who accepts the derivation of Herophile from Hera, defends Φύτω, and connects it with Demeter. But the correct form no doubt is Φόιτω, long conjectured and at last found by K. Mras, *Wiener Studien* 28 (1906), 43ff, in *Cod. Ottoboniensis Graec.* 378. It is not a real name but a descriptive title, meaning 'wanderer' — very appropriate to the later picture of the Sibyl.

31. Menodotus, *Record of the notable things on Samos, ap.* Athen. 15.672E, tells a story of a consultation of Apollo at 'Hybla' by Carians, who had committed sacrilege against the Samian Hera. Wilamowitz, *Gött. Gel. Anz.* 162 (1900), 573 n. 3, proposed to emend to Aulai, near Magnesia on the Maeander. But A. Laumonier, *Les Cultes indigènes en Carie* (1958), 704, argues convincingly for an otherwise unrecorded Apolline oracle-centre on Samos.

32. Strabo 8.6.22; H.G.G. Payne, *Perachora: the sanctuaries of Hera Akraia and Limenia* (1940), 1–19. T.J. Dunbabin, *BSA* 46 (1951), 61, suggests that the large deposit of archaic paterae found in the pool there was to be explained by some practice of divination. E. Will, *Revue de l'histoire des religions* 143 (1953), 145–69, argues unconvincingly for a *nekyomanteion* in the temple of Hera. J. Salmon, *BSA* 67 (1972), 165ff, discusses these theories about the oracle and comes to a negative conclusion about the method, but believes it was practised in the

sanctuary on the harbour from the late eighth century BC. For the Samian Hera derived from Argos, Paus. 7.4.4.

33. Samos occurs in the *Or. Sib.* in the conventional line (3.363; 8.165–6): 'Samos will be sand (ἄμμος) and Delos will become inconspicuous (ἄδηλος).' Cf. 4.91. These all turn on this convenient *paronomasia*, and prove no more for a Sibyl on Samos than on Delos. *Or. Sib.* 3.463 raises a different question: 'Samos also will build royal palaces in due time.' This could be taken as a prophecy of Polycrates' famous palace or of the residence of Augustus on the island. Possibly it may have been applied to each in turn. The earlier datable reference to the Erythraean Sibyl, Callisthenes, *F. Gr. Hist.* 124, f.14.

34. The story of Polycrates' consultation of Delphi, as preserved, is not very convincing, but it may represent their relation; Parke and Wormell, *DO* I, 122; W.G. Forrest, *CAH*, vol. 3.3 (2nd edn, 1982), 317.

35. Hera at Cumae, cf. *infra* pp. 88–9; and on the possibility of an oracular shrine of the Nymphs in the Spiliani cave on Samos, p. 99 n. 39.

4

Cumae

Yet at first sight the crew were not pleased with the view,
  Which consisted of chasms and crags.

It may be significant that the two great cities of Ionia in which we have first traced the presence of Sibyls were rather exceptional in that neither had any important cult of Apollo. Ephesus was dominated by the worship of the local Artemis, exotically oriental in many of its elements. She had no reputation for oracles. In Samos Hera was almost equally dominant and may have had some element of divination in her cult. The only other city where there is clear evidence for a Sibyl in the archaic period was entirely different. It lay in the far west of the Hellenic world and had a cult of Apollo from its foundation. This was Cumae, the earliest colony on the Italian mainland. The sources for the Cumaean Sibyl raise some special problems of interpretation. She is the only Sibyl for whom archaeological evidence dating from the archaic period exists, and, besides occurring in Greek authors, she played a most important role in Latin literature, both in prose and in poetry. But none of the literary references is earlier than the Hellenistic period, though referring back to a legendary Sibyl of archaic times.[1]

The earliest extant allusion occurs in Lycophron's *Alexandra*, where he is describing Italy: 'and Phoebus' mountain, where the priestess maid, the Sibyl, has her awful dwelling-place, a yawning cavern roofed with arching rocks' (Mooney). This cave of the Sibyl can be traced in numerous later descriptions. The vague statement is typical of this extraordinary poem. Lycophron does not mention Cumae by name: such directness would be quite foreign to his style. However, 'Phoebus' mountain' clearly alludes

71

to the hill crowned with a temple of Apollo. The reader would be expected to know of these features at Cumae from some earlier description in a Greek author; possibly Timaeus who had produced a detailed account of the western coast of Italy as part of the introduction to his history of Sicily, although it is more probable that Lycophron's source was the earlier book on the same subject by his adoptive father, Lycus of Rhegium. A grotto to fit the descriptions of Lycophron and later writers was rediscovered by Maiuri in 1932.[2]

However, first we should note a different strand of legend, which describes the Cimmerian Sibyl, a much less renowned prophetess of Campania. The early evidence for her is only found in Latin authors, and she may never have been part of the Greek tradition. Varro, the Roman antiquarian, in his list of Sibyls reckons her as the fourth. This was a hypothetically chronological order, in which she was preceded by the Persian, Libyan and Delphian and followed by the Erythraean, Samian and Cumaean. In this instance Varro named his literary sources as 'Naevius in the books of the *Punic War* and Piso in his *Annals*'. By a conjunction with another fragment, it can be shown that Naevius in his epic followed a legend which reappears later in the anonymous *De Origine Gentis Romanae*. According to this version, Aeneas fled from Troy and reached Italy where he consulted 'the Sibyl who prophesied the future to mortals and lived in the town of the Cimmerians'. His enquiry had been about the state of his fortunes, and no doubt the Sibyl had foretold his settlement in Latium, but she added that he must not bury his kinswoman Prochyta in Italy. This came as a surprise to Aeneas, because he had left her safe and well, but when he returned to his fleet he found her dead. So he buried her in the neighbouring island which was named Prochyta after her. The story was evidently taken over by the Roman annalists who followed Naevius in this. Varro cited Piso, and the anonymous author added Vulcatius and Acilius as sources.[3] But we need not suppose that they had any other version of the legend or added anything significant. It is, then, quite possible that the whole story was an invention of Naevius. He had modelled his epic somewhat on the *Odyssey*. So his hero, like Odysseus, must consult an oracle in the west. Also the motif of Elpenor, the companion, of whose death Odysseus is unaware till he reaches the Other World, suggested to Naevius the notion that the Sibyl might demonstrate her second sight by informing Aeneas of the death of Prochyta.

Vergil again was to borrow much from Naevius, including the consultation by Aeneas of a Sibyl in Italy and the revelation of the death of a companion — this time not Prochyta, but Misenus. But Vergil also imitated the meeting with Elpenor in the Other World by the episode of Palinurus.[4]

Whence did Naevius derive the Cimmerian Sibyl? There was a Greek source which mentioned an oracle-centre in Campania at Lake Avernus, the site inhabited by the Cimmerians. This occurred in Ephorus' description of Italy. It was part of a typical attempt to locate the scenes of the *Odyssey* in the western Mediterranean. In Homer the Cimmerioi are not the horsemen invaders of Asia Minor in the seventh century BC but are simply a people who live in perpetual darkness at the western end of the world. In Ephorus' rationalised version they are located about the neighbourhood of Avernus, and

> inhabit underground dwellings, which they call *argillae*. They come and go to one another by certain tunnels, and welcome strangers into the oracle-centre situated deep below the earth. They make their livelihood from mining and from those who consult the oracle, and the king assigned them contributions. It is an ancestral custom to those concerned with the oracle-centre, that they do not see the sun, but go out from the caverns only at night, and on this account the poet [Hom. *Od.* 11.15] said of them: 'and never does the sun, as he shines, gaze on them'. But later the men were destroyed by one of the kings, because a prophecy had not turned out for him, and the oracle persists, but transferred to another place.[5]

Evidently Ephorus had elaborately worked over his description so as to make a plausible setting for the Cimmerians and for Odysseus' consultation of an oracle of the dead. The way in which those confined to caves managed to subsist without the typical Greek livelihood of farming is painstakingly told. But at the end the destruction of the managers of the oracle and its transfer elsewhere show that at best Ephorus derived his account from some tradition of earlier times about a defunct oracle-centre, and not from any contemporary institution. The recent discovery of the Great Antrum near Baiae provides a possible foundation for some local legend about underground cults, which Ephorus could have worked up to create both his oracle and his Cimmerians.[6]

One difference from Naevius is to be noted. Ephorus never mentions a Sibyl. She seems to be simply an invention of Naevius, while Ephorus' oracle-centre was presumably a place for consulting the dead (*nekyomanteion*), since nothing else would plausibly fit with the visit of Odysseus. Those who managed the oracle are mentioned by Ephorus in a vague plural, and treated as a community, not as a solitary prophetess. This again was necessary to fit with Homer's description of the Cimmerians. Naevius may have been influenced also by surviving local traditions, as he was himself a Campanian. But why did he not leave the Sibyl at her more famous site of Cumae? The explanation may have been that he was faced with a chronological difficulty. Even though Cumae was recognised as the oldest Greek colony on the Italian mainland, it was obvious that it did not antedate the Trojan War. So Naevius had to locate his Sibyl elsewhere. Vergil was also no doubt conscious of this difficulty, but he solved it by another method. He assigned Daedalus as the founder of the temple of Apollo at Cumae, and overwhelmed his readers with an account of the great aviator-artist and his work, before introducing the Sibyl on the scene. Daedalus, the contemporary of Minos, antedated the Trojan War. So the problem in chronology was solved for Vergil, without his sacrificing the location of the Sibyl at the Greek colony of Cumae.[7]

Apart from the Roman poets who wished to connect the coming of Aeneas with Sibylline prophecy, the theme had an appeal to the Hellenistic writers, who wished to connect the rise of Rome with their native mythology. The legend of Aeneas leaving Ilion for Italy may have been at least as old as the late fifth century, but the subject did not attract much interest until the late fourth century.[8] Then what was needed was to supply him with suitable prophecies, such as might be appropriate for the foundation legend of a colony. Here the Greeks adopted two motifs from folk-tale, which both appear to have been native to Latium. One was that the Trojans must wander till they were forced to eat their tables. (This riddle was solved by their eating the flat cakes on which they had laid their food.) The other was to found their city where they encountered a white sow with thirty piglets. The omen of an animal which would guide the settlers to the site of their city was a favourite for Greek colonies, but here it had a special local reference in that the white sow represented Alba (the white city) and the thirty piglets the Latin towns. Both omens occur for the first time in Lycophron, put into the mouth of Cassandra. She does not claim the authorship of the prophecy about eating tables, but describes it as 'a memory of ancient oracles'. The white sow could be regarded as meant to be foretold by her for the first time. In this earlier version she represents Aeneas as shipping the animal with him. As with the other Italian matter in his poem Lycophron is not likely to have been the first Greek actually to write on the subject, but was borrowing from recent prose writers who had described the western Mediterranean and its legends.[9]

When it came to identifying the source from which Aeneas got his guiding oracles, all sorts of traditions were invented. Dionysius of Halicarnassus knew two different versions: one that it had been a response from Zeus at Dodona, when Aeneas had called there on his journey west, and the other that it was given to him 'in the red soil of Ida, where was dwelling Sibylla, a local nymph, who was a prophetess'. Evidently this is the Marpessian Sibyl, who could appropriately be imagined as prophesying to Aeneas before he left the Troad. As Dionysius tells the story of the fulfilment, the sow was about to be sacrificed when it escaped and led the pursuing Trojans inland to the site of Lavinium. Aeneas then recognised in the episode the oracular injunction to follow a four-footed guide. This brings the story into line with the stock Hellenic pattern of a colony founded where a guiding animal rested.[10]

Of extant Roman poets, Tibullus, in an elegy which we have already mentioned, represents a Sibyl as prophesying to Aeneas after the fall of Troy. As is usual for his method, he gives a picture which is colourful but lacking in clear lines. Modern scholars have argued strongly over the question whether the Sibyl is supposed to be addressing Aeneas immediately after he has fled from burning Ilion, and is therefore the Marpessian, or at some unspecified later point in his wanderings, and is therefore the Cumaean. In favour of the latter view is the fact that Tibullus has just previously mentioned the quindecimvir's right of access to the Sibylline books. Also the lengthy prophecy contains no reference to tables eaten or to a white sow, but there is a description of Aeneas' coming to Italy, leading to a forecast of Romulus and the future Roman empire. The *Aeneid* had not yet been officially published, but one senses a hint that Tibullus might have had some inkling of its contents from private readings. His Sibyl ends by stating: 'I sing the truth; so may I continue to chew unharmed the consecrated laurel, and my virginity last for ever.' In this final assertion Tibullus makes her obviously a servant of Apollo, like Vergil's Deiphobe, and not a prophetic nymph.[11]

Vergil re-handled the traditional motifs of the eaten tables and the white sow in a way to suit his own purposes. The prophecies are treated as separate episodes and also their fulfilments occur at different points after the landing on the shore of Latium. Celaeno, the harpy, foretells the omen of the tables. She explains that she had been given this prediction by Apollo, and describes herself as the greatest of the Furies. In other words Vergil is taking over a Sibylline prophecy of ambiguously hostile tone, and assigning it to the inspiration of Apollo. But when it came to describing the fulfilment of the omen, he changed his mind. Instead Aeneas recalls the secrets of the fates (*fatorum arcana*) which Anchises had left him. As S. West has lately suggested, the wording hints that the source was a prophecy of Cassandra. The omen of the white sow is quite otherwise treated. At Buthrotum on the coast of Epirus Aeneas meets Helenus, who, when consulted, leads him to a temple of Apollo and speaks as though inspired by the god. He foretells that the sow and the thirty piglets are to be found by Aeneas on the site of his future city. After the Trojans have landed at the Tiber's mouth, the river-god in a dream advises Aeneas to seek the help of Evander, and, as a token that the dream is to be taken seriously, foretells the omen of the white sow, whose thirty piglets are to signify the thirty years till Alba Longa shall be founded by Ascanius. Here Vergil has substituted an Apolline prophecy of Helenus for the oracle of Dodona, and has adapted the omen of the sow to play a positive part in the action of the *Aeneid*. His motives in altering the traditional legends are not to be easily explained, any more than we can tell how and how far he intended to smooth out the inconsistencies of his provisional telling. At least one can suppose that he did not want to introduce an oracle of the Marpessian Sibyl at the beginning of Aeneas' wanderings, when he intended to make the consultation of the Cumaean Sibyl the central hinge of the work.[12]

There was, however, a quite different legendary thread connecting the Cumaean Sibyl and Rome. This was the story of how the Sibylline books were sold to Tarquinius Superbus. A strange old woman offered him nine rolls for a colossal sum of money. When the king refused, she burnt three volumes and offered him the remaining six for the same price. The Tarquin mocked her as mad; so she burnt three more, and repeated the same offer for the remainder. At this point the king grasped that something serious was involved, and bought the three surviving rolls. Whereupon the woman departed never to be seen again. This legend with minor variations occurs in many sources. Essentially it has no particular features linking it with Cumae, but could be told in perfectly general terms as a cautionary tale about a king and a prophetess. In fact it was probably told in much that way by the earlier Roman annalists. Unfortunately we have no precise evidence which of them told it. Livy chose to ignore it: one may suppose that he rightly felt that it was just a popular story. The most important authority to connect it with Cumae was Varro, the great antiquarian, who also, as we have seen, substituted Tarquinius Priscus for Superbus. He seems to have used more than one source on the Cumaean Sibyl, as he offers three choices for her name: Herophile, which suggests a connection or identification with the Samian or the Erythraean Sibyl; Amalthea, which suggests the nymph or the goat that fostered Zeus; and Demophile, which has no obvious implications.[13]

Actually there is likely to be a faint germ of truth in the folktale. Evidently from the latter years of the regal period there was stored on the Capitol a collection of oracles in Greek hexameter verse. No doubt the Capitol had been chosen as almost the only secure place of storage in primitive Rome. Modern scholars have rightly drawn comparisons with the collection of oracles made by the Pisistratidae about the same period, and stored on the Acropolis.[14] The Tarquin was probably following an excellent principle of Roman statecraft: whenever a possibly dangerous religious phenomenon occurs, reorganise it under official control. One can suppose that at this time Greek oracles were circulating freely in central Italy with Cumae as the ultimate source. The king formed a collection of them, perhaps even by purchase from some *chrēsmologos*, and placed them under the control of a commission of two (originally; later expanded to five and ten during the Republic, and finally to fifteen). This practical piece of politics evolved in folk memory into the somewhat moralistic legend which survives. As such it casts little or no light on the Sibyl of Cumae, except for fitting with the view that Sibylline oracles were extant in Italy in the late sixth century BC. But it is worth noting that the Tarquin's action had no connection with the cult of Apollo. In fact, Rome had no temple of Apollo until 433 BC and then he came not as the god of divination but as the god of healing, to dispel a plague. This suggests that in the sixth century BC the Sibyl in Italy, as probably still in Greece, was not regarded as inspired by Apollo nor associated with his cult.[15]

Apart from the tale of the Tarquin and the Sibyl, Varro may have given other information which was not reproduced by Lactantius. Cardauns calls attention to a fragment preserved in a late grammarian. 'When they were missing a she-goat, they noticed a certain grotto dark and shadowy.' The context has to be supplied by conjecture. Cardauns proposes that the cave is that of the Cumaean Sibyl, and that it was discovered by shepherds in search of a missing she-goat. He compares the legend of the oracular cleft at Delphi discovered by the goatherd, Coretas. Also as Varro appears to have preferred the name Amalthea for the Cumaean Sibyl, Cardauns suggests that she had some legendary connection with goats. This is all very plausible, and may be authentic, but even so it would not be much guidance for the early history of the Cumaean Sibyl. The Delphic legend of Coretas shows no signs of being archaic: instead it was invented to provide an aetiological reason for the use of goats in the Pythian ritual and to explain the Pythia's inspiration rationalistically by the effects of intoxicating vapour. It is not likely to have been produced before the late fourth century and therefore, if the Cumaean legend was modelled on it, the latter cannot have been produced until a century and more after the local Sibyl had ceased to function, as we shall see.[16]

It is possible to discover an alternative legend about the origin of the Cumaean Sibyl. This traced her back to Erythrae as being originally born there and coming to Cumae as an immigrant. The earliest suggestion of it is in the pseudo-Aristotelian *De Mirabilibus Auscultationibus*, a miscellany of marvels compiled at some uncertain date in the third century BC. It mentioned the 'underground chamber of Sibylla the *chrēsmologos*' at Cumae and said 'she was Erythraean, though by some of the inhabitants of Italy called Cumaean, and by some "Melancraera" (Blackhead).' This rather unclear statement would seem to be derived from the same source as Lycophron used in his *Alexandra*. For he knew of the cavern and of Melancraera as a name for a Sibyl. So the probable authority behind these accounts was Lycus of Rhegium, which would fit with the final statement in the pseudo-Aristotle that Cumae was said to be under the control of the Leucanians:

which shows that the source of this passage was written after Cumae fell to the Oscans but before the Romans had taken complete control of Campania.

Livy knew of the story that Sibylla had come from abroad, for when mentioning Carmenta as prophetess, he states casually without further explanation that she was 'before the arrival of the Sibyl'. Servius tells a fanciful story, that when the Sibyl had obtained from Apollo the gift of long life, he had added the condition that she must leave Erythrae and never see it again. She went to Cumae where she lived until she lost all her bodily strength. At last the Erythraeans sent her a letter sealed in the ancient manner with clay. So at the sight of this piece of her native land she succumbed. This is an obvious embroidery on the old folk-tale of the Sibyl who lived till she shrank away to a voice. In the form in which it reached Servius, it was certainly not from a Greek source, for Erythrae is described as an island. But the original notion of the Cumaean Sibyl as coming from Erythrae is probably an explanation framed in the fourth century BC to account for the occurrence of a prophetess of this sort in a distant western colony.[17]

After Varro the next important description of the Cumaean Sibyl in Latin literature occurs in Vergil's *Aeneid*. The passage is one of the great scenes in epic poetry. Vergil here, as throughout his work, had based his account on wide and deep reading, but also, as he was living in Naples when he wrote it, he was in immediate touch with the surviving site. Following to some extent in the steps of Naevius, Vergil made his hero consult the Sibyl at Cumae. She is described as aged — Deiphobe, the daughter of Glaucus — and her relationship with Apollo has no ambiguities. She is called his priestess and is inspired by him. Before she prophesies, she commands Aeneas to sacrifice to the god, and though her inspiration produces in her a great emotional perturbation, there is no suggestion of unwillingness to play her part in the ritual. The response itself is generally not unlike that of a Pythia, except for one detail. She says 'I see wars, grisly wars and the Tiber foaming with much blood.' Here the first person is obviously not meant for Apollo but the Sibyl herself, engaging in that use of second sight which is a typical feature in her prophecies as also in those of Cassandra. In fact Vergil is quite consistent in maintaining the picture that this is a Sibyl, not a Pythia, replying to Aeneas. She is inspired by Apollo, but not completely possessed by the god.[18]

Actually Deiphobe had a double function for Vergil. She was not only the priestess of Apollo, but also of Trivia — that is of Diana in her triple aspects which included the rule of the Underworld. So the Sibyl could lead Aeneas in his journey to consult his father, and, as the route lay through Avernus, she was in one sense not only the Cumaean but also the Cimmerian Sibyl. Vergil's picture of the Sibyl is a brilliant piece of literature, but even more interesting to the historian and archaeologist is his description of her cave. 'The side of the cliff of Cumae is cut out into a vast cavern, into which a hundred approaches lead, a hundred mouths, from which as many voices pour, the answers of the Sibyl.' When the Sibyl speaks, Vergil describes these hundred mouths as opening of their own accord and carrying the responses of the prophetess through the air. Later Greek and Roman writers gave detailed accounts of a similar grotto surviving for some five centuries after Vergil's day. But from the time of the Renaissance, travellers were shown for the Sibyl's cave a very different underground chamber — one of the many vaults and passages excavated in these hills in imperial Roman times. It was only in 1932 that Maiuri uncovered a system of caverns corresponding sufficiently closely with Vergil's account. It consists of a passageway nearly 150 yards in length, some 8 feet wide and 16 feet high, of a curious trapezoidal section, narrowing towards the roof. This vast *dromos* ends in a room, lit by a window on the right and on the left leading into a further chamber. On either side of the doorway into this inner sanctum are rock-cut benches. Also along the passageway, which runs parallel with the cliff face, there is on the right-hand side a series of six openings at regular intervals. These with the window of the main room served to light the area, but one can identify in them what Vergil described with poetic exaggeration as 'the hundred mouths' through which the Sibyl's voice issued. There are also traces of door frames and sockets which show that Vergil's description that the mouths opened when the Sibyl spoke at least corresponded to the way in which the grotto was furnished. Of course in practice, if she were speaking in the innermost chamber, it would be impossible for her voice to carry effectively through the length of the passage and out of the windows and entrance door.[19] But this only proves what one might already have surmised, that Vergil's vivid description was a product of his poetic invention and not based directly on any recent procedure of consultation at Cumae. No literary sources suggest that there was any oracle-centre in use there after the city fell under Roman control. Modern scholars at times imply its continuance or else suggest a revival under Augustus, but there is no ancient authority for these suppositions. Instead it is reasonable to suppose that the oracle ceased at the time when Cumae was captured by the Campanians. Diodorus Siculus under 421 BC records:

> About this same time in Italy the Campanians with strong forces made an expedition against Cumae and conquered the Cumaeans in battle and cut to pieces the majority of those ranged against them. Then after settling down to a siege and making many assaults they took the city by storm. They plundered it thoroughly and enslaved those who were taken and assigned from their own number enough to inhabit it.

This ruthless conquest rather than the death of the aged Sibyl ended the use of the cavern.[20]

The practice of Sibylline divination was abandoned, but the temple of Apollo was maintained as a cult-centre. However, the traditions of the Greek *polis* were seriously interrupted. The only author cited for a local history — Hyperochus — was, as we have seen, a very dubious source and cannot have written before 300 BC at the earliest. All that comes from him about the Sibyl was her personal name, Demo, a shortened form of Demophile, which was one of the three choices offered by Varro. Hyperochus did not reproduce any texts of oracles, and a visit by Pausanias failed to elicit any. All he could record was a story of the temple guides. They showed a stone water-jug (*hydria*) of small size in which they said lay the bones of the Sibyl. This illustrated the legend that before her death she had shrunk to diminutive size, and fits with Petronius' folk-tale that she hung in a bottle (*ampula*) wishing to die. It was appropriate that by Pausanias' time this show was put on for tourists in the temple of Apollo, for by that date and for long before, the Sibyl had been associated solely with Apolline divination.[21]

The story told by the Cumaean guides fitted with the Greek legend of the Sibyl but was quite inconsistent with the Roman tale of the origin of the Sibylline Books. The prophetess who sold them to the Tarquin was old enough for him to treat her as senile, but there is no suggestion that she was dwindling away in size. Also the Roman story usually concludes conventionally with the statement that, immediately after she had disposed of her prophecies, she vanished without trace. Only one alternative account credits her with a sepulchre in Sicily, but no version recognises her entombment in a jar at Cumae. This all serves to show that the Roman legend was quite independent of Greek sources, and was probably already formed before Cumae fell into Roman hands.

The temple guides may also before Vergil's time have been in the habit of leading visitors down the cliff path to inspect the Sibyl's cave. It had evidently been identified as such since at least as early as the time of Lycus in the last quarter of the fourth century BC. If so, it may be to them that Vergil owes the explanation of the windows in the *dromos* as the mouths from which the Sibyl's response issued. But this notion does not appear in literature before the *Aeneid*, and, however fanciful, it must have arisen on the spot at Cumae to explain this striking feature of the grotto. I am inclined, therefore to wonder whether it was not the guides, but Vergil himself, who evolved the idea to suit with his dramatic picture of Aeneas' consultation. Living at Naples when he wrote these lines, he must have had abundant opportunity to visit and study the scene.

Vergil also knew another version of the Sibyl's method of consultation. This was that, instead of delivering her response orally, she wrote it down on palm leaves. Then, as Helenus the prophet had warned Aeneas in advance,

> whatever verses the maiden has written on the leaves, she arranges in order and abandons shut away in the cave. They remain unchanged in position and do not shift from their arrangement. But when the door opens on its hinge a gentle breeze has struck them and disturbed the tender stems. Thereafter she does not trouble to catch them as they flutter in the hollow rock, nor to recall them to their places or combine the verses. The enquirers depart uninformed and hate the Sibyl's seat.

It was because of the danger described in Helenus' warning that Aeneas' enquiry at Cumae ends with the appeal: 'Only do not entrust verses to leaves, lest the confused mockery fly in the clutching breezes. I beg you sing the prophecy yourself.'[22]

The tale of the 'Sibylline leaves' had been told before Vergil by Varro, and the poet had probably derived it from that literary source. Its ultimate origin is uncertain. Written responses which could be drawn like lots (*sortes*) were a common institution in Italian shrines. For instance at Praeneste in the temple of Fortuna the lots were written on oak tablets. More significantly it was said that the prophecies of the Marcii were written on bark fallen from trees. There may have been a magical significance in this use of natural material. For as Norden has pointed out there is evidence for writing spells on leaves.[23] But in this (doubtless legendary) account of the Sibyl's procedure the stress lies on the frustration which her method produced.

This vivid scene could have been enacted at Cumae. For the Sibyl could have spread her leaves on the floor of the adyton at the end of the passage. In fact Maiuri claims to have detected in the jambs of the inner arched entrance to the *adyton* the marks where doors or gates were fitted.[24] But it is not very plausible to suppose that the consultations of the Sibyl had ever taken this frustrating form in real life. Once more we are probably presented with the tales of the guides, which had been developed over the centuries after the practice of Sibylline consultation had long ceased. We may note that the general picture of the Sibyl's procedure is that her responses were frustrating and difficult to grasp. Even the Vergilian picture of her voice booming out of a hundred mouths from an inner cavern certainly suggested to ancient commentators that different words came out of different openings and were hard to combine.[25] Similarly, but much worse, the fluttering leaves each carrying a separate word baffled the enquirer. All this was part of the popular notion that the Sibylline prophetess's utterances were teasing and evasive.

If, instead, we had no accounts of the oracular happenings at Cumae, but had simply to interpret the material remains as they stand, they are susceptible of quite simple explanations. The chambers at the end of the *dromos* are clearly an outer concourse and audience chamber with, leading off it to the left, the innermost holy of holies. The rock cuttings flanking the inner-most doorway, which Maiuri describes as *podia*, were evidently designed as benches on which enquirers could sit on either side, while the prophetess went alone, as we may suppose, into the *adyton* itself. The general arrangement corresponds to those at Delphi or still more at Claros. At Delphi there are no surviving remains to confirm the accounts, but from various references it can be pictured that in the *adyton*, probably to one side, was a small compartment where the enquirers sat during the consultation, while the Pythia was mounted on the tripod in the innermost chamber. At Claros a complex system of passages in the basement of the temple led to a vaulted room where the enquirers sat on benches, which still survive in place. From this room a short corridor led to the similarly vaulted holy of holies where the prophet went to drink the water of inspiration from a spring and to utter his response. This arrangement particularly resembles that at Cumae, but in its present form it belongs to an Augustan restoration. The previous stage may have been less visually like Cumae, as the innermost *sanctum* then was probably unroofed. But even this construction was much younger than that at Cumae, as it cannot have been earlier than 300 BC. What form the sanctuary at Claros exhibited in the archaic and classical periods is quite unknown. Its underground situation in Hellenistic and Roman times is simply due to the fact that the sacred spring was then surrounded by the basement of a large temple. At no time can it have been in a natural cave, as it originally gushed from a flat alluvial plain. Still, the resemblances with Delphi and Claros suggest that the elaborate artificial cavern at Cumae was meant to be used for a similar type of consultation and ecstatic prophecy.[26]

Incidentally one additional feature is not mentioned by Varro or Vergil and does not fit conveniently with their descriptions, but was known to the ancient guides and could have been included in the procedures of Delphi and Claros. Half way down the *dromos* on the inland side was a side passage with three arms leading off it. They were later converted into cisterns and later still used for Christian burials. The author of the *Cohortatio ad Graecos* was shown the place in the third century AD and has left us an accurate account:

When we were in the town [of Cumae], we saw a certain place where we recognised a huge hall cut out of one rock, a very great work and worthy of all wonder. Those who had received the ancestral traditions from their forefathers told how there she [the Sibyl] declared her prophecies. In the middle of the hall they showed us three reservoirs cut out of stone. When they were filled with water, it was there, as they said, that she bathed herself, and taking up her robe walked to the innermost room in the hall, cut out of the same rock, and in the midst of the room, sitting on a chair on a high platform, she uttered her prophecies.[27]

It is quite possible that the cisterns midway down the *dromos*, though altered in Roman times, had originally been a contrivance for providing a ritual bath for the Sibyl and perhaps also for the enquirers. The literary evidence for the Pythia bathing in Castalia is late, but certainly the enquirers had to undergo a ritual purification of this kind. At Didyma, Iamblichus, who appears to be well informed on the local ceremonies, specifies that the prophetess took a bath before the consultation. The Cumaean guides' account of the Sibyl enthroned in the innermost sanctuary uttering her prophecies is much more reasonable than what we get from any other source.[28]

One must admit that it is possible to approach with scepticism the identification of the Sibyl's cave. Maiuri reported no finds of inscriptions or ex-votos, such as would confirm a religious use of the place. But it differs conspicuously both in the style of its cutting and in the whole layout from any of the various Roman passages and store-chambers which had been driven into the hills around it. Also, in spite of Maiuri's comparison with the casemates at Tiryns, it is not suitable in design or in situation to be an archaic fortification. So one is driven back to the favourite recourse of archaeologists when presented with some puzzling artefact — to describe it as an unexplained cult object. But here at least there is an ancient tradition which can be traced from the early third century BC at the latest in favour of the identification. Yet some scholars are upset that the earliest accounts (not Vergil or the pseudo-Justin) do not clearly refer to a rock-cut grotto. They should recall the confusion in scholarship created by the fact that Pliny the Elder and Tacitus both described the *sanctum* entered by the prophet at Claros as a *specus*. This led to the fruitless exploration in 1911 of a cave in the cliff overlooking Apollo's sanctuary, and it was not until Louis Robert from 1951 excavated the basement of the temple that the correct oracular grotto, an entirely artificial structure, was found.[29]

If we accept that the grotto excavated by Maiuri in 1932 was not only Vergil's cavern but also the site of an archaic Sibylline cult, how far can this fit with the ancient traditions? One point is obvious. This was no chance location of a private individual acting spontaneously as a prophetess. The author of the *Cohortatio ad Graecos* was rightly impressed with the colossal scale of the work. A tunnel nearly 500 feet long driven through solid rock, even if it was soft volcanic tufa, was a task requiring engineering skill and a considerable force of labourers. The cutting is all executed smoothly and accurately, with the details of window openings and archways clearly carried out to an exact plan. It would call for the combined resources of a Greek *polis* to achieve this effect. So evidently the prophetess who used it was a public institution.

Secondly, there is the question of date. Maiuri, after referring for analogies to the casemates at Tiryns, the *dromoi* of Mycenaean *tholoi* and the doorways of Etruscan tombs, assigns the trapezoidal gallery to Greek workmanship of the fifth century BC and asserts that 'the *oikos* at the end was evidently enlarged or altered to its present form at a later period, perhaps during the fourth or more probably the third century BC.' Unfortunately, he does not give any detailed examinations of the remains to justify these datings. In particular it would appear that no sherds to provide confirmatory evidence were found in the parts excavated. The periods to which the work is assigned seem to be fixed by nothing more precise than general stylistic considerations, which in view of the lack of analogous datable work are very conjectural.[30]

It is possible to look at the question instead from the point of view of Cumae's history. Here it is first worth remarking that a work on such a scale is only likely to have been produced by an archaic Greek *polis* in one circumstance — when it was under a tyrant. At no other period would a place of the size of Cumae have had the available resources and have been able to concentrate them on such a massive undertaking. Actually the history of Cumae provides at a probable period the individual to plan and achieve such a work, in the person of Aristodemus.

His career is recorded with a few outstanding events dated to precise years in a way which suggests that they are ultimately derived from some local records. The narrative probably comes to us through Cato the Elder, and the selection is influenced by the significance of Aristodemus' tyranny for Roman history. Whether the picture which they give is quite historically accurate would be difficult to demonstrate, but the general outline must be correct. In 524 BC the Etruscans of central Tuscany with Italian allies led an invasion of Campania, which resulted in the foundation of Capua as an Etruscan settlement. This was a threat to the landward territory of Cumae, but the Etruscans were beaten off successfully under the leadership of Aristodemus. Again, in or about 505 BC the Etruscans made a second movement southward, and it is recorded that Aristodemus once more defeated them in a battle at Aricia in southern Latium. This second victory gave him the opportunity to seize the tyranny over Cumae which he retained for some fifteen or more years. His death, probably by assassination, occurred after 492 BC. He had been the supreme leader of a Greek city which under his government was completely dominant in the coastal regions of Campania and Latium.[31]

It was typical of Greek tyrants to inaugurate major public works and introduce cults, particularly of a popular kind. So it would be quite appropriate to assign the excavating of the Sibyl's grotto to such a sponsor. But there are other historical factors which may have interacted in determining the project. For instance, before Aristodemus started to come to power, a Greek colony from Samos had settled some six miles to the south-east of Cumae on the bay of Naples. The site chosen was to become notable later under the Roman Empire as Puteoli (Pozzuoli), but in the sixth century it was known as Dikaiarchia 'the city of just rule', a highly significant name, as the colonists had seceded from Samos to escape the tyranny of Polycrates (traditional date 531 BC).[32]

How far Dikaiarchia maintained an independent existence and policy from Cumae it is hard to tell. It appears never to have produced a coinage of its own. Instead the earliest issue assigned to Cumae carries dual symbols. The reverse has the mussel shell, which was the regular emblem of Cumae: the obverse shows a lion's scalp facing two boars' heads. The boars' heads probably allude to the relic preserved in the Cumaean temple of Apollo, the tusks of the Erymanthian boar, while the lion's scalp is the usual badge of Samos. In this context it can best be explained as indicating some kind of alliance or association between Cumae and Dikaiarchia.[33]

It may seem rather paradoxical if the Samian dissidents from Polycrates were closely associated with the tyrant Aristodemus. But with our dearth of sources from the Greek side it is not possible to tell what factors may have operated on these communities. The threat of the Etruscans may have imposed a united front on the Hellenes. Again, Aristodemus the Soft (*Malakos*) may have been a very different style of ruler from Polycrates. But remarkably their public works had one point in common. The nearest equivalent to the cavern at Cumae, as a feat of engineering, is the still more notable tunnel at Samos, which Polycrates made to guarantee the city's water-supply. The one work was ritual; the other social and military in purpose. But both required advanced technique in rock excavation. Aristodemus may well have been able to make use of citizens of Dikaiarchia with practical knowledge of the latest methods to employ in such work.[34]

The conjunction of Samians and Cumaeans may have provided the technique, but this still leaves unexplained the purpose. Why should the Sibyl need a sanctuary at this particular period? Again the Samians may have contributed something. It has been usual for scholars to suppose that the idea of the Sibyl was carried to Cumae by the original settlers and that they had derived it from Cyme in Aeolis.[35] This source for the Sibyl is possible, though one may note that there is no evidence for a connection between the Sibyl and Cyme before imperial Roman times, by which point it could have been introduced from Erythrae because of the legendary repute of the Cumaean Sibyl. More serious as an objection is the argument which we have already used to suggest that the earliest prophecies of Sibylla were probably not produced before the late seventh century BC. This would have been more than a century after the foundation of Cumae and would, if correct, preclude any idea of a special connection between the Sibyls of Cumae and the Troad.

However, as we have noted, there is good evidence for a Samian Sibyl, whom Varro knew of from Eratosthenes and placed sixth in his chronological order (between the Erythraean Sibyl, dated by the Trojan War, and the Cumaean Sibyl, dated by Tarquinius Priscus (616–579 BC)); otherwise not later than the beginning of the sixth century. It would then have been quite possible that the legendary belief in a Sibyl was not present in Cumae from its foundation, but was introduced from Samos by the colonists of Dikaiarchia.

There is another piece of evidence to point to Samos as the origin of the Cumaean Sibyl. Professor Guarducci was the first to produce a convincing reading and explanation of a bronze disc with an inscription in Euboic script. The form of the letters indicates an origin in Cumae, as would fit with its occurrence in the collection of a local landowner, even though no record of its finding is preserved. The text reads: 'Hera does not permit a supplementary enquiry of the oracle', and as Guarducci proposes, this object is best recognised as an oracular lot (*sors*) meant to be drawn in answer to an enquiry. If so, and if the lot was used for divination in Cumae, it raises the question whether the Sibyl was regarded as under the control and inspiration of Hera. If the *sors* had mentioned the name of the goddess in some general connection — e.g. 'Hera will bless your venture' — it might have been explained away as still being the response of an Apolline oracle-centre. But the evident purpose of the *sors* is to warn the enquirer not to press the subject further, and such a message could only reasonably come from the deity responsible for the operation.[36]

The dating of the *sors* presents a difficulty if Professor Guarducci's estimate is accepted. She proposed the mid-seventh century, but a date considerably later would seem more likely. The forms of some letters would not be found earlier than the sixth century and it could be produced at any date in that period. The fact that the inscription reads from right to left may be due to an archaising religious convention, but it is notable that even on Cumaean coins, which Head dates to *c.* 490 BC, the legend similarly runs retrograde. Accordingly, the *sors* with the name of Hera might well have been inscribed for use in an oracle-centre inaugurated by Aristodemus.[37]

If the Sibyl was introduced to Cumae through Dikaiarchia from Samos, it would not be surprising for her to come in association with the worship of Hera, the great goddess of Samos. We have seen that the evidence for divination in the cult of Hera is limited, but the only plausible interpretation of the bronze inscribed disc from Cumae is that it was intended for such a purpose, and the Sibyl is the most likely to have used it. Again it is perhaps significant that among the three names which Varro knew for the Cumaean Sibyl one was Herophile — 'beloved of Hera'.[38]

There remains one gap in the argument. Neither at Perachora nor on Samos is a sanctuary of Hera combined with a cavern.[39] Why then should Aristodemus have felt it appropriate to create a sanctuary of this peculiar form? Scholars tend to write about Sibyls and caves as though this was a regular conjunction, but, leaving aside Cumae, the evidence elsewhere is slight. Pausanias does not describe any cavern at Marpessus, and other ancient authors are equally silent. At Erythrae a cult-site with inscriptions in honour of the Sibyl has been found, and modern editors call it her cave. But the actual site is not impressive and cannot properly be so described. It consists of a semi-circular cutting 2 metres in diameter with a fountain and a small stone basin artificially constructed. Otherwise, it is not a grotto designed to be entered, like that at Cumae, but is simply a shrine for a water-nymph, the Sibyl's mother, who is so described in one of the inscriptions. These documents do not mention a cave; instead they refer to the rock (*petra*) on which the Sibyl sat when prophesying. For as at Delphi the Sibyl used a rock in the open air for her pulpit and did not utter her oracles from within a cavern. In fact Cumae is the only place where the ancient authorities and the modern remains combine to produce the picture of the Sibyl prophesying underground.[40]

There are some ancient analogies worth noting. The one place where literary evidence shows a cave of the nymphs associated with divination was on Mount Cithaeron. There in the archaic period a cave dedicated to the Sphragitid nymphs was the scene of prophetic ecstasy, taking hold of ordinary individuals. In the classical period and later it was still a site of cult, but the practice of divination lapsed. At the sanctuary of Gē (the Earth Goddess) near Aegira in Achaea, the priestess, when about to prophesy, 'descends into a cave'. But there is no further description of the ritual, and the site has not been identified. The oracle of Trophonius at Lebadeia could be regarded as another highly specialised instance of the same belief, that one could receive a divine revelation by entering the earth in some consecrated place. It is not clear whether at Aegira the prophetess spoke from within the cave or emerged to give her oracle. At Trophonius the enquirer, who acted as his own medium, had to emerge and be resuscitated, before he could speak. The only examples of a prophetess speaking from within a cave occur in accounts of the Pythia at Delphi, but it is significant that they all are found in Roman authors, who may have been influenced more or less directly by the tradition of the Cumaean Sibyl.[41]

So as far as Greek traditions are concerned, we are led back to Cumae again in search of an explanation. If the cave is not easily accounted for on Greek analogies, what native Italian beliefs and practices might help to explain it? The origin of Sibylline prophecy in the spirits of fountains and streams would fit naturally with the thought of the primitive Latins. They too worshipped goddesses of flowing springs and attributed to them the power of conveying revelation and also of driving human beings to distraction. Such a deity associated with a site in Rome was Carmenta, primitive enough to have a *flamen* of her own. Her name is derived from the Latin for 'song', which could be used of prophetic verse. Later mythology worked her into the pattern of Hellenising legend, making her the mother of the Arcadian

Evander who was guided by her oracles to settle on the Palatine. Again, Egeria, the nymph presiding over a fountain just outside the Porta Capena, was credited with advising Numa in his law-making. Even in Juvenal's time she still had *speluncae* (grottos) at her spring, which were then artificial constructions, but these had taken the place of the natural water-worn rocks whence the spring issued. This will have been no more a Sibyl's cave than the fountain-head at Erythrae. Essentially these were not highly institutionalised cults but natural shrines where the deities spoke to their chosen worshippers.[42]

Speech was highly important as a divine manifestation. The Latins did not draw a distinction between a god's spoken prophecy and destiny itself. By derivation *fatum* could be the word foretelling the future or the decree which determined it. The Sibylline oracles were regularly called the *Libri Fatales*. There is even some indication that the Sibyls and the Fates could be confused. In the Forum beside the rostra there stood in imperial times three statues of Sibyls. Pliny the Elder, who records them, clearly was a little puzzled at the plural and dated them together with the statue of Attus Navius, the augur, to the reign of Tarquinius Priscus: which really means that he had no evidence for their origin. What he does state is that they were restored, one by Sextus Pacuvius Taurus, plebeian aedile, and the other two by Marcus Messala (presumably the famous Corvinus). In other words these three antique female statues were restored as Sibyls in the period of the Augustan revival. This would not prove that they had originally been images of Sibyls, and it is very significant that in later times they gave the name of Tria Fata — the three Fates — to the locality. One may well argue that this was an instance of the survival and re-emergence of an original name. At any rate it shows how easily the concept of the Sibyl could be accepted into Roman tradition.[43]

Another element of the Cumaean cult was also very typical of Italian practice — the use of *sortes* (lots) for divination. There are two instances at the beginning of the Second Punic War when they are mentioned at Caere and Falerii because of the spontaneous omens which they produced. In each instance there is reason to believe that they were in a temple of Juno, who was regularly identified with Hera. One can see that, even if the Sibyl came to Cumae without any previous practice of cleromancy, her association with Hera might easily have led in Italy to her adoption of the lot in divination.[44]

This survey of the possible affinities of the Sibyl and her practices with their Italian equivalents shows how easily she could fit into the context. But from none of these could she acquire the institution of divination in a cavern. The only Italian example of this is the oracle of the Cimmerians as described by Ephorus, but it is very difficult to assess as a parallel, because, as we have already noted, that historian had written up his account so as to make it fit a passage in the *Odyssey* as interpreted in the most plausible fashion. But even if much has to be discounted as Ephorus' distortion of a popular legend, it is reasonable to suppose that there was some basis of fact, and the discovery in 1962 of the Great Antrum north of Baiae serves to confirm this possibility with material evidence.[45]

The minimum basis of fact to Ephorus' account would be that near the lake of Avernus there had been a subterranean sanctuary used for divination. It need not have been an oracle of the dead. That interpretation of the obsolete cult could be part of Ephorus' contrivance to fit the place with the *Odyssey*. Actually he was not the first to draw the connection. In Sophocles already there were suggestions of this localisation. So it may have been made by the Greek colonists in the fifth century at the latest. Ephorus' king who destroyed the Cimmerian oracle and transferred the practice of divination elsewhere may be a distorted echo of Aristodemus' foundation of the Cumaean cult. But anyway for his purpose Ephorus needed to find a different site for his Cimmerians, and not at Cumae.[46]

Unfortunately the Great Antrum itself contains nothing to determine its date. If it can be associated with the small square temple just south of the entrance, it would be late archaic, after 550 BC. Otherwise it would not be very different in date from that suggested above for the Cumaean cave, but might be a little earlier. Also, if it was excavated at the time the temple was built it would look like the work of Greek colonists rather than native Italians. In fact the plausible idea would be to attribute it to the Dikaiarchean settlers, and explain its suppression as an act of Aristodemus when asserting his dominance. Alternatively the Antrum might have preceded the temple, and it might represent a native cult of underground worship taken over by the Greeks. But the lack of certainty in dating makes it impossible to treat the Antrum as more than a possible antecedent to the Cumaean cave.

The arrangement of the Sibyl's cave suggests that a form of ecstatic prophecy was practised there, and this was the tradition adopted by Vergil. But the bronze disc, if correctly identified as a *sors* and associated with the place, indicates a different method — that of cleromancy, which, as we have seen, is more typical of local Italian cults, particularly of Juno. But there would be no improbability in supposing that both methods of divination were being practised in the same place at the same period. Contemporaneously at Delphi it is likely that both were in use in the late sixth century. The only point where Cumae would seem to differ from the usual Apolline oracle-centre is that there is nothing to indicate how the prophetic state was induced in the Sibyl. At Delphi it was supposed to be produced by sitting on the tripod and inhaling the vapour from the sacred cleft (the *stomion*). At Claros the prophet drank from the sacred water in the *adyton*. At Didyma the prophetess had contact with the sacred spring. But there is nothing in the *adyton* at Cumae which appears intended to produce this effect. At most the ritual bath taken in the annexe to the passageway before giving the response might have been supposed to evoke inspiration. Vergil's account seems to attribute the prophetic state simply to the prayers of the enquirer delivered after a sacrificial offering to Apollo, who responded by inspiring the Sibyl. There may have been a primitive belief that the mere contact with Mother Earth by entering a cavern was of itself inspiring, as apparently at Aegira. But, if so, the seats outside the *adyton* are hard to explain, for presumably they were meant for the enquirers. Perhaps, however, they represent a sophisticated later stage.[47]

To recapitulate, we assume the existence at Avernus of a native Italian cave-sanctuary which may have been used for divination. This later had imposed on it by Naevius the legend of a Cimmerian Sibyl, but originally had no Sibylline connection. The settlement of the Samian colonists at Dikaiarchia introduced the legend of the Sibyl as prophetess and Hera as the goddess who inspired her. Aristodemus on becoming tyrant applied the resources of Cumae to create a new cavern sanctuary to be an oracle-centre. The cult practices may have been derived both from Avernus and from old Greek traditions. The title of Sibyl and the idea of a woman as ecstatic prophetess of Hera were adopted from the Samian colonists. But the difference from the Sibyls elsewhere in the Greek world was that the Cumaean prophetess became an official state institution, who responded to enquiries instead of issuing spontaneous revelations. The most likely explanation of this transformation is to suppose that

Aristodemus saw it as in his interest to sponsor such an oracle-centre. It must have been founded to some extent in conscious rivalry with Delphi, then at the height of its power and influence. The Etruscans had formed direct contact with the Pythian Apollo even before the time of Aristodemus, and the city of Caere had gone so far as to dedicate a treasury in the sanctuary at Delphi. Hence Aristodemus, who was the chief obstacle to Etruscan expansion southward along the Campanian coast, may have deliberately chosen to create his own independent source of religious guidance and encouragement. If it seems strange that the Pythian Apollo might support barbarians against Greeks, one need only remind oneself of the somewhat parallel situation in Asia Minor earlier in the century, where obviously Delphi had supported the Lydian monarchy even when it was extending its dominance over the Greek cities of the coast.[48]

The picture of the development of the Cumaean Sibyl has to remain largely hypothetical and can only justify itself as a way to explain the various anomalies of our evidence. The transformation of the Sibyl into the mouthpiece of an oracle-centre was not imitated elsewhere. In Asia Minor and on the Greek mainland the existing places of consultation were too well established to give room for a rival institution, but the original function of Sibylla as a source of spontaneous revelation reflecting on contemporary events had still much scope for activity in the fifth century.

Notes

1. Cumae, Strabo 5.4.4. For Apollo as personally guiding the colonists, Vell. Pat. 1.4.1; Stat. *Silv.* 4.8.45. On the colony, T.J. Dunbabin, *The western Greeks* (1948), 2ff; J. Boardman, *The Greeks overseas* (2nd edn, 1980), 168–9. There is no legend of a Delphic response for the foundation, unlike so many later western colonies. So it may have been founded before Delphi established itself in this field of activity.

2. Lycoph. *Alex.* 1277. For Lycophron, cf. *supra* pp. 16–7. For Lycus, *F. Gr. Hist.* 570. His *Concerning Sicily* was addressed to an Alexander, probably the king of Epirus (343–331 BC). The subject would suit his western interests. Lycus may have settled in Alexandria in his later years, where he was involved in some feud with Demetrius of Phalerum. There, if not earlier, he will have become associated with Lycophron. His history appears from the fragments to have concerned itself much with such marvels as the Sibyl's cave. Hence it is probably also the source of the reference to that subject in the pseudo-Aristotelian *De Mirabilibus*

Auscultationibus (95, 838a5. Cf. *infra* pp. 78–9), as is shown by the reference to Cumae as in the control of 'the Lucanians' (i.e. the Samnites). This would not apply after the Romans took it over (conventional date 338 BC — Livy 8.14.11). Timaeus may have reproduced this material borrowed from Lycus, but this is not a necessary hypothesis. For somewhat different views and a survey of modern literature on the controversial subject of the sources of the *Mir. Ausc.*, P.M. Fraser, *Ptolemaic Alexandria* (1972), 1.771.

3. Varro *ap.* Lactant. *Div. Inst.* 1.6.9 (cf. *supra* p. 33). Naevius, *Bellum Punicum* fr. 12 (Strezelecki). Piso, fr. 41 (Peter). Servius, *Verg. Aen.* 9.17 (Naevius, fr. 13). Auctor, *De Orig. Gent. Rom.* 10 (which Peter did not include). *F. Gr. Hist.* 813 f.B (C. Acilius). For Prochyta, cf. also Dion. Hal. 1.53.3.

4. Elpenor, Hom. *Od.* 10.552; 11.51. Misenus, Verg. *Aen.* 6.149; 162. Palinurus, Verg. *Aen.* 6.337.

5. Ephorus, *F. Gr. Hist.* 70 f. 134 (Strabo 5.4.5). There is no archaeological evidence for ancient mines in the Phlegraean plain. The location of Odysseus' *nekyomanteion* at Avernus is at least as early as Aeschylus, *Psychagogoi*: cf. *Kölner Pap.* 3.125, J.S. Rusten, *ZPE* 45 (1982), 33–8. Cf. also Sophocles fr. 748 (Pearson); Ps. Scymn. 238; Max. Tyr. 8.8; R.J. Clark, *Catabasis: Vergil and the wisdom-tradition* (1978), 64–5.

6. R.F. Paget, *In the footsteps of Orpheus* (1967); *PBSR* 35 (1967) 102ff; *Vergilius* 13 (1967), 42ff; C. Hardie, *PBSR* 37 (1969), 17ff; C. Hardie, appendix in R.G. Austin's commentary on Vergil, *Aeneid* VI (1977), 279ff. For an opposite view, F. Castagnoli, *Atti dei Convegni Lincei* 33 (1977), 78.

7. Daedalus at Cumae, Verg. *Aen.* 6.14. He may have taken the idea from Sallust, who, however, had made Daedalus land first in Sardinia (Serv. *Verg. Aen.* 6.9).

8. Hellanicus, *F. Gr. Hist.* 4 f. 84. For a rather too sceptical discussion, see N. Horsfall, *CQ* 29 (1979), 372ff.

9. Lycoph. *Alex.* 1250–62.

10. Dion. Hal. 1.55.4. Dionysius' source for Dodona may have been Varro (Servius, *Verg. Aen.* 3.256): see H.W. Parke, *The oracles of Zeus* (1967), 148. The Marpessian Sibyl probably came from some Greek author. One late source attributes the prophecy to the Delphic oracle: Parke and Wormell, *DO* II, no. 593.

11. Tib. 2.5.19–64. Cf. *supra* pp. 35–6. As delivered in the Troad, F. Cairns, *Tibullus. A Hellenistic poet at Rome* (1970), 66. As Cumaean, B. Cardauns, *Hermes* 89 (1961), 357–66. For chewing the laurel for the purposes of inducing divination, Parke and Wormell, *DO* I, 26.

12. Celaeno, Verg. *Aen.* 3.230. *Fatorum arcana*, Verg. *Aen.* 7.123; S. West, *CQ* 33 (1983), 134. Helenus, Verg. *Aen.* 3.359. *Deus Tiberinus* and the sow, Verg. *Aen.* 9.42–85.

13. Varro *ap.* Lactant. *Div. Inst.* 1.6.9.

14. Hdt. 5.90.2; 93.2; 7.6.3.

15. J. Gagé, *L'Apollon romain* (1955), 10ff. The first temple, Livy 4.25.3. The extracts from the Sibylline Books, probably forged 207–200 BC, contain no references to Apollo as inspirer, but suggest an origin in Cumae (*F. Gr. Hist.* 257 f.36 p. 1181, 11.53ff.).

16. B. Cardauns, *M. Terentius Varro, Antiquitates rerum divinarum*, fr. 57 and commentary. Coretas, Parke and Wormell, *DO* I, 20.

17. [Aristotle], *Mir. Ausc.* 95, 838a5; Livy, I, 7.8; [Justin], *Cohortatio ad Graecos*, 38; Serv. *Verg. Aen.* 6.321; Martianus Capella, 2.169 (garbled, as usual). For Lycus of Rhegium, cf. *supra* p. 72.

18. Verg. *Aen.* 6.35ff. The classical commentary was produced by Edward Norden (1903), and the most up-to-date by R.G. Austin (1977). Glaucus, unique to Vergil as the Sibyl's father, may be the fisherman of Anthedon, who became a prophetic sea-god and was worshipped in Chalcis, Cumae's metropolis. N.K. Rutter, *Campanian coinages 475–380 B.C.* (1979), 15, notes the occurrence of a male marine deity on the coinage of Cumae. The name Deiphobe for a Sibyl is not found before Vergil.

19. Verg. *Aen.* 6.42. It is unfortunate that the only publication *in extenso* of his excavations produced by Amadeo Maiuri was in the popular series 'Guide-Books to Museums and Monuments in Italy' (no. 32). I use the third revised edition, *The Phlegraean Fields* (1958), translated by V. Priestley, 123–32. For recent discussions of the relation between Vergil's description and the remains, see R.G. Austin's edition; F. Castagnoli, *Atti dei Convegni Lincei* 33 (1977), 41ff; R.J. Clark, *Latomus* 36 (1977), 482ff. Even in recent times scholars have cast doubts on the connection: R.F. Paget, *JRS* 58 (1968), 168 n. 49; J. D'Arms, *Vergilius* 15 (1969), 59. M. Napoli, *Atti del Quarto Convegno di Studi sulla Magna Grecia* (1965), 105–8, regarded the *adyton* of Maiuri's grotto as Byzantine and identified the Sibyl's grotto in the immense cavern below the lower acropolis. But I regard Clark's article as proving that Maiuri's discovery was what Vergil believed to be the Sibyl's cave.

20. For assertions of the revival of the cult, see, for example, H. Comfort, in R. Stillwell (ed.), *The Princeton encyclopaedia of classical sites* (1976), 251, *s.n.* Cumae: 'though restored by Augustus, the Sibyl's official cult collapsed within the next century'. Cf. Maiuri (*supra* n. 19), 132. The capture of Cumae by the Campanians, Diod. 12.76.4; Livy, 4.44.12. The absence of the Sibylline cult in the late Republic is proved by the fact that the detailed accounts of the embassies sent to collect fresh Sibylline books after the fire of 83 BC do not record any visit to Cumae.

21. Hyperochus, *F. Gr. Hist.* 576; Paus. 10.12.8; Petronius, *Sat.* 48.8. For the temple of Apollo, Paus. 10.12.8; 8.24.5; Coelius Antipater fr. 54 (Peter) = Serv. *Verg. Aen.* 6.9 — a wooden statue of Apollo there, not less than 15 feet high, which was notorious for giving omens by weeping or sweating. See Cic. *Div.* 1.98 with Pease's note. The temple is usually recognised in the remains on the lower (S.E.) end of the acropolis. Maiuri (*supra* n. 19), 115, states that it was identified by an Oscan inscription found in the 1912 excavations, but this was never published and is now lost (Clark (*supra* n. 19) 483, n. 8). The remains consist mostly of an Augustan restoration and a Christian adaptation. SHA *Clod.* 5.3 describes how the pretender had earlier made a dedication there and received a *sors Vergiliana* in response. But I regard this as one of the fantastic fictions which recur in these *Lives*. The Sibyl's cave lies at a lower level and southward from the acropolis.

22. Verg. *Aen.* 3.441ff; 6.74ff.

23. Varro *ap.* Serv. *Verg. Aen.* 3.444; 6.74. Servius suggests that the Sibyl might either have written in hieroglyphs, 'as we see on the obelisk at Rome', or in a code in which 'one letter signified something'. But these details are not from Varro and are not implied in Vergil's account. *Sortes* on oak tablets, Cic. *Div.* 2.85; cf. Plaut. *Cas.* 384. The prophecies of the Marcii, Symmach. *Ep.* 4.34.3. For spells on leaves, Norden on *Aen.* 6.74, and *P. Oxy.* VI, 886.15ff. The forger of the extract from the Sibylline Books (200 BC) had some tradition that the Sibyl of Cumae wrote on leaves (*F. Gr. Hist.* 257 f.36, p. 1182 1.65), but it is not clear whether the Vergilian legend is implied, or whether, as H. Diels, *Sibyllinische Blätter* (1890), 57 n.4, supposed, the reference was to lot-oracles written on leaves.

24. Maiuri (*supra* n. 19), 128. But was this door an original fitting or a later addition?

25. Servius (*Verg. Aen.* 6.43) discusses the number of one hundred for *ostia*, and decides that it is a definite number put in place of an indefinite. In the discussion he relates it to the number of words (*sermones*) in the Sibyl's responses.

26. For Delphi, see G. Roux, *Delphes; son oracle et ses dieux* (1976), 134ff and figs 7 and 8. Claros has not been fully published, but cf. for example, L. Robert, *Les Fouilles de Claros* (1954); L. Robert in C. Delvoye and G. Roux, *La Civilisation grecque de l'antiquité à nos jours* I (1969), 305–12.

27. Maiuri (*supra* n. 19) 126 and fig. 77. [Justin], *Cohortatio ad Graecos* 38. The pseudo-Justin in the immediately following passage mentions the 'bronze flask' containing the Sibyl's remains. Cf. *supra* p. 41.

28. For purifications at Delphi, see H.W. Parke, *BCH* 102 (1978), 214. For the preliminary bathing of the prophetess at Didyma, Iambl. *Myst.* 3.11.

29. For descriptions of the Sibyl's cave, Verg. *Aen.* 6.42; [Justin], *Cohortatio ad Graecos* 37; Lycoph. *Alex.* 1279; [Aristotle], *Mir. Ausc.* 95, 838 a5. For the *specus* at Claros, Pliny, *HN* 2.232; Tac. *Ann.* 2.54. For the hillside cave, T. Macridy and C. Picard, *BCH* 39 (1915), 39–41, and for Robert's excavation, cf. *supra* n. 26.

30. Maiuri (*supra* n. 19), 124; 132.

31. Dion. Hal. 7.2.4ff; Livy, 2.14.5–7; 2.21.5; 2.34.4. Diod. 7.10. Aristodemus' death, Plut. *Mor.* 261 E (a very romanticised account, perhaps derived from Hyperochus). For modern discussions of Aristodemus, M.B. Combet Farnoux, *MEFR* 69 (1957), 7ff; N.K. Rutter, *CQ* 21 (1971), 55–61; T.J. Cornell, *MH* 31 (1974), 193–208; M. Frederiksen, *Campania* (1984), 95ff. Aristodemus in this connection, C.G. Hardie, *PBSR* 37 (1969), 17ff. A.G. McKay, *Cumae and the Phlegraean Fields. Ancient Campania* I (1972), 142–59, attributed the Great Antrum at Baiae to Aristodemus, and the temples of Zeus and Apollo, and the Sibyl's cave, to the restored aristocracy after the naval battle of Cumae, using the captive Etruscans (474 BC).

32. Euseb. *Chron.* 185 (531 BC). Steph. Byz. Ποτίόλοι. Cf. T.J. Dunbabin, *The western Greeks* (1948), 344; A.J. Graham, *CAH* vol. 3.3 (2nd edn, 1982), 181. The date appears to be based on a synchronism with one of the dates for the establishment of Polycrates' tyranny, just as it was also used for the departure of Pythagoras from Samos. The

connection between the colony and the tyranny is no doubt correct, as proved by its name, but this does not prove that it went out in the first year of the tyranny, whenever that was. Evidently no local record of the foundation date was preserved.

33. B.V. Head, *Historia Numorum* (2nd edn, 1911), 236, dating *c.* 490 BC. Rutter (*supra* n. 18), nos. 1–2, 14–16, 18, 141, 143–4, assigns to his earliest group, dated *c.* 475–470 BC. He proposes the hypothesis that some Samian colonists, familiar with coinage, were expelled from Zankle by Anaxilas in 490/89 and took refuge in Cumae. But if so, why was the coinage delayed for fifteen years? There is no literary evidence for these refugees. It seems simpler to suppose a connection with Dikaiarchia, for which there is evidence. Also need the crisis (for there was also a gold coinage about this time) have been in 475 BC (the battle of Cumae, 474 BC) rather than under Aristodemus? For the Erymanthian boar, Paus. 13.24.5.

34. See M. White, *JHS* 74 (1954), 40–1 for a calculation which would suggest that either the tunnel was begun before Polycrates' accession, if this is dated to 532/1, or else he may have begun to rule before that date. For the arguments in favour of the second hypothesis, see B.M. Mitchell, *JHS* 95 (1975), 75–91, who tends to reduce the time for the tunnel's construction.

35. E.g. A. Rzach, *RE* 2a (1923), col. 2094; K. Latte, *Römische Religionsgeschichte* (1960), 160 n. 1. The earliest certain evidence of the Sibyl at Cyme is on imperial coinage, F. Imhoof-Blumer, *ZFN* 20 (1897), 279, no. 32 (Antonine bronze). An earlier uninscribed coin of the Flavian period might represent her. Close relations between Cyme and Erythrae at that time are shown by the use of the same dies for coinage.

36. M. Guarducci, *Bullettino della Commissione Archeologica Communale di Roma* 72 (1946–8), 130–41. R. Renehan, *Rh. Mus.* 117 (1974) 193–201, proposes to read ἦρι μαντεύεσθαι ('do not enquire in the morning'). But this appears to imply a general instruction about oracular procedure rather than a specific reply on a *sors*. As to supplementary enquiries, oracle-centres differed. At Delphi it was exceptional (Parke and Wormell, *DO* I, 34), but at Didyma in Imperial times it was quite usual (A. Rehm, *Didyma II: Die Inschriften* (1958), nos. 496, 501, 504). Presumably at Cumae it was possible to draw a second lot, and if one got this one, one had in effect drawn blank. For examples of *sortes* with latin inscriptions, A. Degrassi, *Inscriptiones Latinae Liberae Rei Publicae*, II, nos. 1070–87.

37. L.H. Jeffery, *The local scripts of Archaic Greece* (1961), 238, and further information by letter.

38. Varro, cf. *supra* p. 31. Rutter (*supra* n. 18), 11, notes the occurrence of a female head on a coin of his Group I: 'an important religious figure', not Sibylla, possibly Hera, but without special headgear or attributes.

39. Hera is usually regarded as the chief example of an Olympian goddess associated with the heavens, but like most Greek deities she could have a chthonic aspect. For a rather exaggerated and old-fashioned argument on these lines, S. Wide, *Archiv f. Rel.* 10 (1907), 259ff. E. Will updates the arguments with an unconvincing theory of a *nekyomanteion* in the temple of Hera at Perachora, cf. *supra* p. 69 n. 32. On

the question of a cavern in Samos associated with the worship of Hera, I consulted Dr Herman Kienast with particular reference to the cave of Spiliani, which contains a sanctuary of the Panagia. (I had vivid memories of the place from a visit paid in 1929, when I had no idea of this line of research.) It is, of course, obviously likely that the Christian shrine was preceded on the same site by some pagan cult, but as Dr Kienast kindly confirmed, there is no evidence for Hera. However, he called my attention to G. Dunst, *AM* 87 (1972), 162; a fragment of an archaic *kore* dedicated to the Nymphs, found in the neighbourhood of the cave. Dunst also cites other inscriptional evidence for shrines of the Nymphs on Samos and the fact that Anacreon called Samos ἄστυ Νυμφέων (448, Page). It is possible that when the Sibyl was adopted by the Samians, she might appropriately have been localised in an existing cave sanctuary of the Nymphs under the supremacy of Zeus: Appendix I, p. 176.

40. The Erythraean inscriptions, *IGR* IV, nos. 1532, 1540, 1541; H. Engelmann and R. Merkelbach (eds), *Die Inschriften von Erythrae und Klazomenae* II (1973), 225–6. The Grotto, P. Corssen, *AM* 38 (1913), 1ff.

41. The Sphragitid nymphs, Appendix I, p. 181. For the archaeological evidence of the cult of nymphs (with or without Pan) in caves, P. Amandry, *BCH*, Suppl. IX, *L'antre corycien*, II, 404–8. The only instance which provides evidence pointing to divination is the vast accumulation of *astragali* in the Corycean cave. Aegira, Pliny, *HN* 28.147; Parke and Wormell, *DO* I, 10. Trophonius, Paus. 9. 39, 5ff. The Pythia's cave, Parke and Wormell, *DO* I, 19 and n. 6. The only Greek author of Hellenistic date, Lycophron, *Alex.* 208, is no evidence for the Pythia entering a cave and may be a deliberate ambiguity.

42. Carmenta, Livy, 1.7.9 (*ante Sibyllae in Italiam adventum*). Egeria, *speluncae* at the Porta Capena, Juv. 3.12. *Spelunca* at Aricia, Lactant. *Div. Inst.* 1.22.1.

43. The Sibyls' statues, Pliny, *HN* 33.22; R.E.A. Palmer, *Roman religion and Roman empire* (1974), 100. *Tria Fata* as a locality first in Cyprian, *Ep.* 21 (AD 250) and later quite frequently, Otto, *RE* 6 (1909), cols 2050–1.

44. Livy 21.62.5 (Caere); 22.1.11 (Falerii). Palmer (*supra* n. 43), that these temples are to be identified as Juno's. For example of *sortes* inscribed in Latin, *supra* p. 98 n. 36.

45. Cimmerii, *supra* p. 73. The Great Antrum, *supra* pp. 73–4 and n. 6.

46. Soph. fr. 748 (Pearson) (Bekker, *Anecd.* 414, 13). The other reference is in Max. Tyr. 8.8, to whom it was a *nekyomanteion*, which had provided a *mis-en-scène* for Homer, but with no mention of Cimmerians.

47. Delphi, Parke and Wormell, *DO* I, 18 (the use of the lot); 19ff (modes of inducing inspirations). Claros, Tac. *Ann.* 2.54. Didyma, Iambl. *De Myst.* 3.11. Aegira, Parke and Wormell, *DO* I, 10.

48. Parke and Wormell, *DO* I, 143 (Caere); 1.28ff (Lydia).

5

The Sibyl in the Classical Period

It will sigh like a thing that is deeply distressed
And it always looks grave at a pun.

Down to the end of the sixth century BC we have examined the
spread of Sibylline oracles among the eastern and western Greeks
and the particular prophecies concerned with events in those
regions. There is in this period no evidence for a Sibyl on the
Greek mainland, and no sign even that Sibylline prophecies were
circulating there. But one historical event happening in the
Peloponnese in the sixth century was said to have been foretold
by the Sibyl. So although it is not a very convincing example, it
had better be considered first before going on to deal with Hellas
in the fifth century. Pausanias in describing the dedications at
Delphi spends much space on the Spartan monument commem-
orating their victory at Aegispotami, whose bronze statues were
the most prominent works of classical art surviving near the
entrance to the sanctuary. He ends by quoting oracles of Sibylla
and Musaeus about the battle, which we shall discuss later, and
follows them by a brief notice of a dedication of the Argives which
he encounters next on his route, linking it up by a second
reference to a Sibylline oracle:

> As for the contest between the Spartans and the Argives
> near the territory of Thyrea, Sibylla also foretold it, that it
> would end in a draw. But the Argives, claiming that they
> had been superior in the action, sent to Delphi a horse of
> bronze to represent the Wooden Horse. It is a work of
> Antiphanes of Argos.

Pausanias would suggest that the Argive monument was to commemorate the famous Battle of the Champions about 545 BC. But it is most unlikely that a dedication for a mid-sixth century victory would have been erected at this place in the sanctuary, and the attribution of the work to Antiphanes (probably derived from an artist's inscription) would indicate that it must have been produced in the late fifth or early fourth century, and therefore must actually have been a monument to a victory in the wars of 421 or of 395 BC. No doubt the dedicatory inscription simply stated that it was the spoils of the Argives from the Lacedaemonians.[1]

For our present purpose it does not matter that the monument was misdated by Pausanias. This error does not invalidate his citation of a Sibylline oracle about the Battle of the Champions. Evidently by the second century AD at least, a prophecy of this famous event was to be found in the Sibylline corpus. The question is: was it written in the sixth century BC in close conjunction with the historical occurrence, or was it inserted at some later date as a literary embellishment? Since Pausanias for once did not furnish a quotation, decisive evidence is lacking. But it is worth considering the arguments available.

As we learn from Herodotus, one of the well-known synchronisms of ancient history was that the battle of Thyrea took place when Croesus went to war with Cyrus. In fact Herodotus implies that the failure of the Spartans as allies to assist Croesus on his expedition across the Halys was because they were preoccupied with their border war with the Argives. Even so, when they heard that Croesus was besieged in Sardis, they were preparing to come to his aid until the news of his capture put an end to their expedition. If, as we have seen, there is some reason to believe that the Sibyl's prophecies were deeply involved in the fall of Lydia, then it would possibly have been appropriate to insert a reference to the Battle of the Champions so as to account for the failure of Croesus' mainland allies to come to his assistance. Herodotus' account suggests a Spartan apologia for their absence, and as such it may have been circulated immediately after the Thyrean campaign and may have been incorporated early into the Sibylline picture of events.[2]

The alternative argument may be to draw attention to the fact that so far as other evidence goes the Sibyl did not concern herself with mainland events until well into the early half of the fifth century when her prophecies first reached Athens. By then the Battle of the Champions had little significance in the pattern of history. But it became popular again by the Hellenistic period through its scope for sensational treatment in epigrams.[3] One might argue that at this late point it was vamped into the Sibylline oracles for literary effect. This hypothesis cannot be refuted, but I would myself prefer to believe in the early origin of the *post eventum* forecast of the battle.

Sibylla is never quoted by classical authors in connection with Marathon or Xerxes' expedition, which may seem a strange omission in the face of such dramatic events. But this may be because up till that period Sibylline oracles as such were produced only in Aeolis and Ionia, and viewed from these regions Marathon did not appear catastrophic, and Xerxes' expedition, on which so many conscripted forces from the eastern Greeks had served, may have been a rather ambivalent subject for prophecy. Instead, as we have seen, Herodotus quoted Bacis with prophecies of the battles of Artemisium, Salamis and Plataea. The two latter are highly specific and detailed. Indeed Herodotus was convinced that the forecast of Salamis was a test-case proving the authenticity of such prescience. But we need not doubt that they were all actually composed in this form after the event. Once more, however, one could argue that these quasi-Sibylline oracles were rather anti-Apolline in tendency. Bacis, inspired by the Nymphs, was much more explicit about Greek victories than any of the utterances of the Pythian Apollo. Also Bacis' words may have helped the Boeotians in their efforts to counter the prejudice of the rest of Greece against the charge of Medism, as showing them expecting triumph for the Hellenic cause.[4]

The first reference to Sibylla in a mainland Greek author occurs in Aristophanes, and it is possible that it was not before the Peloponnesian War that her oracles reached Athens in a relevant form. Undoubtedly that conflict created a field in which all sorts of popular divination flourished. Thucydides, unlike Herodotus, was obviously unconvinced of the power of sooth-sayers to foretell events. But he regarded their activities as one of the symptoms of the war-neurosis which he had made it his task to describe. So twice in the early part of his work he calls attention to the subject. First of all, before the general outbreak of hostilities, he tells how all Greece was in a state of high excitement. 'Many prose prophecies were told and many oracle-mongers sang in verse among the peoples about to go to war and also in the other cities'. Again, at the time of the first Spartan invasion of Attica, when there was sharp dispute in Athens over what action to take, 'oracle-mongers were singing all manner of oracles to which each individual was excited to listen'. After these two early notices he does not refer to the subject until retrospectively after the news of the Sicilian disaster reached Athens. Then, as he records, 'they were enraged with the oracle-mongers and prophets and all those who by divination had given them hope of taking Sicily.' Thucydides probably thought it beneath the dignity of his subject to name individual oracle-mongers or the alleged authors of their oracles. He only refers by name to Delphic responses and always in rather impressive contexts.[5]

Very different is Aristophanes, who fully confirms the picture of oracle-mongers as familiar and easily caricatured members of contemporary society, but also mentions them by name and the sources of their prophecies. His second extant play (*The Knights*, 424 BC) turns largely on the importance of oracles. The central character, the Demos, as a somewhat dotty old man, is described as 'being crazily eager for the Sibyl'. Otherwise Sibylla is not mentioned in the comedy. Instead the prophecies are attributed to Bacis (or his elder brother Glanis, a figure of parody invented by Aristophanes). Apollo is also often mentioned, especially under his cult-title Loxias. Bacis is named in two other plays — the *Peace* (421 BC) and the *Birds* (*c.* 415 BC) — where oracle-mongers appear as actual characters quoting his prophecies. Only in the *Peace* is the name Sibylla used (twice) for the sake of a joke. The oracle-mongers are caricatured in a conventional way as glib, intrusive and gluttonous. Also it is assumed throughout that their oracles are preserved in writing and not merely passed by word of mouth. The slaves in the *Knights* filch the Paphlagonian's book of oracles, and in the *Birds*, when the oracle-monger is challenged, his stock retort is to proffer his text with the phrase: 'take hold of the booklet'. The general impression left is that Bacis is still the most familiar source of prophecies in Athens, but Sibylla was also establishing herself.[6]

One single verse is transmitted to us which is assigned to a Sibylline oracle of this period. Addressing Athens the prophetess speaks: 'As a leather bottle you will be immersed, but it is not heaven's will that you sink.' This might have been produced whenever Athens was in danger, at any time in the fifth century before the end of the Peloponnesian War. But it was most likely at the beginning of that conflict. For the rather ludicrous comparison of Athens to a leather bottle caught the fancy of the writers of comedy. They made the simile more ridiculous by substituting 'bladder' (*molgos*) for 'leather bottle' (*askos*), and introducing the notion of beating associated with it. The first joke of this kind occurs in Aristophanes, *Knights*, which could then give a *terminus ante quem* of 424 BC for the circulation of the Sibylline prophecy. The comparison in its more dignified form of 'leather bottle' was also incorporated in a legendary response attributed to the Pythia. She was supposed to have used it in a beautiful address of encouragement, in which she replied to Theseus about the future of his city: 'Be not too distressed and lay your plans. For as a leather bottle you will ride the waves, even in a swelling surge.'[7]

This is the first extant instance of what was no doubt a frequent phenomenon — the cross-fertilisation between Sibylline prophecies and other oracular responses. The process can be seen working in the opposite direction in Aristophanes' *Birds*, where the *chrēsmologos* claims to be quoting 'an oracle of Bacis expressly speaking with regard to Cloudcuckooland', and proceeds to quote two lines obviously modelled on well-known Pythian responses. Of course one may discount this as just part of Aristophanes' foolery, but it probably reproduces accurately enough the way in which effective phrases from oracles tended to pass from one collection or context to another, irrespective of their original source.[8]

Apart from Aristophanes the only classical author of fifth-century Athens who is known to have named Sibylla in his writings was Euripides, and significantly enough he mentioned her, not in a tragedy, but in a satyr-play. The context can only be rather conjecturally reconstructed, but it is of considerable importance in the development of the tradition of the Sibyl.

Sibylla was mentioned by Euripides in his *Busiris*, a satyr-play in which the prologue was spoken by Lamia. She was a figure in folk-tales, whom some early Greek mythographer had mentioned as rising from the ground in woods and glades. To Athenians she was a female demon who stole infants from their mothers. Appropriately her first words were: 'Who does not know my name, execrated by man — Lamia the Libyan by race?' Euripides may well have been the first to conceive the fantastic notion of putting this horrific figure on the stage. He made her the daughter of Poseidon, and therefore plausibly connected with Libya, of which Poseidon was the chief god according to Greek belief. Also this gave a link with the chief character of the play, for Busiris, the wicked king who sacrificed all strangers when they reached his land, was himself by legend the son of Poseidon. In the prologue Lamia explained that she was the mother by Zeus of Sibylla, and this is the reason why the play is mentioned in later authors, to whom it became their authority for the existence of a Libyan Sibyl. No other evidence for this mythical figure exists. So it is best to suppose that she was entirely the product of Euripides' fantasy. One may conjecture that she had a useful function to perform in the plot. It was necessary, so as to provide a motive for Busiris' horrible practice, that he should have received a prophecy that he would be killed by a foreigner. No doubt before Euripides it had been sufficient for this warning to come from an unnamed oracle, as so often in Greek legends. But also it is reasonable to suppose that Euripides felt that he could make the play more effective if the forecast was attributed to Sibylla and she was made a daughter of Lamia and native to Africa. Lamia herself is not known to have any previous connection with Libya, but as a demon she could be suitably pictured as having her home in a desert, and her opening lines suggest that Euripides used her to create the atmosphere of horror and savagery which would fit his play.[9]

We may accept the picture of the Libyan Sibyl in Euripides as pure literary fantasy with no basis in historical fact. It might, indeed, be cited as evidence that, when Euripides wrote his play, the ordinary Athenian had no very clear notion of a locality associated with Sibylla, and so was prepared to accept for the purposes of the drama any imaginative suggestion. Also if Euripides chose to give Sibylla such a mother as Lamia, it is evident that he had a view of Sibylline prophecy not much more favourable than that of Aristophanes. Unfortunately there is no evidence on the date of the production of the *Busiris*. It might have been after the Sicilian disaster, when disillusionment with oracle-mongers was at its height.

At the beginning of the war Sibylla had been quoted as giving Athens a somewhat qualified encouragement in a fashion not normally attributed to her. At the end of the war in much more typical style she was cited as foretelling Athens' final defeat. Pausanias, after describing Lysander's monument erected at Delphi for the victory of Aegispotami, quotes four lines from what was evidently a longer passage of Sibylline prophecy: 'And then Zeus, the thunderer from on high, whose might is greatest, will place on the Athenians mournings of heavy groans: on their ships of war battle and hostility as they perish by crafty devices, by the baseness of the herdsmen.' The reference in the last line was explained by Pausanias, who doubtless reproduced the traditional interpretation, as alluding to the treachery of two of the Athenian commanders, Tydeus and Adeimantus, who were alleged to have accepted bribes from Lysander for the betrayal of the fleet. This explanation of the disastrous capture of the Athenian navy was not generally approved by the historians of antiquity, but was evidently circulating as a popular belief within ten years of the battle. As the consequences of the battle of Arginusae had shown, the average Athenian of the period preferred to attribute national disasters to the crimes of individuals rather than to general incompetence. So one can well believe that the Sibylline oracle would be accepted in that sense as referring to Aegispotami, and might have been forged after the event with that purpose. But actually, as far as quoted by Pausanias, the prophecy is so lacking in specific detail that one need not necessarily assume that it was concocted with knowledge of what happened. If any producer of oracles wished to picture disaster for Athens, a naval defeat was the obvious event to forecast and though the noun 'baseness' (*kakotēs*) could appropriately be applied to treachery, it could be more general in meaning, covering cowardice in face of the enemy or even mere incompetence. But as Sibylline oracles by this date were familiarly expected, it was inevitable that one with reference to the final defeat of Athens would be created, if it could not be found already in circulation. In the same context Pausanias cites an oracle of Musaeus with a very similarly vague forecast of disaster for Athens.[10]

It is noteworthy that in the fifth century references no attempt is made to localise Sibylla except in Euripides' legend, which not only transported her from Asia to Africa but also provided her with a much more exalted pedigree — not a peasant and a nymph, but Zeus himself as father, and a goddess, however monstrous, as mother. But this was her first introduction into high literature and it had been imagined for a particular literary purpose. What did the Athenians ordinarily think of as the Sibyl's home? Not apparently Athens itself, which is perhaps stranger than one might expect, if one fails to notice how the Athenians managed to annex other popular prophets. Musaeus was probably Orphic and came from Thrace, before Attic tradition linked him by various genealogies with Eleusis and the Mysteries. Bacis was originally Boeotian, but later it was said that there was a second prophet of the name — an Athenian.

Perhaps this myth was developed by the oracle-mongers during the Peloponnesian War when it would make his prophecies more acceptable to an Athenian audience, who might well feel inimical to a prophet from their hostile neighbour.[11] But Sibylla shows no sign of having been adopted by the Athenians. It may have been at this time then that the legend was invented that Sibylla was a native of Erythrae. The connection of the prophetess with Samos must already have lapsed. For if it had persisted until well into the fifth century, it could scarcely have been forgotten, so as to justify Eratosthenes' statement that he had rediscovered her. On the other hand Erythrae's claim to be the birthplace of Sibylla was evidently firmly established by the time of Callisthenes. For just after 334 BC he could write of Athenais (a local woman who was uttering prophecies about Alexander's divine birth), that she was like the ancient Sibyl of Erythrae. It seems reasonable to allow at least a couple of generations between the historical Athenais and the creation of the legend of this Sibylla, and therefore put the association of the latter with Erythrae not later than 400 BC and possibly a good deal further back into the fifth century.[12]

In developing the legend of a local Sibylla Erythrae had two directions from which it took material. Its immediate rival was Marpessus, or rather Gergis, the *polis* in whose territory Marpessus lay. Gergis had not been included in the Athenian Empire, and at the turn of the fifth century it was combined with Scepsis under a local prince loyal to the Persians. Dercyllidas, the Spartan general, in 398 BC won it over to the Hellenic side, but it will have relapsed shortly afterwards into Persian control. This is the only faint glimpse which we get of its history in the period. But evidently it laid a serious claim to be the home of Sibylla, for about this time it began to issue its first coinage with, as the only types, on the obverse her head; on the reverse a seated sphinx. The latter type was intended to allude to her oracles as enigmatic utterances. Barclay Head classified the coinage in two issues: one 400–350 BC, the other 350–241 BC. If the earliest of these dates can be taken as approximately correct, it gives some indication when Gergis became aware of Erythrae's claim and decided to reply by striking coins. In antiquity the significance of the types was evidently recognised. For, centuries after the issue had ceased, Phlegon mentioned it: a rare instance of a local coin type recorded in literature. Also he noted another demonstration of Gergis' claim: that in their sanctuary of Apollo was what they said was the tomb of Sibylla. It is unlikely that this tradition dates back to the beginning of the Sibyl's legend, as it stresses her connection with Apollo, disregarding the nymph of Marpessus, and also appears to contradict the possible early legend of her shrinking to diminutive size. By the late fifth and early fourth century, Apollo was so dominant in oracular divination that it would be natural to associate the Sibyl closely with him.[13]

In another way, too, the origin of Sibylla from a nymph was being superseded. For there are traces of a legendary genealogy which would derive her instead from the royal house of Troy. According to it Dardanus fled from Samothrace to the Troad, where he married the two daughters of Teucros, the Cretan, who had settled there as king. By one, Bateia, he had sons, Erichthonius and Ilus, from the latter of whom the kings of Ilion descended; by the other wife, Neso, he had a daughter, Sibylla. This legend appears first in an indirect allusion in the *Alexandra* of Lycophron, but evidently was already established. It must have been produced to favour the belief that the original Sibyl belonged to the Troad in very primitive times, but also it conveniently substituted for a peasant father a royal ancestor, which would suit better, if the Marpessian Sibyl was to find a place in high literature. It was probably invented by one of the logographers of the fifth century.[14]

This genealogy ignored Sibylla's original statement that she was born of a nymph, but, as we have already seen, the Erythraeans retained it, but in a doctored form which substituted their city for Marpessus as her birthplace. In fact they went further, and for the first time the man is given a name, Theodorus, and is described as a local shepherd. The birth of Sibylla was located on a hill in the territory of Erythrae; a spring was identified with her mother, a Nais; and a rock beside it was shown on which she sat to sing her oracles. The Erythraeans accepted the legend of the Sibyl's longevity and introduced another element into the story: the child immediately after her birth began to speak, uttering prophecies.[15]

We have noted already that the personal name, Herophile, which may have originated in Samos, was often attached in literary sources to the Erythraean Sibyl. But actually the evidence from Erythrae itself never names her thus: instead she is simply called Sibylla, as if it was her personal name. The earliest local evidence is a calendar of sacrifices datable to the first half of the second century BC, in which Sibylla appears as the recipient of an offering. (It is interesting to notice that Erythrae is the only place where the Sibyl received worship). Again on the imperial bronze coins of Erythrae in the second century AD the legend describes her as 'Sibylla' or even 'Thea Sibylla'. Also the long verse inscription of the time of the emperor Lucius Verus, set up near her grotto, only names her similarly. It is perhaps therefore significant that when Strabo twice cites Callisthenes as mentioning her — probably the earliest literary allusion — he simply calls her Sibylla. Again when Varro records her as the fifth in his list of Sibyls, and cites Apollodorus of Erythrae, a local historian, who 'asserted she was his citizen', he does not give her any personal name. Instead Varro transfers the name Herophile to be one of three possibly belonging to the Cumaean Sibyl.[16]

The use of Sibylla as a name for their Sibyl was part of the Erythraeans' claim that she was the first and only one, in opposition to the Marpessians. But Heraclides of Pontus who originally attempted to settle this contested claim by accepting the separate existence of both Sibyls, was also the first author of whom we know that he applied Herophile to the Erythraean Sibyl. It was evidently convenient for him to use a different name for her from the Marpessian. He probably found Herophile actually in some of the current oracles which he used as sources (the name was certainly there in the time of Pausanias). But also he was evidently unaware of the Samian Sibyl, who was forgotten until rediscovered by Eratosthenes. So the name Herophile was conveniently available for him to attach to the Erythraean prophetess, where it stuck in later authors, in spite of the fact that the Erythraeans themselves show no sign of ever having adopted it.[17]

In one other detail it is possible to see the influence of Erythrae on the Sibylline oracles: in the alleged forecasts of the Trojan War and of Homer's account of it. As Pausanias describes it, the subject of the Sibylline oracle was Helen: 'how she would be brought up in Sparta for the ruin of Europe and Asia, and how Ilion would be taken for her sake by the Greeks'. This contrasts with the account given by Apollodorus of Erythrae about his native Sibyl: 'she prophesied to the Greeks, as they were on their way to Ilion, that Troy would perish.' Pausanias indicates a prophecy produced before the birth of Helen, which could be used as evidence of a Sibyl long antedating the Trojan War, while Apollodorus implies a prophetess contemporary with the expedition, who is perhaps to be pictured as actually intercepting the

Grecian warriors on their route. The version known to Pausanias also appears to lie behind that which Solinus quotes from Bocchus: that the Delphic Sibyl prophesied 'before the Trojan War, of whom he demonstrates that Homer inserted many of her verses in his work.' Similarly Diodorus Siculus described Homer 'appropriating many of her [the Delphic Sibyl's] verses to adorn his poetry'. This account of Homer's action contrasts strongly with that in Apollodorus, who said that the Sibyl prophesied that Homer would tell many lies about the Trojan War.

Of these two contrasting treatments of the subject the version that the Sibyl antedated the Trojan War and that her work was plagiarised by Homer could be the earlier and could belong to the Marpessian tradition. For Pausanias, who cites it as far as the date of the Sibyl is concerned, follows it by quoting the lines which give Marpessus as her birthplace. The version in which the Sibyl was contemporary with the Trojan War, and Homer is a liar, is fully documented for Erythrae as it comes from Apollodorus. The explanation of the difference may be a local feud. Erythrae faced the capital of Chios across a narrow stretch of sea, and there were old traditions of hostility between the neighbouring states. So it would not be surprising if some Erythraean poet, when composing a Sibylline oracle, took the opportunity to make the attack on Chios' poet more pointed and venomous. Elsewhere, for instance at Delphi, the milder version continued to be current. The third book of the *Oracula Sibyllina* gives a prophecy of the birth of Helen. Obviously its prophetess could not pose as contemporary with the Trojan War. But also it proceeds to combine both versions of the attack on Homer, accusing him both of mendacity and plagiarism and mentioning Chios as his alleged birthplace. It is not surprising if the author of the third book in this way shows a dependence on the Erythraean tradition, for at the colophon he named Erythrae, though only to disown it in favour of Babylon as birthplace. Yet Lactantius, when citing his version of Book 3, normally refers to it as the Erythraean Sibyl; and it evidently belonged to that tradition.[18]

The establishment of the Erythraean Sibyl is the first instance where a new claim to such a local prophetess can be traced, but it was to be followed by a succession of others. The nearest in date and the next in importance was at Delphi. As we have seen, Heraclides of Pontus, who was the first scholar whom we know to have drawn a distinction between the Marpessian and the Erythraean Sibyls, was also the first to mention the Delphic

Sibyl. For though she is a familiar figure in later literature, there is no evidence for her earlier than the late fourth century BC. She was associated with a rock in the sanctuary, on which she was described as standing or sitting to sing her oracle. It was a natural outcrop situated below the terrace on which the temple stood, in the area of the sacred precinct, which had been left untouched probably because it was traditionally dedicated to the Earth goddess, the original deity at Delphi.[19]

Heraclides gives us the three lines which formed the opening words of the Delphic Sibyl, introducing herself and her subject to her audience. They are remarkable verses, quite unlike the general run of Sibylline oracles. First of all, we may note that nowhere else does the Sibyl begin in this way with a direct address to a particular audience. Her oracles are usually uttered as general prophecies, and if she wishes to deal with a particular people, they are normally referred to in the third person by the name of their *polis*. Even if the city is addressed, it is still usually by its name in the singular, and not in the person of its inhabitants. Evidently whoever composed this Sibylline oracle pictured the Sibyl as perched on her rock addressing an actual gathering of Delphians. In this respect the form used is much more like that of the Pythia replying to an enquiry, and suggests that the oracle in its lost continuation had some specific message to convey.

Secondly, the Sibyl is not speaking in her own person but as the mouthpiece of the goddess Artemis. This is a complete divergence from the usual Sibylline practice in which the prophetess, however unwilling to speak, still retains her own personality. It looks as though Heraclides was conscious of this as a peculiarity, for his description of the Delphic Sibyl, as paraphrased by Clement, was that 'she was a Phrygian called Artemis'. This would suggest that she was a mortal woman, who happened to be named after the goddess. If Heraclides had used this interpretation to explain away the oracle, it will not do. No mortal could describe Apollo as 'my very own brother', unless of course she was an impostor — a woman, named Artemis, pretending to be the goddess. But this fanciful complication is unnecessary. Instead, the reasonable way to interpret the oracle is to suppose that whoever wrote it meant that the goddess Artemis had inspired the Sibyl by taking full possession of her in the manner in which Apollo inspired the Pythia. This second resemblance to the manner of a Delphic response can best be explained by supposing that the verses were produced at Delphi by some poet who was much more familiar with the local methods of prophecy than with the typical utterance of a Sibyl.

What then were the circumstances in which someone familiar with Delphi as an oracle-centre wished to produce a Sibylline oracle specifically designed to be spoken there? If only Clement or Heraclides had continued the quotation to include some part of Artemis' message, we might have been able to answer confidently. As it is, the only clue we have is the positive statement that Artemis was angry with her brother. This certainly suggests that the oracle was not a kindly prophecy, but in the manner appropriate to Sibyls contained some bitter and hostile forecast. This would, indeed, explain why the author chose the Sibyl as the mouthpiece, and even why Artemis, and not Apollo, was represented as the deity who spoke; although here again we may note a third typically Delphic feature: Artemis claims that her oracle expresses the mind of Zeus himself in the same way that the Pythian Apollo often does.[20]

If one assigns this composition to the fourth century BC at some date which would still allow for it to be quoted by Heraclides, there were various events in that period worthy of Sibylline prophecy. For instance, the Third Sacred War with the occupation of the sanctuary by the Phocians and the melting-down of the treasures was a shocking event. But it is fairly well documented in our surviving evidence, which contains no reference to Sibylline oracles. Much more likely as a subject is the destruction of Apollo's temple in 373 BC. This horrendous event is so imperfectly recorded in our ancient authorities that it is still uncertain what exact form the disaster took. Some connection with the appalling earthquake on the north Peloponnesian coast, dated to that year, is probable, though never clearly stated in our sources. Delphi may perhaps have escaped serious loss of life, and so the events there have been overshadowed by the tragic fate of the inhabitants of Helice and Bura in Achaea. A response of the Delphic oracle was invoked to explain the divine retribution behind their deaths, but there is no suggestion that the Pythian Apollo had given any forewarning of the ruin of his own temple.[21]

This unforeseen disaster striking at the sanctuary of Apollo himself would provide just the appropriate occasion for concocting a Sibylline oracle foretelling the future destruction of the temple by an earthquake. Then it could be disclosed that this ancient prophecy foreseeing and explaining the catastrophe had just been discovered. The choice of Artemis as the angry messenger of Zeus cannot fully be explained. It would have been awkward to represent Apollo as forecasting the destruction of his own temple, but the Sibyl was perhaps not felt by the Delphians to be of sufficient standing to convey such a grim message in her own person. The Sibyl's rock was already part of the traditional area consecrated to the Earth goddess, which had been left inviolate. So, although I do not believe that it had actual associations with a Sibyl before the fourth century BC, it may have been the proper haunt of the Earth goddess's prophetess in primitive times. This tradition may have made it easier to assign the rock to the Sibyl, herself a nymph's daughter.

The actual identity of the Delphic Sibyl may have originally been left vague, judging from Heraclides' reference: she had come from Phrygia, and was more ancient than Orpheus. Later, as her existence was accepted, different accounts of her ancestry were produced. The earliest is in Diodorus Siculus: the Epigoni, when taking Thebes, captured Daphne, the daughter of Tiresias, and in accordance with their vow presented her as first-fruits of the spoil to the Pythian Apollo. She had acquired prophetic skill from her father, which she developed further at Delphi, and wrote various oracles so excellent that Homer borrowed from them to embellish his poetry. This account is a thoroughly typical Hellenistic fiction, combining different archaic legends with a certain degree of mild rationalism. The motif of a prophetic daughter of Tiresias dedicated at Delphi by the Epigoni is taken from the epic of that name. It was there used as the foundation legend for the Apolline oracle-centre at Claros. The prophetess in the *Epigoni* was named Manto, but in Diodorus the name is Daphne, which in view of the close association between the bay tree and the Delphic oracle made a convenient substitute. Also though Diodorus does not record it, the Hellenistic author may have been aware of the resemblance in that both maidens had resisted the amorous advances of Apollo. But all this material as an account of the Delphic Sibyl could easily have been put together by an author without any close connection with the place.[22]

Legends with a much closer Delphic association are known from Plutarch. In his dialogue on the failure of the contemporary Pythia to utter responses in verse, when the learned interlocutors in their ascent to the temple reach the place where they are in sight of the Sibyl's rock, Plutarch inserts the explanation that 'the first Sibyl sat on it, when she had come from Helicon after being brought up by the Muses. But some say she came from the Malians, being the daughter of Lamia, the daughter of Poseidon.' These legends are quite unrelated to that in Diodorus, and may be actually earlier than it in origin, even though they do not occur in any author until two centuries later in date. They look like the efforts of scholarly Delphians to provide a proper origin for the local Sibyl without having to import her from Phrygia. Clearly the legend which brought her from the Malians was later than Euripides' *Busiris*. Euripides' genealogy is literally retained: the Sibyl is the daughter of Lamia, the daughter of Poseidon. But it is implied that this Lamia is not the monster of Greek folk-tale but the eponymous heroine of Lamia, the chief *polis* of the small state of Malis in central Greece. Also by this process of taking over the Libyan Sibyl, the Delphians could claim that their local prophetess was the first of that name.[23]

With such respectable ancestry as descent from the foundress of a neighbouring community, a member of the Amphictyony, the Sibyl could be safely welcomed by the most conservative Delphians. The alternative legend, which Plutarch put first for preference, does not explain her parentage but simply states that she was brought up by the Muses in their home on Mount Helicon. The Muses had an ancient traditional cult at Delphi, originally associated with the worship of the Earth goddess and attached to a sacred spring in her sanctuary. The Sibyl's rock stood just below it. So all the cult-sites were in convenient proximity. Also it was very apposite to imagine that the prophetess who spoke in hexameter verse had been the foster-child of the Heliconian Muses. They had promised to inspire Hesiod so that he could sing of both past and future. As for the Sibyl's parentage, it would be highly suitable if Apollo had been her father in view of his close association with the Muses in the fourth century: he appeared with them on the east pediment of the restored temple. Pausanias knew a passage in his corpus of Sibylline oracles, in which the prophetess asserted that she was a daughter of Apollo, and the *Suda* listed a tradition that the Sibyl was the daughter of Apollo and Lamia. These fragmentary traditions fit with the alternative Delphic legends of the Sibyl and serve to fill out the genealogy there left incomplete.[24]

Besides recording legends of the Delphic Sibyl's origin, Plutarch in the same dialogue put into the mouth of Sarapion, the poet of Stoic leanings, a mention of the legend about her death. He recalled the verses in which she sang of herself, that not even after death would she cease from prophecy, but that she herself shall go round and round in the moon, having become the face shown on it; while her breath mingled with the air shall be carried in audible rumours and omens, and as from her body transformed in the earth grass and timber grow up, consecrated animals shall feed on it and retain all manner of colours and shapes and qualities in their entrails, from which the presages of the future come to mankind.[25]

This is the earliest occurrence in literature of this rather extraordinary myth, which attempts to make the Sibyl herself the physical source of various forms of divination. The actual verses which Sarapion quoted are partly preserved for us in an extract from Phlegon's book on longevity.[26] After citing instances of centenarians and older from the Roman census records, he appends even more remarkable cases from literature, ending with the Erythraean Sibyl who

lived a few years short of the thousand, as she herself says in her oracle as follows: 'But why indeed all-lamentable for others' sufferings, do I utter in prophecy divine oracles, holding on to my fate of madness? Why do I taste its painful sting, retaining my grievous old age in the tenth century, raving among mortals and speaking unbelievable things, and having foreseen in a vision all the unendurable griefs of mankind? Then also seized with jealousy of my gift of prophecy the son of famous Leto, filled in his baneful heart with emotion, shall loose my spirit, chained within its miserable body, when he has shot through my frame with his flesh-smiting dart. There indeed my spirit, having flown into the air, mingled with the breath shall send to the ears of men audible omens involved in complex riddles. My body in unseemly manner shall lie unburied on mother earth. For no mortal man shall sprinkle soil on it or hide it in a tomb. Down the broad paths of the ground my black blood shall trickle, as the passage of time shall dry it. From thence shoots of much grass shall spring up, which, when the herds have grazed it down, shall sink into their livers and show the purposes of the immortal gods by prophecies, and birds in their feathered robes, if they taste my flesh, shall convey true prophecy to men.'

This quotation both omits part of what Sarapion paraphrased and adds at the beginning details which he had not included. Particularly, it shows that the proper context for this personal statement by the Sibyl came at the end of her oracle, where she expressed her weariness of prophesying other people's troubles. This will therefore have formed the colophon to a book of oracles like the ending of Book 7 of the *Oracula Sibyllina*. But Phlegon, whose main interest lay in the life of ten centuries claimed by the Sibyl, stopped short of the last lines. Sarapion's paraphrase shows that they described how the Sibyl herself was raised to the moon and continued to prophesy as she was carried round with it.

Plutarch made use again of this legend of the Sibyl as the face of the moon in his dialogue *On the delay of divine vengeance*. There, in a passage closely modelled on the myth of Er in Plato's *Republic*, Thespesius, who has passed into the world after death, is led by his guide near the oracle of Night and the Moon, which is responsible for true and false dreams.

> But then he heard, as he passed by, a woman's high voice foretelling in verse among other things the time (as it appears) of his own death. The daemon [his guide] told him that it was the voice of the Sibyl, who sang of the future, as she was carried about on the face of the moon. Accordingly, he wanted to hear more, but was thrust back, as in an eddy, by the onrush of the moon, and caught but little. Among these was something about Mt Vesuvius and the destruction of Dikaiarchia, and a tag-end of verse about the emperor of that time: 'though good, through sickness he shall leave his rule'.[27]

In this passage Plutarch is working from existing passages of Sibylline oracles combined by his own fantasy. The Sibyl as the face of the moon uttering prophecies as it goes on its orbit is taken from the colophon of the oracle which he made Sarapion paraphrase in the *De Pythiae Oraculis*. Also elsewhere in that dialogue it had been suggested that the Sibylline oracles produced in the far past had foretold the recent happenings connected with Cumae and Dikaiarchia — evidently meaning the eruption of Vesuvius. So Plutarch had not invented these words of the Sibyl, but simply selected them again as a convenient example of a true prophecy for Thespesius to hear. Only one element of the prophecy does not occur elsewhere — the description of the just emperor who dies from illness. This obviously could apply to Titus, the emperor at the time of the eruption, who died a natural death just two years later.[28] If, as seems clear, Plutarch is quoting from a Sibylline oracle current when he wrote, this passage must have been composed after AD 81.[29]

In view of the way in which Sibylline oracles retained and accumulated material over the centuries, it would not be surprising that the same corpus which included prophecies of events from AD 79 to 81 ended with a colophon derived from a much earlier time. The colophon itself is difficult to date. Its style and diction could not be earlier than the Hellenistic period. Also this is the dating which would be suggested by its general thought. The archaic legend of the Sibyl's end had been based on the folk-tale motif of dwindling away to tiny dimensions, and was perpetuated at Cumae where the container of her body was exhibited. Gergis had shown the Sibyl's tomb as part of its claim to possess at Marpessus the birthplace of the original prophetess. This probably dated from the late fifth century BC, and when Gergis lapsed into insignificance, the claim to possess the tomb was transferred to the sanctuary of Apollo Smintheus under the patronage of Alexandria Troas. The Roman legend of the Sibyl and the Tarquin usually ended in the manner of a folk-tale by the sheer disappearance of the prophetess, but one late version suggested that she was buried in Sicily, where a tomb was shown at Lilybaeum.[30]

The Phlegon fragment is entirely different from these legendary stories of tombs. Its Sibyl is not buried at all, but is absorbed physically into the universe, and by this process she provided a quasi-rational explanation for divination by audible omens, by observing birds and by inspecting the entrails of sacrificial victims. It is difficult to tell whether the theory was merely a poetic fantasy or whether it was meant at least to some extent to provide a reasonable cause for these phenomena. At any rate it suggests a philosophical source, and with its stress on universal sympathy would fit particularly well with the Stoics. This may have been a motive for Plutarch to put the paraphrase of it into the mouth of the poet, Sarapion, whose beliefs, as we saw, lay in that direction. Elsewhere also Plutarch uses him to cite poetry as evidence. So he was doubly suitable to be shown as citing these verses.

If we accept this as a quasi-Stoic composition, it could belong to the third century BC at the earliest. One is then reminded of Chrysippus and his attempt to produce a comprehensive survey of divination and his interest in the Pythia and the Delphic Sibyl.[31] These verses might have been written under his immediate influence. (Phlegon had cited them as the utterance of the Erythraean Sibyl, but in his day, as Pausanias shows, composite collections of oracles were in circulation under different names of which the Erythraean was the most famous.) Delphi had no legend about a local Sibyl's tomb. So perhaps this oracle may have been produced originally to fit with their prophetess. Certainly Sarapion treats it as the words of the woman who spoke from the rock at Delphi.

There are also extant some lines of a Sibylline oracle in which the speaker claims to be the daughter of Lamia and so appears to be the Delphic Sibyl. They occur in the thirty-seventh speech in the collection of Dio Chrysostom, a very euphuistic composition which is usually attributed not to Dio but to Favorinus (c. AD 125). In a flowery passage in praise of Corinth the orator mentions a legend that Poseidon and the Sun-god, Helius, had both claimed possession of the city. They had agreed to refer the decision to Briareus as arbiter. He made a division of the territory, assigning the isthmus to Poseidon and Acrocorinth to Helius. The orator, after telling the legend and justifying it by rational arguments, concludes by citing in support a reference in a Sibylline oracle: 'Blest is the prosperous neck of Ephyre, the pine-clad daughter of Oceanus, where Poseidon, the begetter of my mother, Lamia, established a contest first with Helius, though he alone carried off the honours.'[32] It appears at first sight that the Sibyl was referring to the contest for possession of Corinth between Poseidon and Helius. But the orator goes on to describe the contestants in the first (legendary) Isthmian games. So the passage, if he explains it correctly, is really referring to their foundation, attributing it to Poseidon in partnership with Helius, though the celebrations were only in honour of Poseidon. He goes on to enumerate the victors in the various events, who are mostly Argonauts, which shows what date was chosen for the first Isthmia. It is not clear, however, whether these details were taken from the Sibylline oracle, which may have gone no further on the subject than the end of the quotation. What the address to Corinth originally meant and what was its context is quite beyond recovery. All one can say is that it appears as though the Sibyl, instead of expressing her usual form of gloomy prediction, was greeting Corinth with well-omened eulogy. At the latest this must have been written before the city was sacked by the Romans in 146 BC and, if the legend of the Delphic Sibyl as the daughter of Lamia belongs to the mid-fourth century BC, this oracle might have been produced at any date between those two limits.

There is only one precisely datable event in the fourth century that is explicitly connected with a Sibylline prophecy. This was the battle of Chaeronea. According to Plutarch the Pythia had foretold the result in dire prophecies which he does not quote, but

> also there was an ancient oracle which was recited out of the Sibyllines: 'As for the battle on Thermodon, may I be far away from it as an eagle in the clouds and the upper air, to behold it only. The vanquished weeps, but the victor is destroyed.'[33]

If applied to the battle of Chaeronea this could be taken as referring allusively to the severe casualties and to the fate of Philip II, assassinated only two years after his victory. It all turns on the indication of the locality contained in the reference to Thermodon. Plutarch saw that there was a problem here. Chaeronea was his native city, and he knew that those who interpreted the oracle in this sense said that the Thermodon was a small river which fell into the Cephisus in that neighbourhood. But Plutarch was not acquainted with any river there of that name. The only one which he could find on the battlefield was a stream called Haimon, which flowed near the Greek camp. So, in order to preserve the credit of the oracle, he conjectured that the original name of the river had been Thermodon, but that it had been changed to Haimon after the battle because of the blood (*haima*) which had filled it. This is a most unconvincing piece of special pleading.

Evidently within the lifetime of the combatants the problem of applying this oracle had already been raised, and another even more unconvincing solution had been propounded. Duris of Samos, a notoriously imaginative historian, denied that the Thermodon in the prophecy was a river. Instead he explained that some soldiers digging on the battlefield for the purpose of setting up a tent had found a stone statuette inscribed 'Thermodon'. It showed a male figure bearing a wounded Amazon. The river Thermodon in Pontus was traditionally the scene of the battles of the Amazons. So the statuette was evidently imagined as a representation of the river god carrying away an Amazon wounded in battle. Tombs of Amazons legendarily associated with their invasion of Greece were shown in antiquity in Thessaly and Megara, and Plutarch knew of one in the territory of Chaeronea near the Haimon. So this statuette was supposed to be accounted for in this way, but it is all probably a fairy-tale composed by Duris to justify the application of the Sibylline oracle to the battle of Chaeronea and the assassination of Philip.[34]

Actually an earlier context can be found for the oracle, which fits it much more convincingly. Already Herodotus had quoted an oracle of Bacis, which claimed to foretell the destruction of a Persian army 'on the Thermodon and the grassy Asopus'. He was clear on the reference to the battle of Plataea not only because of the well-known river Asopus, but also because he could identify the Thermodon as a stream flowing between Tanagra and Glisas. That this identity is not a fiction is proved by the fact that some six centuries after Herodotus, Pausanias records the Thermodon by name in this locality. If we take the Sibylline verses as originally contrived to appear to foretell a sanguinary battle and a victor who would subsequently perish, they can apply appropriately to Plataea. Apart from the Persians, the Greek losses on both sides were heavy, and Pausanias the regent, after winning a dazzling reputation came to a tragic end some twelve years later. The *vaticinium post eventum* would have been produced soon after the latter event. The problem that remains is whether the verses were originally written in the name of Sibylla. If they were, they are the only Sibylline verses known to deal with an event of the Persian War. But alternatively they might have been originally a product of Bacis. The Boeotian seer might well have had other verses attributed to him on the subject of Plataea besides those which Herodotus quoted. Whichever was the original author, the prophecy was revived as a Sibylline forecast of the battle of Chaeronea. The heavy Greek losses and the sudden assassination of Philip of Macedon only two years later gave a highly suitable context. The sole difficulty was the Thermodon as a geographical indication. Only by ingenious fictions could it be worked into the topography of the battle, but it is typical of human perversity that this was achieved and won acceptance.[35]

Notes

1. Paus. 10.9.12. Earlier discussions of the archaeological evidence are superseded by J. Pouilloux and G. Roux, *Énigmes à Delphes* (1963), 60ff. No inscribed stone can be assigned to this dedication. One might ask whether these quotations from Sibylla were part of the stock patter of the second-century AD guides. But I believe it was typical of them to quote rather banal unauthentic Delphic responses (e.g. Parke and Wormell, *DO* II, no. 483) while Pausanias deliberately inserted oracles derived from his extensive reading; here so as to provide a literary link.

2. Hdt. 1.82.3.

3. E.g. *Anth. Pal.* 7.430; 431; 526.

4. Bacis in Hdt. 8.20.1 (Artemisium); 8.77.1 (Salamis); 9.43 (Plataea). Cf. Appendix I pp. 182–3. Xerxes' expedition, with a rhetorical reference to his bridging the Hellespont and cutting through Athos, occurs briefly in *Or. Sib.* 4.76–9. The conjunction of the two achievements cannot be traced as a commonplace earlier than Lys. 2.29 and Isocr. 4.89. Geffcken also compares Lycoph. *Alex.* 1414–5. The fourth book of *Or. Sib.* was originally of Hellenistic date, adapted by a Jew in the late first century AD: for bibliography see J.J. Collins, 'Sibylline oracles' in J.H. Charlesworth (ed.), *The Old Testament pseudepigrapha* I (1983), 381 n. 1.

5. Thuc. 2.8.2; 21.3; 8.1.1. For legendary oracles from Delphi and an omen discouraging the Sicilian expedition, Parke and Wormell, *DO* I, 198 and II, nos. 166 and 167. See also H.W. Parke, *The oracles of Zeus* (1967), 136 (Dodona); 216 (Ammon). Thucydides mentions Delphic responses explicitly: 1.25.1; 103.2; 118.3; 126.4; 134.4; 2.17.1; 3.92.5; 5.16.2; 32.1. Also unspecified contemporary oracles: 2.54.2; 5.16.3 (which he emphasises as the only positive fulfilment). The Athenian delegates to Melos may be expressing Thucydides' view that those who took refuge in oracles were engaging in wishful thinking (5.103.2).

6. Ar. *Eq.* 61 (the Demos). *Pax* 1052ff (Hierocles of Oreus). Sibylla, *Pax* 1095 and 1116. *Av.* 959ff (*chrēsmologos*). Books of oracles, *Eq.* 116; *Av.* 974, 976, 980, 986 and 989. For a more detailed discussion of *chrēsmologoi* in this period, see J. Fontenrose, *The Delphic oracle* (1978), 145ff.

7. Plut. *Thes.* 24.5 (Sibylline oracle and the Pythia's response to Theseus). Cf. Parke and Wormell, *DO* II, no. 154 with Ar. *Eq.* 963 and other references.

8. Ar. *Av.* 968 and Parke and Wormell, *DO* II, no. 46.1. Ar. *Av.* 978 and Parke and Wormell, *DO* II, no. 121.3. Fontenrose (*supra* n. 6), 154ff, discusses the phenomenon, but only from the viewpoint that recurrence of phrases in Pythian responses and other oracles proves the unhistoric nature of the Pythian responses. This theory imposes a one-way system on what was probably a two-way traffic.

9. Lamia in association with Naiades and sea-nymphs, Dion. Hal. *Thuc.* 6, who cites these as examples of mythical beings in previous authors rejected by Thucydides. Cf. Eugon of Samos, *F. Gr. Hist.* 535 f 1. It used to be supposed that Euripides' play was called *Lamia* because of the ambiguity in Varro's citation (Lactant. *Div. Inst.* 1.6.8): *secundam (Sibyllam) Libycam, cuius meminit Euripides in Lamiae prologo* ('in Lamia's

prologue' or 'in *the* Lamia's prologue'). On this see A. Nauck, *Tragicorum Graecorum Fragmenta* (2nd edn, 1889), 506; Snell, *Suppl.* p. 7 corrects the title to *Busiris* on the evidence of *P. Oxy.* xxvii, 2455. 19. For Poseidon as the god of the Libyans, e.g. Hdt. 4.188. For Busiris as the son of Poseidon, Pherecydes, *F. Gr. Hist.* 3 f 17 (Sch. Ap. Rh. 4. 1396). For the Libyan Sibyl as a daughter of Zeus and Lamia, the daughter of Poseidon, Paus. 10.12.1 and cf. *supra* pp. 37–8.

10. Paus. 10.9.11. For the 'treachery' theory, Xen. *Hell.* 2.1.52 (who names Adeimantus, but appears to reject this version); Lys. 14.38 (395/4 BC, who names Adeimantus); Diod. (Ephorus?) 13.106 (with no mention of treachery). Plut. *Lys.* 11.1 only mentions it as a suspicion in the mind of Alcibiades. κακότης in the phrase δι' ἡγεμόνων κακοτῆτα is a favourite in *Or. Sib.* See 3.366 with Geffcken's note.

11. Musaeus: for the different traditions of his origin, Harpocration *s.n.* Bacis. cf. Appendix I, pp. 178–80.

12. Callisthenes, *F. Gr. Hist.* 124 f 14 (Strabo 17.1.43).

13. Gergis, J.M. Cook, *The Troad: an archaeological and topographical study* (1973), 347ff; B.V. Head, *Historia Numorum* (2nd edn, 1911), 545. Head fixes the final date by the statement in Strabo 13.1.70 that Attalus I (241–197 BC) destroyed Gergis in an unspecified year and transferred the inhabitants to a site on the head-waters of the Caicus. But see Cook (*supra*) 350–1, for archaeological evidence against taking this too literally. Phlegon, *F. Gr. Hist.* 257 f 2 (St. Byz. Γέργις) correctly describes the types of Sibylla and sphinx on the coins of Gergis and adds: 'they say that the grave of Sibylla is in the sanctuary of the Gergithian Apollo.'

14. Arrian, *F. Gr. Hist.* 156 f 95. This is the only record of Dardanus as the father of Sibylla. The mythographers were more interested in Bateia (alternatively called Arisbe) as the explanation of a Homeric difficulty, or as the ancestress of the Trojan royal house. For the daughter of Neso, Lycoph. *Alex.* 1465.

15. The Erythraean claim, cf. *supra* pp. 152–3. Paus. 10, 12.7 (where the site of her birth is on the hill, Corycus). Theodorus also in *IGR* IV. 1540; *Inscr. Eryth.* 224 (where the hill appears to be named Cissotas) and 226. The *Suda*, Σ335 gives Hermippus as the authority for Theodorus, but which Hermippus remains uncertain; also Aristocrates and Hydales and Crinagoras, as other possible parents, but whether of the Erythraean Sibyl is not certain. Infant prophecies in the former inscription (and Sch. Pl. *Phaedr.* 244 B) are simply attributed to Sibylla without mention of Erythrae. Proclus, *In Tim.* vol. III, p. 159 (Teubner), 288D and p. 282, 352E. For a discussion of the site in Erythrae, P. Corrsen, *AM* 32 (1913), 1ff.

16. *Inscr. Eryth.* no. 207, 1.73. F. Imhoof-Blumer, *Monnaies Grecques* (1883), nos. 63 and 63a. Callisthenes, *F. Gr. Hist.* 124 f 14 (Strabo 17.1.43; 14.1.34). Apollodorus of Erythrae, *F. Gr. Hist.* 422 f 1 (Lactant. *Div. Inst.* 1.9.7, etc.).

17. Heraclides Ponticus, cf. *supra* pp. 24–6. For later attributions of the name Herophile to the Erythraean Sibyl, Plut. *Mor.* 401B; Paus. 10.12.7 (but he applies the name alternatively to the Marpessian); Isidorus, 8.8 (but he appears to derive this from the colophon of the third book of the *Oracula Sibyllina*); *Suda*, H 541. Other occurrences: Varro *ap.*

Lactant. *Div. Inst.* 1.6.6 (the Cumaean); Tib. 2.5.68 (where the identity of Herophile is not made clear); Nic. Dam. *F. Gr. Hist.* 90 f 67.2 (where she is fetched from Ephesus); Martianus Capella, 2.159 (p. 67 Dick) (where in a corrupt passage she appears to be the Marpessian). For Herophile as the Samian Sibyl, cf. *supra* pp. 65–6.

18. Paus. 10.12.2. Apollodorus, *F. Gr. Hist.* 422 f 1. Bocchus, fr. 1 (Peter) (Solinus, 2.18). Diod. 4.66.5. *Or. Sib.* 3.419. For an alternative tradition that the Erythraean Sibyl was contemporary with the foundations of Rome, Augustine, *De Civ. D.* 18.23. For wars of Erythrae and Chios, e.g. Alcaeus, fr. 444 (Lobel and Page), G.L. Huxley, *The early Ionians* (1966), 48–9; and their general hostility, J.M. Cook, *CAH* vol. 3.3 (2nd edn, 1982), 217.

19. Heraclides, fr. 1 (Trespe), fr. 130 (Wehrli) (Clem. Al. *Strom.* 1.21.384P). For the text of the oracle, cf. *supra* p. 26. For the Sibyl's rock, G. Roux, *Delphes, son oracle et ses dieux* (1976), pl. xxxv.

20. For the Pythian Apollo as the mouthpiece of Zeus, H.W. Parke, *The oracles of Zeus* (1967), 49ff.

21. The Third Sacred War, Parke and Wormell, *DO* I, 216ff. The earthquake of 373 BC, Parke and Wormell, *DO* I, 213ff.

22. Diod. 4.66.5; cf. *Epigoni* (*Homeri Opera*, ed. T.W. Allen, vol. 5, p. 116) and Sch. Ap. Rh. 1.308. For the bay laurel at Delphi, Parke and Wormell, *DO* I, 3 and 26.

23. Plut. *Mor.* 398C. Euripides, cf. *supra* pp. 104–5. For Lamia, the eponym, Schwenn, *RE* 12 (1924), col. 546 no. 2. For Chrysippus and the Delphian claim to the earliest Sibyl, cf. *supra* p. 33.

24. For the Muses and Delphi, H.W. Parke, *Hermathena* 130/131 (1981), 104ff; Hes. *Theog.* 32; Paus. 10.12.2; *Suda*, Σ 355 (on which see n. 15 *supra*).

25. Plut. *Mor.* 398C; paraphrased in Clem. Al. *Strom.* 1.15.358P, who appears to have erroneously attributed the Sibyl's verses to the authorship of Sarapion.

26. Phlegon, *F. Gr. Hist.* 257 f 37 (p. 1188).

27. Plut. *Mor.* 566D. For 'Mt Vesuvius and the destruction by fire of Dikaiarchia' cf. Plut. *Mor.* 398E: 'these recent and strange disasters in the neighbourhood of Cumae and Dikaiarchia, sung of long ago and hymned by the Sibylline Oracles'. Plutarch in both passages must be referring to the eruption of Vesuvius (AD 79), but Cumae and Puteoli (Dikaiarchia) were not seriously damaged. The appropriate places were Pompeii and Herculaneum. Either Plutarch has made a topographical slip, or the verses of the oracle itself may have been vague in their apparent geographical reference. Had it been worked up *post eventum* from some forecast of damage to Cumae and Dikaiarchia originally suggested by the near presence of the solfatara? Plutarch's dialogue *On the face of the Moon* curiously contains no mention of the Sibyl: it probably occurred in the lost beginning.

28. The Jew who in the second century AD produced *Or. Sib.* 5 had a quite other view of Titus, and believed his sudden death was a divine vengeance for his part in the Jewish War (408–13). Cf. the equally unhistoric *Or. Sib.* 12.117–29, produced later, where, however, he is described as good.

29. For a chronology of the dialogues in Plutarch's *Moralia*, see especially C.P. Jones, *JRS* 56 (1966), 61–74.

30. Cf. *supra* pp. 41; 81 (Cumae); pp. 51–2 (Gergis); p. 40 (Alexandria Troas); pp. 76–8 (the Sibyl and the Tarquin); p. 48 n. 25 (Lilybaeum).

31. Chrysippus, cf. *supra* p. 33.

32. Dio Chrys. 37.13. The contest of Poseidon and Helius is mentioned as a Corinthian tradition by Pausanias (2.1.6 and 4.6) who supplies particulars of the division. It is also mentioned as a subject for theatrical dancing by Lucian, *De Salt.* (45), 42. The first line of the oracle is very corrupt. I translate Arnim's emendation. For πιτυώδης, cf. Strabo 8.6.22, who uses the same uncommon adjective of Poseidon's grove at the isthmus; perhaps a conscious echo of the Sibylline oracle. For Poseidon and the Isthmia, cf. also Ap. Rh. 3.1240 with Sch. (Musaeus, *F. Gr. Hist.* 455 f 1). It would, of course, be possible to argue that this Lamia was the monster, and the Sibyl the Libyan, derived directly from Euripides. But this seems to me improbable and not appropriate to the dignified tone of the passage.

33. Plut. *Dem.* 19; 21.4. cf. *Thes.* 27.6. Zenob. 4.78. Gemistius Pletho 2.24.

34. Duris, *F. Gr. Hist.* 76 f 38 (Plut. *Dem.* 19).

35. Hdt. 9.43.1. cf. Paus. 9.19.3. For the phrase 'an eagle in the clouds and upper air' cf. 'an eagle in the clouds' in the Delphic response, Parke and Wormell, *DO* II, no. 121.3. But one should note that the scholiast on Ar. *Av.* 978 believed the phrase occurred in the oracles of Bacis. The explanation in Zenob. 2.50 fits this context rather than the Delphic oracle. For Bacis, cf. Appendix I.

6

The Sibyl in the Hellenistic Period

You may charge me with murder — or want of sense —
(We are all of us weak at times):
But the slightest approach to a false pretence
Was never among my crimes.

With the conquest of western Asia by Alexander, the whole mould of Hellenic civilisation was broken, and it spread out into directions which it had scarcely touched before. Also internally the balance of society was displaced, and the relation of the citizen of the *polis* to his world was transformed. All these changes had their effect on the production of Sibylline oracles. To start with, Alexander's amazing career invited the creation of prophecies. In the restored democracy of Miletus the Apolline oracle at Didyma was revived and proceeded to foretell his triumphs. At Erythrae a new prophetess, called Athenais, arose to announce Alexander as the offspring of Zeus and to recall by her vaticinations her legendary predecessor, Sibylla. But also Sibylline oracles appeared in at least one new direction. As we have seen, Varro listed as his first and most ancient Sibyl the Persian, and cited an otherwise unknown writer of Alexander's deeds, named Nicanor, as his authority.[1] This vague reference does not enable us to determine the date or subject matter of these prophecies, but they are an illustration of the fact that the Sibylline oracles, which had begun in a distant corner of north-west Asia Minor and had spread south and west through the Hellenic world, were later to swing back to Asia, and find ultimately a new development in their original continent and in Africa.

Meanwhile in another direction the Hellenistic wars of the third century provided the subject matter of a new prophetess —

Phaennis the Chaonian. She would not be known to us if it were not for Pausanias, who in his diligent reading of books of divination had come across her prophecies. He lists her, after the end of his catalogue of Sibyls, together with the Dove-Priestesses (*Peleiai*) of Dodona, as 'women who prophesied through divine inspiration, but were not called Sibyls by men'. Phaennis, as he explains, 'was the daughter of a man who had been king among the Chaones' and was dated to the time 'when Antiochus had just come to power after the capture of Demetrius' (i.e. 281 BC).[2] Presumably, these statements about her paternity and date were derived from passages in her oracle, where, like Sibylla, she had given her name and parentage, and described her birthplace. Also in a Sibylline manner she referred to events in the Seleucid kingdom as though they were contemporary, so as to give an apparent date for her prophetic utterance.

The Chaones were one of the three major tribes inhabiting Epirus. They had been dominant in the fifth century BC, but in the fourth and third centuries the sovereignty over Epirus had passed to the Molossi. However, the tribes seem to have survived as subordinate units. So there may have been nothing wrong in Phaennis describing herself as a daughter of a Chaonian king, but her suggestion that she produced her oracle in 281 BC is fallacious. Pausanias later quotes seven lines from it, which he treats as a forecast of the defeat of the Gauls in Asia Minor by Attalus I (238/237 BC):

> Then the baleful host of the Galatae, having crossed the narrow strait of the Hellespont, shall boast, and they shall ravage Asia in lawlessness. But God will lay many more horrible things on all those who dwell by the sea for a little while. For soon the son of Cronos will raise up an ally for them, the dear child of the heavenly bull. He shall send a day of destruction on all the Galatae.

The 'son of the bull' was evidently Attalus: Pausanias cites a similar phrase from a Delphic oracle addressed to him. So the event alluded to is Attalus' victory over the Gauls, but Pausanias is too credulous in supposing that the oracle was genuinely prophetic.[3]

This is the only real quotation from Phaennis' book. Zosimus in his *New history* (written early in the fifth century AD) tried to attribute to 'Herophile, the Erythraean Sibyl, or Phaennis of

Epirus' some oracular verses which he quoted. Actually they were probably two responses issued by Apollo Chrēstērios of Chalcedon, but, because they dealt with the Gallic invasion of Asia Minor, Zosimus thought Phaennis a likely authoress.[4] Evidently he knew of her from Pausanias but had no direct access to her work, which had probably gone out of circulation in the intervening centuries. Apart from these references there are no traces elsewhere in ancient literature of Phaennis' oracle. So we cannot tell whether she dealt with other events in the third century BC.

Clement of Alexandria in his catalogue of Sibyls lists without comment 'the Thesprotian', and she appears again in the *Suda* with the rather obvious further statement that she produced oracles.[5] This may all come from the same source, but whether she should be identified with Phaennis is dubious. Pausanias is positive that Phaennis was not called a Sibyl, but one might read his statement as a deliberate contradiction of some authority who had classed her as one. More serious may be the point that the Chaones were quite distinct from the Thesproti and so Phaennis could only be called Thesprotian by a very loose transfer of epithets. Thesprotia was specifically the district in which at Dodona the oracle-centre of Zeus was situated. So one might more plausibly suppose that in the Hellenistic period a legend of a Sibyl connected with that sanctuary was developed on the same lines as the Delphic Sibyl. Dodona had a practice of imitating its greater rival, Delphi.[6]

That this was a common practice of the time, for oracle-centres to acquire legends about local Sibyls, is illustrated again by the existence of the Colophonian Sibyl, who was similarly associated with Apollo of Claros. She, too, appears in Clement's list and in the *Suda*, but the latter has much more independent information about her. 'She was also called Lampusa, the daughter of Calchas, and she published prophecies and oracles in hexameters and other things.' That this legendary figure was already created early in Hellenistic times is proved by the fact that Lycophron knew of her. He compares Cassandra in oracular frenzy to a 'Bacchante (*Mimallōn*) of Claros'. The legend that she was a daughter of Calchas, from whom she evidently inherited her prophetic powers, was founded on the story in Hesiod of the contest between Calchas and Mopsus at Claros. Calchas, as was foretold, had died there on meeting in Mopsus a greater diviner than himself. So it was fancied that he had a daughter who had lived on where her father was buried. Pausanias also knew of the Colophonian Sibyl, but in his practice of reducing these prophetesses to the minimum number, he identified her with the Marpessian Sibyl, whom he named Herophile. For he listed Claros together with Samos, Delphi and Delos as the places which she had visited.[7]

Several other Sibyls can be found as mere names or designations in Clement, the *Suda* and similar sources. It is probable that if we had more information about them, we would find that they too had been created in the Hellenistic period. A Macedonian and a Rhodian prophetess would be appropriate to the importance of these states at that time. Also we have already discussed the evidence for Babylonian, Hebrew and Egyptian Sibyls as examples from the world outside the Hellenic homeland. They illustrate how this form of literature spread into all the parts of the world where Greek was spoken.[8]

It is perhaps significant that the quotations from oracles of this period which survive are concerned with what is a new subject, natural phenomena, rather than with particular battles. It was not that the third and second centuries BC were lacking in warfare. Many epoch-making victories were won on land and sea. But war in the Hellenistic period had generally ceased to be an activity directly involving the ordinary citizen. It was a matter for professionals, and was not the clash of citizen armies over their boundary fields but the campaigns of monarchs about the sovereignty of vast provinces. This change in popular involvement is perhaps to be seen mirrored in the failure of evidence for Sibylline oracles mentioning particular battles, and the occurrence instead of oracles either foretelling the fall of kingdoms or else the dire effects of natural phenomena.

The most picturesque and complicated of these Sibylline extracts is the passage quoted in one of Plutarch's Pythian dialogues (the *De Pythiae Oraculis*) as an example of the perfect prophecy. The subject of discussion emerges at a point which we have already mentioned. A group of scholars accompanying a distinguished stranger round the sights of the Delphic sanctuary has just reached the Sibyl's rock and has mentioned the legends connected with her birth and death. This leads to a dispute about the genuineness of her prophetic powers. Boethius, who was inclined to Epicureanism, maintains that

Sibyls and Bacides in an arbitrary fashion cast and scatter

128

into the ocean of time names and phrases of all manner of disasters and coincidences. This previous saying of theirs is a deception, even if later, when some events happen accordingly, there is truly such an occurrence.[9]

Sarapion, a poet with Stoic leaning, takes up the challenge and maintains that the authenticity of prophecies can be proved by the circumstantial details which correspond with the subsequent event. He first quotes as an example the Delphic oracle warning Sparta against a lame kingship, which he interprets as referring to Agesilaus' disability, and follows it with seven hexameters, which he connects with the Romans and their defeat of Philip V.[10]

> But whenever the race of the Trojans shall have got the upper hand in contest with the Phoenicians, then unbelievable events will happen. The sea will shine with unquenchable fire, and, after thunder-claps, water spouts upwards will rush through the wave, mingled with a rock-mass, and it will be made firm there — an island never before named by men; and worser folk by force of hands shall conquer the stronger man.

Sarapion does not name the source of either prophecy. It is only from elsewhere that we know that the Lame Kingship oracle was delivered by the Pythia and had already been used seventy years before Agesilaus' reign in a debate on Spartan policy. The oracle about the Second Macedonian War is not quoted by any other author. So the fact that it is grouped with a Delphic response might be taken to prove that it had the same origin. But it is noteworthy that Sarapion follows it up with a briefer example: 'also the fact that to the Romans similarly five hundred years before was foretold the time when they would fight against all nations at once. This was the war against the slaves in rebellion.'[11] Here Sarapion is evidently alluding to Spartacus' revolt (73–71 BC) and dates the utterance of the prophecy to *c.* 570 BC. There is obviously no possibility that this could have been a response of the Pythia to a Roman consultation at such a date, but it could very well be a Sibylline oracle. In fact the round figure of five centuries may have been meant to indicate that this prophecy was supposed to be found in the Sibylline Books of the Roman state. The Sibyl who sold them to the Tarquin could be roughly dated that length of time before Spartacus' rebellion. The contents of the Sibylline Books could only be known after a formal consultation by the *quindecimviri*, when authorised by the Senate. Our limited sources for the period do not mention such an act, but it would be quite likely that the Books were consulted at such a time of general alarm, and that an oracle from them would be made public, if it would be calculated to allay popular disquiet.

Anyway, it is evident that Sarapion was quoting his examples of perfect forecasts from any oracular source that came to hand, and the verses on the Second Macedonian War may also be Sibylline rather than Pythian in origin. This is not to say that they came from the Roman Sibylline Books. Their underlying tone is not such as would ever have been issued by Roman magistrates. Instead they could appropriately come from a Greek Sibyl. There are also further arguments which make this attribution more plausible. First of all, there is nothing in the form of the verses to suggest that they are in answer to any enquiry. In itself this is a rather indecisive point, as it is true of a number of other probably authentic Pythian responses. But one must recognise that the whole content of the oracle would suit a Sibylline context. Particularly, as Fontenrose has observed, no historical responses from Delphi contain predictions of natural phenomena.[12] Such a generalisation is somewhat risky, but in this instance it is supported by the large number of extant Pythian oracles. By contrast the *Oracula Sibyllina* contains numerous predictions of natural disasters.

If we accept the conclusion that this prophecy occurred in a collection of Sibylline oracles, it describes in horrific detail a volcanic eruption which occurred in the submarine crater between Thera and Therasia. This event is mentioned in four other places in ancient literature, and where details are given they correspond closely.[13] Also the date is fixed in the fourth year of the 145th Olympiad (summer 197 – summer 196 BC). The first clause about the victory of the Trojan race over the Phoenicians plainly alluded to the end of the Second Punic War (201 BC). The only obscurity lies in the final sentence where 'the stronger man' and 'the worser folk' are deliberately not identified. Sarapion, without wasting words on justification, names Philip V and the Romans: that is, the battle of Cynoscephalae. Modern scholars are agreed that the battle took place in early June 197, which strictly would put it in the third year of the 145th Olympiad, and therefore make it precede the eruption, if that is accurately dated in the fourth year.[14] But the implication of the oracle is that the natural marvel preceded the human event, and Justin, the only ancient author to record the eruption in a historic sequence, inserts it between Philip's acceptance of a two-month truce, so that he might negotiate peace with the Senate, and the Senate's refusal, which was followed by the campaign of Cynoscephalae. The truce is dated by Walbank from November to January, 198/7.[15] This would leave some six months in the first half of 197 for the eruption to occur, if it was to precede the battle. It is possible that the oracle was written in this period, after the sensational eruption had attracted public notice and when the final result of the war was still in suspense. Flamininus in the campaign of 198 had clearly been gaining some superiority over Philip, and therefore the forecast may have been drafted with the prospect of a Macedonian defeat. But though the use of the singular might suggest the king, and the plural the alliance of his opponents, it was conveniently vague, and if the result had turned out differently, another interpretation could have been produced. However, the pattern underlying the oracle is essentially literary rather than historical. The end of the Second Punic War is to be followed by unbelievable happenings — fire in the sea and waterspouts that rush upwards. These perversions of nature are to be linked with another contradiction in human affairs — the stronger will be overcome by the worse.

It is quite probable that Plutarch's source for this Sibylline oracle was Poseidonius, who certainly had written extensively about the new island near Thera as an example of his theory of the operative effect of gas (*spiritus*) in earthquakes and eruptions. As a Stoic philosopher he was prepared to accept the possibility of divine revelation through prophecy, and attempted to provide a rational cause. So he may well have chosen these Sibylline verses as an illustration of the possibility of exact prediction.[16] If so, it would be highly appropriate for Plutarch to represent Sarapion, a Stoic in sympathy, as borrowing the example from such an authority. Also it may explain why Plutarch did not feel it necessary, in order to make his point, to go into any detailed discussion of the historicity of the predictions. He was echoing a passage in a well-known philosopher.

Another Sibylline oracle is extant which refers in a much more open manner to the Second Macedonian War and a Roman victory. It occurs in Pausanias and Appian with one major difference between their versions.[17] That in Pausanias runs as follows:

> You Macedonians who boast in the dynasty of the Argeadae, Philip when he rules shall be to you a blessing and a bane. Indeed the earlier shall place monarchs over towns and peoples, but the younger shall lose all honour, when he has been subdued by men both from west and east.

Evidently it is implied that this prophecy to the Macedonians was issued before the accession of Philip II, for Pausanias by his paraphrase interprets it as foretelling his creation of a Macedonian empire which Philip V was to lose. 'The men of west and east' are the Romans and Attalus I of Pergamum. No doubt this was the Sibyl's meaning. Appian's version was probably a later variant. By altering the last line to read: 'and after being subdued he shall perish here by men from the west', it omits any reference to Rome's allies and attributes the destruction of Philip V to the Romans alone. This looks like a later modification, when Pergamum had been absorbed in the Roman empire and the end of the Macedonian monarchy could be referred to in a loose phrase.

The oracle itself is probably a *post eventum* product of the period immediately after Cynoscephalae. It might have been produced as propaganda just before it, but it has too much of the tone of an epitaph on Macedonian imperialism for this dating. The phrases used are typically allusive. Philip II's spread of power is described in terms of setting up tyrants to rule as his subordinates, and Philip V's fall from empire is not treated as a transfer of sovereignty to Rome, but simply as his loss of honours. This is worth noting because in the apocalyptic literature which was to develop greatly in the next two centuries a different interpretation in terms of successive monarchies was to be put on this event.

Returning to Sibylline prophecies of natural disaster, the remainder are very vague in content and reference compared with the description of the eruption at Thera. For instance, when dealing with Sicyon, Pausanias mentions its devastation by an earthquake, and adds, 'it also damaged the towns in the region of Caria and Lycia, and the island of Rhodes was so severely shaken, that it appeared that the oracle of the Sibyl with reference to Rhodes had been fulfilled.'[18] Unfortunately Pausanias gives no chronological indication for the disaster, except that it must have been after Demetrius had transferred Sicyon to its later site, and it seems to imply that the effects remained visible down to the time of Pausanias' own visit. Earthquakes on Rhodes are difficult to identify because the island was very subject to that kind of disaster. The most likely is perhaps the one nearest to Pausanias' own day: in 138 AD in the reign of Antoninus Pius. Pausanias certainly knew of this instance, for he mentions it elsewhere in a eulogy of the emperor for his benefactions.

There are two passages in the *Oracula Sibyllina*, either of which Pausanias might have had in mind. In the fourth book in a sequence of disasters there occurs: 'and you, Baris, shall fall and Cyzicus, when cities shall slide with earthquakes, as the land is shaken, and evil shall come last to the Rhodians, but greatest.'[19] Though it is not specifically stated, the context would suggest an especially terrible earthquake for Rhodes. The hexameter verse mentioning the island appears to have become traditional, for it recurs again in isolation in Book 8. The likelihood is that Pausanias did not encounter it in either of these books, of which Book 4 shows signs of Gnosticism and Book 8 of Christianity, but in some earlier collection of Sibylline oracles.

Curiously the two lines which precede the passage which we have quoted in Book 4 are the only actual words of the *Oracula Sibyllina* to be quoted by an extant classical author. They are concerned with another form of natural phenomenon — an alluvial deposit. Strabo cites the verses twice: in Book 1 when discussing this geological feature in general, and again in Book 12 where he follows in detail the course of the Pyramus from its source in Cataonia to its mouth in Cilicia: 'It shall be to men who shall be at the time, when Pyramus the river with broad eddies by silting up its beach shall reach to holy Cyprus.' Strabo does not describe it as a Sibylline prophecy, but vaguely writes of an oracle being delivered, as though these two verses were all that was produced. This is probably to be explained by the hypothesis that he took them from some previous writer on geology or geography, who had confined his quotation to these lines and not named their context. But the first words of the quotation seem to be alluding to some disaster which the Sibyl asserts will take place when the Pyramus completes its alluvial deposit. The minor differences in wording between Strabo and the corresponding passage in the *Oracula Sibyllina* can be taken as clearly showing that, though they had a common source in the farther past, their transmission was quite independent.[20]

Notes

1. Didyma and Athenais of Erythrae, Callisthenes, *F. Gr. Hist.* 124 f 14 (Strabo 17.1.43; cf. 14.1.34). For Athenais, cf. *supra* p. 28. For the Persian Sibyl, cf. *supra* pp. 32–3.

2. Paus. 10.12.10. For the Chaones, N.G.L. Hammond, *Epirus* (1967) 685.

3. Paus. 10.15.2. I translate in line 2 Sylburg's emendation αυχήσει, as the best so far proposed. For Attalus I as ταυρόκερως, cf. Parke and Wormell, *DO* II, no. 431.1. For the date of his victory, E. Will, *Histoire politique du monde hellénistique 1* (2nd edn, 1979), 297.

4. Zosimus, 2.37. Cf. H.W. Parke, *CQ* 32 (1982), 441. Phaennis is also mentioned in Tzetzes, *Chiliades*, 7.548; 9.820; both passages merely derived from Zosimus.

5. Clem. Al. *Strom.* 1.21.398P; *Suda*, Σ 360.

6. For Dodona imitating Delphi, H.W. Parke, *The oracles of Zeus* (1967), 76.

7. Clem. Al., *loc. cit.*, n. 5. *Suda*, Σ 357. Calchas' contest and death, Hesiod, fr. 160 (Rzach). Lycophron, *Alex.* 1464. Paus. 10.12.5, and cf. *supra* p. 127.

8. Clem. Al. (*loc. cit.*, n. 5) lists, besides those already discussed, Phyto, as well as the Samian Sibyl, with whom she is elsewhere identified; Taraxandra, who is perhaps the Phrygian; the Macedonian (Μακετίς, for which form, cf. Strabo 10.4.10); and the Thessalian (cf. *infra*). The *Suda*, Σ 355, besides those already discussed, lists the Sicilian (because of the Sibyl's tomb at Lilybaeum; cf. *supra* p. 48 n. 25); the Lucanian (perhaps the Cumaean, as the Pseudo-Aristotle described the Lucanians as in possession of Cumae, cf. *supra* p. 78); and the Rhodian. The *Suda*, Σ 356, Sibylla Elissa (probably some Semitic Sibyl); Σ 358, the Thessalian, who was also called Manto, the daughter of Tiresias, cf. *supra* p. 46. For the Hebrew, Babylonian and Egyptian Sibyls, cf. *supra* pp. 41–4.

9. Plut. *Mor.* 399A, cf. *supra* pp. 113–7. For Boethius as an Epicurean, cf. the retort at Plut. *Mor.* 399E and 700D, where he is represented as using explicitly Epicurean arguments.

10. For other references to the Lame Kingship oracle, cf. Parke and Wormell, *DO* I, 181; 207. Xenophon (*Hell.* 3.3.3) describes it simply as Apolline; Paus. 3.8.9 says 'from Delphi'. The oracle about Philip V is listed as Delphic in Parke and Wormell, *DO* II, no. 357; cf. I, 275. But here it is argued instead that it is Sibylline. Sarapion was the recipient of the dedication of the dialogue *On the E at Delphi* (Plut. *Mor.* 384E) and acted as host in *Quaest. Conviv.* (*Mor.* 628A). For his Stoic leanings, cf. *Mor.* 400B.

11. Plut. *Mor.* 399D. According to Varro's list of Sibyls an oracle about 570 BC would have been produced by the Marpessian Sibyl, cf. *supra* p. 34. But Plutarch shows no knowledge of the Roman chronological scheme. The reference to the oracle as given 'to the Romans' is best taken as referring to the Cumaean Sibyl and her books.

12. J. Fontenrose, *The Delphic oracle* (1978), 161; Q 238. Herodotus (6.98.3) quotes a written oracle without further attribution: 'I shall shake

Delos, also, though it is unshakeable.' He regards this as fulfilled by an earthquake which followed on the departure of Datis from the island in 490 BC. Thucydides (2.8.3) is probably not talking about the same earthquake: see A.W. Gomme, *A historical commentary on Thucydides* II (1956), 9. The use of the first person indicates that it is spoken by a god — Zeus or Apollo? This makes it unlikely to be Sibylline.

13. Strabo 1.3.16; Pliny, *HN* 2.202 (with the Olympiad dating); 4.70; Just. *Epit.* 30.4.1; Seneca, *Qu. Nat.* 6.21.1, mentions the eruption that had occurred at Thera in his own day (AD 19 according to Pliny, *HN* 2.202).

14. Cf. F.W. Walbank, *A historical commentary on Polybius* vol. 2 (1967), 579. Polybius does not mention the eruption.

15. Cf. Walbank, *id.*, n. 14 560.

16. Strabo 1.3.16, the account of the eruption, followed by a citation from Poseidonius for an earthquake at Sidon (*F. Gr. Hist.* 87 f 87, with Jacoby's commentary). Seneca similarly, after referring to the most recent eruption, quotes Poseidonius on the effects of *spiritus*. As Poseidonius lived till at least 60 BC, he could also have included the reference to the revolt of Spartacus, even though his history did not extend so far.

17. Paus. 7.8.9; App. *Mac.* 2.

18. Paus. 2.7.1. Demetrius transferred Sicyon to a new site in 303 BC (Diod. 20.102). On earthquakes on Rhodes, Hiller von Gaertringen, *RE* Suppl. 5 (1931), col. 785, shortly before 219–18 BC, when the Colossus was overthrown (Pol. 5.88 states that the Rhodians managed the occasion so well that it turns out to their advantage); col. 812, AD 138. Cf. Paus. 8.43.4 (Antoninus Pius' benefaction); Aristid. *Or.* 45, addressed to the Rhodians on this occasion; Dio 69.4; SHA *Anton.* 9.1. Cf. *CIG* no. 2721 (Stratonicea) for another benefaction of Antoninus after an earthquake, perhaps on the same occasion. Inscriptions from Rhodes (*IG* XII, 1.708 and 9026) and Telos (XII, 3.30) refer to earthquakes without giving any precise dating.

19. *Or. Sib.* 4.99–101. Baris is introduced by Badt's emendation in place of the MS reading Σύβαρις (cf. Pliny *HN* 5.147). *Or. Sib.* 8.160. There are also elsewhere in the *Or. Sib.* two very threatening prophecies about Rhodes: 7.1–3, where the kind of destruction is unspecified; and 3.444–8, where the reference is exclusively to enslavement.

20. Strabo 1.3.8; 12.2.4; *Or. Sib.* 4.97–8. In both passages Strabo's readings are line 1 εὐρυοδίνης and line 2 Κύπρον, where *Or. Sib.* gives ἀργυροδίνης and νῆσον. It is usual, following Meineke, to emend the Strabo reading to suit with *Or. Sib.* in line 1, but to retain Κύπρον in line 2. I would prefer to retain Strabo's readings throughout, including the unique epithet εὐρυοδίνης instead of the conventional ἀργυροδίνης. All readings in line 2 give προχέων where Sterrett's emendation προχόων is preferable. Eustathius (*Dionys.* 867) and Tzetzes (*Chil.* 7.572–5) reproduce the lines from Strabo.

7

The Sibyl in Pagan Rome

Erect and sublime, for one moment of time.
  In the next, that wild figure they saw
(As if stung by a spasm) plunge into a chasm,
  While they waited and listened in awe.

We have followed the Sibyl throughout the passages in Greek and
Roman literature where her oracles are referred to or quoted.
With the collapse of the Macedonian and the Seleucid empires
before the might of Rome a change came over the Sibyl's
prophecies. Like the river Aidoneus in her native Marpessus, her
works plunged underground, and their course can scarcely be
glimpsed until they gradually emerged in the world of Christian
apologetics. In this hidden passage they were joined by various
strange tributaries, which coloured and changed the composition
of the stream, so that when it emerged it is difficult to separate the
original classical elements from the later accessions.

It is best to examine first the general references which indicate
the position which Sibylline and similar prophecies held in
Greco-Roman society at different times and the effects which they
produced. Our sources are sparsely scattered but give some
positive indications. For instance, when Mithridates in 88 BC
made his triumphant conquest of Asia Minor from the Romans,
Poseidonius, who had lived as a contemporary of the events,
recorded later that Athenion described to the Athenian assembly
how 'oracles from everywhere are prophesying (for Mithridates)
the rule over the inhabited world.' This reference to oracles is
vague and might apply simply to the responses given from cult-
centres. But in view of the contemporary decline of such shrines it
is tempting to see in it an indication of the dissemination of

136

Sibylline prophecies from different places, and there is matter in the *Oracula Sibyllina* which scholars have assigned conjecturally to the Mithridatic period.[1]

On 6 July 83 BC, while Sulla was fighting his way up Italy, the temple of Juppiter Optimus Maximus on the Capitol was destroyed by fire and the original deposit of Sibylline Books stored there perished. What the collection had contained can only be surmised. The consultation of the books is recorded on some fifty dated occasions in our ancient authors between 496 and 100 BC. Most of these instances probably were derived from the *Annales Maximi* and had some historic foundation. But all we are given by these entries are accounts of some plague, famine or prodigy which provided the impulse for the consultation, and some details of the ritual practised for stopping the plague or famine or 'procuring' the prodigy in accordance with the Sibylline books. The words of the oracle are never quoted. If the *Libri Sibyllini* actually contained this kind of material, they must have been notably different from any of the Sibylline oracles from which we have quotations, or also from the Judaeo-Christian *Oracula Sibyllina*. These foretell disasters without offering any ritual methods to avert them. A much nearer analogy to the apparent contents of the *Libri Sibyllini* would probably have been found in the books of 'purifications' (*katharmoi*) or 'initiations' (*teletai*), which are attributed to Epimenides and Musaeus. But since they were also credited with 'oracles' (*chrēsmoi*), it is reasonable to suppose that miscellaneous collections of this sort of material may have been circulating in Italy from the late sixth century and may have formed the nucleus of the deposit on the Capitol.[2]

The only verbatim text from the *Libri Sibyllini* is preserved in Phlegon's *Book of wonders*, an odd assortment put together in the reign of Hadrian. This offers an oracle which the *decemviri* read and expounded from the books in 125 BC on the occasion of the prodigious birth of a hermaphrodite. Hermann Diels, who examined the text in great detail, makes a convincing case for the conclusion that it really consists of two oracles, which had been originally fabricated in 207 and 200 BC on the occasion of two similar prodigies. There is good evidence to show that on the occasion of these two previous consultations, ritual in accordance with the Sibyl's prescriptions was performed. So one can take it that in 125 BC the *decemviri* simply extracted from the books the oracles actually written some eighty years earlier, and on this later occasion, if not previously, they had obtained the Senate's authority to publish the texts, so as to allay any public alarm by proving that the Sibyl had foreseen the prodigy and provided the proper remedy.[3]

The dating of the oracles to the Second Punic War is sufficiently indicated by some references to contemporary dangers and their remedies. Also the peculiar use of acrostics in the text, which we shall discuss shortly, at least proves that they cannot have been composed before the Hellenistic period. The second oracle by its detailed reference to the foundation of Cumae shows that its author thought that the *Libri Sibyllini* were the product of the Cumaean Sibyl — a belief which does not appear in the annalistic tradition but is seen first in Varro. The author shows one noteworthy contact with a Cumaean legend which was later to reappear both in Varro and Vergil. For he implies by a casual reference that the Sibyl committed her oracle in writing to leaves. Also he makes no suggestion of Apolline inspiration, but stresses the cult of Hera at Cumae. One may consider whether the author, whose knowledge of the colonisation of Cumae is historically sound, had some accurate tradition also of its cults, even if he was guilty of a typical exaggeration in assigning the Sibyl to such an antiquity that she could prophesy its foundation.[4]

The Phlegon text was no doubt released to the public in 125 BC. Whether other extracts also had been made available at other times or had evaded security is uncertain, but that what actually passed as Sibylline oracles were in circulation in the Sullan epoch is proved by the happenings when the Roman Senate set out to restore the lost collection. In the tumult of the Civil War it was to be expected that no immediate steps could be taken to re-establish the corpus, and it was not till seven years later in 76 BC that the consul Caius Curio proposed the appointment of a commission to go to Erythrae in search of Sibylline oracles. It is interesting, but not surprising, to notice that Erythrae was evidently regarded as the original home of Sibylla. But the results probably proved disappointing, for the commissioners returned with only about a thousand verses, which they had copied there from private sources. If the original collection had run to the three books of the conventional length, then presumably a thousand verses would be barely a third in bulk and would seem an inadequate replacement. So probably further expeditions of collectors were sent to search for utterances of the Sibyls. This would explain how elsewhere the collection is described as derived from cities in Italy — probably the colonies of Magna

Graecia — and Samos, Ilium, Africa and Sicily. These different localities suggest that, besides the Erythraean Sibyl, the Senate may have attempted to collect the oracles of the Samian, Marpessian and Libyan prophetesses. Some of these may have come from the official texts preserved by city authorities, but it is only mentioned expressly that some were from private individuals.[5]

The sacred college of the *quindecimviri* was entrusted with the task of editing this collection, from whatever Sibyl they were derived.[6] What criteria they used are not explained, except in one particular. They were able to detect and expunge certain verses as interpolations, because they were convicted by their failure to fit the acrostic pattern used. What this meant is illustrated by the Sibylline verses quoted by Phlegon. In these the letters forming the first line of the oracle are identical with the initial letters of the first and following lines, so that the same words can be read horizontally and vertically. Any interpolated line would break this tight pattern, and it may have been as a precaution against such tampering that the device was applied. But also it served to give a strongly magical effect to the composition.

Cicero knew of these acrostics as a feature of the Sibylline oracles, but the conclusion which he drew from them was that the Sibyl could not have been in a frenzy when she produced such verses, as they could only have been composed with deliberate thought. Modern scholars have used the occurrence of acrostics for another purpose: to suggest a limiting date for the composition of these oracles. There are no extant examples of this sort of pattern from the archaic or classical periods of Greek literature, but it was quite a favoured practice in the Hellenistic age, together with other devices of word-play. Most often the initials formed a cryptogram of the author's name. But Aratus used the device of horizontal and vertical identity at the beginning of the second part of his *Phaenomena*. Also the Sibylline oracle preserved in Phlegon shows this arrangement applied continuously throughout all the 70 verses quoted. If Phlegon can be trusted that this was the oracle reported to the Senate in 125 BC, this example antedates the destruction of the original collection, and so shows that the acrostic as a method of guaranteeing the security of the text was used before the post-Sullan restoration. On the other hand it also shows, as we have seen, that the Sibylline books which were alleged to belong to the time of the Tarquins contained oracles which cannot have been composed in this form until well into the Hellenistic period.[7]

The general picture which we get from the account of the post-Sullan restoration is that the Senate found it necessary to collect the materials from as wide a range of sources as they could. There was no possibility of simply going to Cumae and copying the sanctuary's records. Here one must remind oneself that the connection with Cumae may not even have been accepted in the seventies of the first century BC. For although the forger of the Phlegon oracle believed it at the beginning of the second century, it first occurs in Varro and the authors derived from him. So the Senate in 76 BC may have regarded the Sibyl who sold the books to the Tarquin as a wandering prophetess, connected uncertainly with various places, and perhaps only one of several individuals so described. So far as Cumae was concerned, they may have approached it fruitlessly. Two centuries later Pausanias could not find any traditional material there. On the other hand Erythrae had managed to raise and maintain the predominance of its claim to have been the home of Sibylla. So it is not surprising that it is prominently mentioned at this point in our accounts. But it would seem that Sibylline oracles were to be found at various places throughout the Roman empire. There is no indication that the ambassadors went farther beyond its boundaries — for instance, to Antioch or Alexandria — in their search.[8]

It is not suggested by our ancient authorities that the Senate made any search in Rome itself for texts of Sibylline prophecies. Probably the reason for this omission was because strictly Roman citizens were not supposed to possess copies of Sibylline oracles, since they were a carefully guarded monopoly of the state. But we have evidence soon after, that individuals could claim to have private information of this kind. When, on 3 December 63 BC, Publius Lentulus Sura was brought before the Senate charged with conspiracy against the Republic, Cicero reported how, on the testimony of the Allobrogian ambassadors, he had boasted to them that he was fated to rule Rome. 'In accordance with the Sibylline fates and the responses of the *haruspices*, three Cornelii were to rule the city: Cinna and Sulla were the Cornelii before him, and he was to be the third.' Cicero's rather odd expression 'the Sibylline fates' may have been meant to leave undefined whether Lentulus' information was supposed to have been obtained by some leak from the state repository or whether alternatively he claimed to have his own source of Sibylline prophecy. More important is the point that, while Cicero may have meant to shock the people with this picture of a traitor guided by divine forecasts, he does nothing to indicate that the claim to possess such information was in itself extraordinary.[9]

In the abundant evidence for the half century after the Catilinarian conspiracy there are no contemporary references to the private circulation of Sibylline oracles. The books themselves were officially consulted on two occasions and their contents used conveniently for political purposes. At these times rumours of their contents tended to circulate even before the official report had been delivered to the Senate. The lack of contemporary mention of the circulation of unofficial *Sibyllina* is probably to be taken as an indication of the vulgar level at which they were handled. Certainly, later, Lucan includes them in the catalogue of horrors which precede the outbreak of the Civil War together with monstrous prodigies and the prophecies of the Galli: 'And dreadful lays of the Cumaean seer are spread among the people.' This statement, although in a passage obviously written up for dramatic effect, may, like much else in the *De Bello Civili*, have come not entirely from Lucan's imagination but from a notice in a lost book of Livy.[10]

The *Libri Sibyllini* like everything else in the Republic fell under the reforming hand of Augustus. In 28 BC he completed and consecrated the great marble temple of Apollo on the Palatine as a thanks-offering for the victory of Actium. This was taken as the occasion to transfer the Sibylline books from the custody of Juppiter to two gilded bookcases in the new temple. In one way this could be regarded as a process of rationalisation. When the oracles had first been received, if it was in the Regal period, there was no temple of Apollo in Rome, and we cannot be sure that the Cumaean Sibyl, if the oracles were attributed to her, was even associated with that god. Hera, identified with Juno, Juppiter's partner in the Capitoline Temple, may have been the deity who inspired that Sibyl. But actually the choice of the original site for storage was probably dictated simply by the need for maximum security. Five centuries later the situation was very different. Apollo was accepted as the inspirer of the Sibyl, and also as the patron god of Augustus. His cult was being deliberately enhanced by the *princeps* while Juppiter Optimus Maximus, as the traditional deity of the Republic, was being allowed to fall somewhat into the background. The transfer of the Sibylline books to the Apolline temple on the Palatine both placed them in the precinct of the god who inspired them and also brought them near to the residence of Augustus, the new focal point of the state.[11]

It was later in his principate that Augustus felt able to grapple with the more difficult problem of the unauthorised circulation of popular oracles. At last, on the death of the holder Lepidus, he was able in 12 BC to assume the position of *pontifex maximus*, and with it the control of religion. He issued an edict that 'since much empty matter was published under a famous name', by a fixed date all prophetic books (*fatidici libri*) in Greek and Latin were to be surrendered to the *praetor urbanus*. These were examined, and those that were anonymous or of unsuitable authorship, amounting to more than two thousand volumes, were burned. A minority, of unstated amount, were classified as genuinely Sibylline and were retained. Evidently they were incorporated into the official collection. The edict was meant to guarantee that no unauthorised oracles were in circulation, for it specified that after the stated date, private individuals must cease to possess them. Some later episodes, however, show that, as one might expect, prophecies of this sort might be temporarily eradicated but would crop up again.[12]

In AD 19 the populace of Rome were disturbed by prophetic verses which passed as Sibylline: 'When thrice three hundred years have passed over, the Romans shall perish through civil war and Sybaritic folly.' As the last word starts a new line of verse, these are clearly only an extract from a somewhat longer poem. The nine hundred years are based on the idea of a thousand as forming a complete epoch and that the final century would introduce a great change. This would be quite in accord with some passages in the *Oracula Sibyllina*, though these particular verses are not found there. Why the populace should have been led to believe that AD 19 was at this point in the epoch is not explained. One can only conjecture that in some way it was implied that the Sibyl had uttered this prophecy nine centuries before. Anyway, Tiberius intervened. He declared the verses to be spurious and held another investigation of all books of oracles in circulation. 'Some he rejected; others he approved.' Otherwise following Augustus' example he burnt the majority but accepted some as authentically Sibylline and confiscated them to be added to the official collection.[13] Tacitus did not notice these events in the *Annals*, perhaps because they had little importance when viewed from his rather exalted social standpoint as a historian. But in AD 32 he recorded in detail a curious episode which may have interested him because it illustrated the relations between the Senate and Tiberius. Quintilianus, a tribune of the plebs, reported to that body that Caninius Gallus, one of the *quindecimviri*, had accepted a book of prophecies which passed as Sibylline. A motion approving this action was carried on a division, but this called forth a letter from Tiberius, dispatched from Capri, in which he mildly rebuked the tribune, as a young man unaware of ancient custom, but put the blame on Gallus, who was old in the knowledge of the established procedures, which he had ignored in accepting this book of uncertain authorship. Instead of being discussed at a poorly attended meeting of the Senate, it should have been read and assessed by the masters of the college, and submitted to a vote of the full body of the *quindecimviri*. Tiberius reminded the Senate of the precedent set by Augustus' action in 12 BC. So the book which had caused all this fuss was referred to the *quindecimviri*, and is not heard of further.[14]

Again, in AD 64 after the fire of Rome, the populace blamed Nero, and the memory was revived of the oracle current under Tiberius forty-five years earlier about the destruction of Rome in the nine hundredth year. Perhaps the imperial court was seen as fulfilling 'the Sybaritic folly' of the prophecy. To assure the people of the future, the emperor issued a statement that these verses could not be found in the Sibylline books. This denial could be given with more certainty because there had just been an official circulation of the books on the subject of the fire, which had produced instructions for the conventional atonements of Vulcan and other deities. But the people were not put off and simply substituted another hexameter line alleged to be Sibylline: 'Last of the sons of Aeneas a matricide shall reign.' As Dio Cassius in recording these events noted, the prophecy was to prove correct. Nero was to be the last of the Julio-Claudian dynasty. But Dio was uncertain whether to regard it as a genuine Sibylline oracle or whether instead to suppose that the populace itself had been divinely inspired to produce this forecast. As Suetonius' account of the same period shows, the *plebs urbana* was given to circulating verses about Nero, which were usually satirical, but not prophetic. One example was the single line: 'Nero, Orestes, Alcmaeon, all matricides.' This pasquinade was so popular that later authors actually attributed it to the Delphic Pythia as an Apolline response — which serves to show how easily such flying verses could be converted into oracles.[15]

The examples which we have discussed show Sibylline oracles, or what passed as them, circulating at Rome in popular, even vulgar, classes. But at the same time the works of the Hellenistic prophetess were having considerable impact on higher literature. The earliest instance which we know of was in the works of Alexander Polyhistor. A native of Miletus, he had been brought to Rome as a slave at the time of the First Mithridatic War, presumably as the property of one of the proscribed, and so obtained his citizenship and his gentile name, Cornelius, by the dispensation of Sulla. He devoted himself to a life of scholarship, probably under the patronage of one of the great Roman families, and produced what are described as 'numberless books', which earned him his nickname of Polyhistor ('Much researcher'). His main theme was the chronicles of the various Asiatic peoples, with whom the Romans were now coming into more frequent contact owing to the campaigns of Pompey, Caesar and Antony. There is no evidence that he was acquainted with Asian or Semitic languages, but by diligent search he would amass the information required from the numerous local historians, who during the Hellenistic period had written in Greek about their native antiquities. Among these compilations which he published was a 'Chaldaean History' which was largely derived from Berosus of Babylon, who himself had employed cuneiform sources.

After reproducing the Babylonian narrative of the Flood, Alexander inserts an account of the Tower of Babel, referring to the Sibyl as his authority. His prose paraphrase corresponds closely with the passage on the subject in Book 3 of the *Oracula Sibyllina*, and there can be no doubt that Alexander had before him a version of this oracle. This was one of the parts where the prophetess (who subsequently in the poem claimed to be Noah's daughter-in-law) writes of an event in the past tense, as though it had taken place in her lifetime. The story of the Tower of Babel is generally told on biblical lines, except for the detail that God destroys the building by a mighty wind in addition to distracting the builders by the confusion of their language.[16]

This citation by Alexander Polyhistor proves that a version of the third book of the *Oracula Sibyllina* had reached Rome by the mid-first century BC. But unfortunately there is nothing to prove when exactly Alexander published his Chaldaean History: it may have appeared as late as after 45 BC — the date of Varro's *Antiquitates*, which would explain why the latter shows no knowledge of it. It is usually supposed that Alexander cannot have lived long after 35 BC. It is therefore possible to suppose that this version of the third book was also accessible to Vergil at the time when he was writing the *Fourth Eclogue*.[17]

In discussing the relation of this poem to the Sibyl we are undertaking a task very different from what we have dealt with so far.[18] For the *Fourth Eclogue* is a masterpiece of European literature, whose value is scarcely affected by the extent to which it casts light on the Sibylline oracles. We need not doubt that in designating her song in the prefatory verses as *Cumaeum Carmen*, Vergil was implying that this poem must be read as a Sibylline prophecy. One ancient commentator was inclined to offer the alternative interpretation that the reference was to Hesiod and his account of the ages named after the metals.[19] But it is hard to believe that 'Cumaean' would not at once suggest to the Roman reader the Sibyl of Cumae rather than the poet of Ascra whose family came from Aeolian Cyme. The lack of obvious resemblance to the *Oracula Sibyllina* should not force one to accept this alternative, which still remains the less appropriate. The *Fourth Eclogue* is no mere translation or paraphrase of a Sibylline oracle. Rather it is a transposition of Sibylline motifs into a pastoral key.

The interpretation of the poem is sometimes clouded by the different purposes and diverse levels of thought which it contains. It is a graceful compliment to a valued patron, and also more obscurely it is a courtly tribute to the all-powerful Triumvirs. But further, it expresses the intense longing of contemporary Italy for a new age of peace and prosperity, and in giving utterance to this human feeling it rises above its own limitations of space and time, so that its symbolism throughout is infused with universality. The Middle Ages were not wholly misled in reading into it some at least of the significance and emotion proper to a contemplation of the Incarnation.[20]

This achievement is far away from the crude productions of Sibylline literature, to which at most it is indebted for some motifs. For instance, it is not in the Greco-Roman tradition of Vergil's day to expect the impending arrival of a Golden Age. The Golden Age as the primal epoch of a distant past was commonly accepted by poets and philosophers, and the cyclic view of time might therefore imply its return. But this was usually combined with the view that the universe must pass through a stage of destruction before the process would start again with a Golden Age. Even if it was accepted that this was the pattern of the future, the Romans were not expecting an end of the world to happen suddenly or in their lifetime.[21] No doubt similarly the original Greek Sibyls had not included this contingency in their oracles, but when these were borrowed as a model by their Jewish imitators, the motif of the impending Golden Age was one of the elements which they introduced, taking it from the Messianic expectations of the Hebrew prophets. Here it is significant that Vergil not merely presupposes the immediate advent of the Golden Age, but also endows it with some of the special features of the Jewish Sibyllines. The picture of the lion lying down with the lamb has suggested Vergil's 'herds will not fear mighty lions', and he goes even further than the prophet and the Sibyl in not merely taming but killing his snakes. It is strange, however, that we cannot find in the *Oracula Sibyllina*, as transmitted, the main theme of the *Eclogue*, though it does appear in a simple form in Isaiah. This is the idea of the Divine Child, born of mortal parents, but with whose growth and maturity in some mystic way the Golden Age is linked. Nothing like this is found in previous classical literature, and, while Vergil might have imagined the concept by himself, in view of his explicit description of this eclogue as a Sibylline prophecy, one would expect some element of the main motif to come from that source. It is too improbable that he had followed back the *Oracula Sibyllina* to their roots in the *Septuaginta*. All one can say is that, if Vergil knew a Sibylline oracle, which like Book 3 of the *Oracula Sibyllina* reproduced Isaiah on the peace among animals, his version may also have paraphrased the prophecy of a child Emmanuel. Of course the Augustan poet has given the concept a very different colouring in the explicit references to Greek mythology and Roman institutions.[22]

The Servian commentary on the *Fourth Eclogue* shows no sign of an acquaintance with the Jewish *Sibyllina*. It alleges connections with Sibylline oracles, but they appear to have a more classical colouring than what is now extant. For instance the Sibyl, according to Servius, 'divided the age by metals and also told who ruled over which age, and wished the Sun to be the last, that is the tenth'. In some points this corresponds to our *Oracula Sibyllina*: in others it differs completely. The tenth generation is a favourite point of reference in the texts, but there is no systematic pattern of ages with clearly defined rulers, and the division by metals is never mentioned. At one place in the third book there is mention of a 'king from the sun, sent by God, who will stop all the earth from evil war'. Actually all this is rather distantly connected with the *Fourth Eclogue* where to call the ideal age golden is a commonplace in this context. This is the only mention of metals and no tenth age is so identified. Servius can only maintain a connection with his Sibylline oracle by stressing the interpretation of the Sun as the Ruler of the Golden Age — *tuus iam regnat Apollo*. But this does not specially fit the context in the *Oracula Sibyllina*.[23]

The fact is that we cannot fully identify Vergil's Sibylline sources, and this must not be regarded as too surprising, since we have often noticed how fluid and variable was the Sibylline tradition. For our purpose, in tracing the passage of that tradition down the ages, it may be more significant to note that Vergil expected a reference, even indirectly, to the Sibyl through a mention of Cumae to produce some echo in the minds of his readers. As we have seen, there is some evidence that such prophecies circulated in Rome during the Ciceronian and the Augustan periods, and no doubt at least as much under the rule of the Triumvirate, when folk must have been constantly asking what the future held.

Vergil's personal answer took its place in the literature of the world, but it made much less immediate impression on the Augustan and Silver Age writings than his other account of Sibylline prophecy. The sixth book of the *Aeneid* became the model for descriptions of oracular consultations and served to establish the Cumaean Sibyl as a familiar figure in Roman literature. Lucan, in his great set-piece of Appius Claudius' consultation of the Pythia, creates his picture of the prophetess's frenzy after Vergil's Sibyl and converts the *adyton* of the Delphic temple into a vast cavern on the Cumaean pattern.[24] Later Statius in the *Silvae*, to celebrate the completion of the *Via Domitia*, imagines an epiphany of the Sibyl, who hails the road as the fulfilment of one of her own oracles. One or two phrases are borrowed from the *Aeneid* to describe her state of inspiration. Elsewhere Statius writes of her cavern as one of the entertaining sights of the neighbourhood.[25]

Also the longevity of the Sibyl becomes a favourite motif, often with a touch of exaggeration or humour. Propertius prays that even a Sibylline age cannot change his mistress's face, and assures her that such an epoch will not alter his love. Ovid, describing the festival of Anna Perenna, when those who celebrated it counted the cups of wine they drank and prayed for as many happy years, assures us that one can find men whose years would equal Nestor's and women who are Sibyls by the number of their potations. In the fourteenth book of the *Metamorphoses* Ovid used the *Aeneid* as a framework into which he could insert episodes of transformation. After paraphrasing Aeneas' consultation of the Sibyl and the descent of Avernus, on the way back (which Vergil had passed over in a few lines), Ovid represents Aeneas as vowing to build a temple to the guiding prophetess. But she refuses the dedication, explaining that she is not a goddess nor immortal. Instead she tells the story how she was to live as many years as she had held grains of dust in her hands. This was to be a millennium, and when she spoke to Aeneas she had lived seven centuries and had still three centuries to come. By the end she would be reduced to a mere voice. It was this transformation which justified her inclusion in the *Metamorphoses*, but although Ovid writes with his usual light touch, on this occasion he avoids the flippancy with which he treats other legends. Other poets, however, could use the Sibyl's longevity in less dignified contexts. Martial taunts a bawd in a mock epitaph that she will not equal the Sibyl in age: she will fail by three months. In slighter connections also, any reference to Cumae brings with it a reference to the prophetess. When Juvenal's friend in the third *Satire* decides to abandon Rome for retirement, he goes to Cumae and adds one citizen to the Sibyl. Even the red pottery produced in the town evokes from Martial an allusion to 'the chaste Sibyl'. The frequent poetic references are in marked contrast to earlier periods: neither Lucretius nor Catullus nor Horace had found any occasion to mention her.[26]

Notes

1. Poseidonius, *F. G. F. Hist.* 87 f 36 (= Ath. 5.50.213B). Cf. *Or. Sib.* 3.350ff, on which see B.C. McGing, *The foreign policy of Mithridates VI Eupator King of Pontus* (1986), 102ff.

2. On the *Libri Sibyllini* see A. Rzach, *RE* 2A (1923), cols 2105ff and Appendix II. Epimenides and Musaeus, Appendix I, pp. 174–8 and pp. 178–80.

3. Phlegon, *F. Gr. Hist.* 257 f 36, X. H. Diels, *Sibyllinische Blätter* (1890), 77–103. 207 BC: Livy 27.37.5; 200 BC: Livy 31.12.6.

4. References to contemporary situation, Phlegon (*supra* n. 3), ll. 24–5; 69. Acrostics, *infra* p. 139. Foundation of Cumae, Phlegon (*supra* n. 3), l. 53 (cf. Livy 8.22). Writing on leaves, Phlegon (*supra* n. 3), l. 65. Hera at Cumae, Phlegon (*supra* n. 3), ll. 55–6.

5. The most authoritative statement is Fenestella, *Annales* fr. 18 (Peter) = Lactant. *Div. Inst.* 1.6.14. As he gives the names of the three commissioners, his account is probably derived ultimately from the text of the *Senatus Consultum* in the *Acta Senatus*. Cf. Lactant. *De Ira Dei* 1.22.

Also Varro *ap*. Dion. Hal. 4.62.5; Tac. *Ann*. 6.12.4 (where the other places are listed). Cf. Lactant. *Div. Inst*. 1.6.9.

6. Editing the oracles, Varro *ap*. Dion. Hal. 4.62.6; Tac. *Ann*. 6.12.4.

7. Acrostics, Varro *ap*. Dion. Hal. 4.62.6; Cic. *Div*. 2.112. Phlegon *F. Gr. Hist*. 257 f 36, X. For a detailed discussion of the use of acrostics in Greek verse, see E. Vogt, *A & A* 13 (1967), 80ff. The only acrostic in the *Oracula Sibyllina* is a Christian interpolation (8.217–50), but it only reads vertically, unlike Aratus, *Phaen*. 783–7.

8. Varro and the Sibyl of Cumae, *supra* pp. 33–4. Pausanias at Cumae, *supra* p. 37. Erythrae, *supra* p. 52.

9. Cic. *Cat*. 3.9; 11 reporting to the people the events in the Senate earlier in the day. Cicero combines 'the Sibylline fates' and 'the responses of the *haruspices*', and associates with these two sources the prophecy of the three Cornelii, and a forecast that the tenth year after the acquittal of the Vestal Virgin and the twentieth after the burning of the Capitol, would prove fatal for the city and the empire. The intervals of ten years were a favourite Etruscan motif and probably belong to the forecast of the *haruspices*. The acquittal of the Vestal Virgin, Ascon., *In Toga Candida*, 82; Oros. 6. 3.1. Cicero later worked the subject into a rhetorical figure (*Cat*. 4.2). Sallust (*Cat*. 47.2), distinguishes the prophecy of the three Cornelii, which he attributes to the *Libri Sibyllini*, from the forecast 'that the twentieth year after the burning of the Capitol would be bloodstained with civil war', which he assigns to the *haruspices*. It is plausible enough that after both horrific events, the burning of the Capitol and the accusation of the Vestal Virgin, *haruspices* may have been officially consulted. The prophecy of the three Cornelii would obviously not have been the kind of matter officially revealed from the Sibylline books, although Sallust, unlike Cicero, refers to them explicitly, as does Quintilian (5.11.30), which is probably derived from Sallust.

10. 56 BC, the Sibylline books forbid the restoration of the king of Egypt by use of an army: App. *Syr*. 51; *B. Civ*. 2.24; Dio 39.15.2; 55.3; 56.4; 59.3; 60.4; 61.4; 62.3; Cic. *Fam*. 1.1.3; 1.7.4. Cic. *Fam*. 1.4.2 refers to the Sibylline intervention as 'a trumped-up religious pretext'. 45/4 BC, the rumours that Lucius Cotta had found in the *Libri Sibyllini* a prophecy that the Parthians could only be conquered by a king: Cic. *Att*. 13.44.1 (if this vague reference to Cotta bears this meaning — see D.R. Shackleton-Bailey, *Cicero's letters to Atticus*, vol. 5 (1966), no. 336 p. 382). Otherwise all sources refer to an intended announcement on the Ides of March, 44: Cic. *Div*. 2.110; Suet. *Iul*. 79.3; Plut. *Caes*. 60–2; App. *B. Civ*. 2.110; Dio 44.15.3. As this oracle was never officially reported to the Senate, it must derive from a leak in security, or what was taken as such. For modern discussions, see A.S. Pease, *M. Tulli Ciceronis de Divinatione* (1963), 528; S. Weinstock, *Divus Iulius* (1971), 340 n.l. For popular circulation at this period, Lucan 1.564; Dio 41.14.4.

11. Dio 53.1.3 (28 BC), completion and dedication of Apollo's temple. Suetonius (*Aug*. 31) combines in one sentence the assumption of the Pontificate, the edict against unauthorised prophecies and the transfer of the Sibylline books to the Palatine. But Sir Ronald Syme has suggested to me that this need not be taken as sound chronological evidence that all these events took place together in 12 BC. Suetonius was more interested

in grouping his subject matter together than in observing precise dating. The references elsewhere to the Sibyl would be much better explained if the books had been transferred at the dedication of the temple of Apollo. This would account for Vergil making Aeneas vow a marble temple to Apollo and Trivia, and promise in that connection a place for the Sibyl's oracles (*Aen.* 6.69ff). Also Tibullus (2.5) begins his address to Messalinus on becoming *quindecimvir* by invoking Apollo to come to his temple, and proceeds to write at length on the Sibylline prophecies; *supra* pp. 35–6.

12. Suet. *Aug.* 31; Tac. *Ann.* 6.12 (where, in spite of the indicative tense, I take the *quia* clause to be an echo from the original edict).

13. Dio 57.18.4, discussed by R.F. Newbold, *Athenaeum* 52 (1974), 110ff. For the importance of the tenth century, cf. Servius, *Verg. Ecl.* 4. 4. The Cumaean Sibyl divided time into ten *saecula*, each with its appropriate metal and the power which ruled over it (the tenth and last belonged to the sun). But Servius links this with Vergil's Golden Age, instead of with the fall of Rome. For ten γενεαί as the length of time, *Or. Sib.* 4.20. Elsewhere ten γενεαί are only the interval between significant events: e.g. the Flood and the generation of Cronos (*Or. Sib.* 3.108).

14. Tac. *Ann* 6.12. Tiberius may have disliked Sibylline oracles. The only other mention of them in connection with him in the *Annales* is when he vetoed a proposal to consult them about a flood of the Tiber (1.76.1).

15. Dio 53.18.3. The official consultation, Tac. *Ann.* 15.44.1. Suet. *Nero*, 39. Parke and Wormell, *DO* I, 284.

16. Alexander Polyhistor, *F. Gr. Hist.* 275 f 79. Berosus, *F. Gr. Hist.* 680 f 4, p. 382. Jacoby's commentary is lacking, but if he implied that Berosus quoted the Sibyl, he must be wrong: P. Schnabel, *Berossus und die babylonisch-hellenistische Literatur* (1923), 139. But Schnabel is not convincing in arguing that there was a Chaldaean Sibyl as the source and predecessor of the Jewish Sibyl (i.e. the author of Book 3). The Tower of Babel, *Or. Sib.* 3.97–105. The Sibyl and Noah, *Or. Sib.* 3.823–7. The identification of Moso (Alexander f 70) as a Sibyl is groundless, as shown by Jacoby.

17. It is usual to argue that Vergil became acquainted with the Sibylline Oracles because his patron, Pollio, was particularly interested in Herod and Judaism: L.H. Feldman, *TAPA* 134 (1953), 73–80. But D. Braund, *CQ* 33 (1983), 240–1, has lately shown that there is no sound evidence for these alleged Jewish interests. Nor is there any evidence for a connection between Alexander Polyhistor and Pollio. But in one passage, in *Aen.* 10.388, Servius believed Vergil was indebted to Alexander for a legend.

18. In dealing with the *Fourth Eclogue* I am greatly dependent on R.G.M. Nisbet, 'Vergil's *Fourth Eclogue*: easterners and westerners', *BICS* 25 (1978), 59–78. I find myself generally in agreement with his conclusions. For a very different analysis of the poem, reducing the Sibylline element to a minimum, G. Williams, *Tradition and originality in Roman poetry* (1968), 274–84.

19. Probus, *Verg. Ecl.* 4.4. Hes. *Op.* 109ff.

20. For the feelings of the time, Hor. *Epod.* 16 with even more desperation. The bucolic elements there are borrowed from Vergil (see Williams (*supra* n. 18), 276), and another fantasy, the Earthly Paradise in

the West, is substituted for the Golden Age. Instead of the Sibyl, Horace himself is the *vates* (line 66). The medieval interpretation of the *Fourth Eclogue* was, as often, anticipated by St Augustine (*De Civ. Dei* 10–27).

21. As an Epicurean, Lucretius envisages the collapse of the world as possible at any time (5.104), but is more inclined to detect a process of slow decay (2.1164ff). That the Golden Age could return in current time is first expressed by Vergil: see B. Gatz, *Weltalter, goldene Zeit und sinnverwandte Vorstellungen* (1967), 25 n. 56.

22. Peace among animals, Verg. *Ecl*. 4.22–5; *Or. Sib*. 3.722–95; Isaiah 11:6–9. Emmanuel, Isaiah 7:14–17.

23. Servius, *Verg. Ecl*. 4.4. Cf. *supra* n. 10. The tenth generation, e.g. *Or. Sib*. 3.168. The king from the sun, *Or. Sib*. 3.652. But as Gatz (*supra* n. 21), p. 7, says, the decade in period reckoning is as much Etruscan as Sibylline.

24. Lucan, 5.71–224, with an explicit comparison with Cumae at 1.184. The account of Appius' consultation may be derived from a lost book of Livy, for the story appears in Valerius Maximus (1.8.10), excerpted probably from that source. Silius Italicus (13.20) curiously transforms the consultation of the Cumaean Sibyl into a *nekyomanteion*.

25. Stat. *Silv*. 4.8.24; 114ff (also 3.5–95). Statius was born at Naples.

26. Prop. 2.2.15; 24.3. Ov. *Fast*. 3.531; *Met*. 14.130ff; Mart. 9.29.3; 14.114.2 (cf. Tib. 2.3.48; Juv. 3.2).

8

The Sibyl in Christian Literature

But much yet remains to be said.

As we have seen, from the time of Vergil the Cumaean Sibyl was
a familiar figure in Latin poetry. It is therefore significant that
when the Sibyl first appears in the Christian Fathers, it is in a
context with a consciously literary flavour. Hermas, the brother
of Pius (bishop of Rome, *c.* AD 148) produced a work of which the
first part contained an account of a series of visions in which the
author received moral and spiritual instruction. The first two
begin by Hermas going on the road to Cumae. In the first, after
he has been rebuked by a heavenly apparition of a woman with
whom he has been in love, he sees before him 'a white chair of
great size made of snow-white wool; and there came an aged
woman in shining garments with a book in her hand, and she sat
down alone and greeted me'. She gave him a message from God,
a mixture of encouragement and warning to him and his
household, and then said: 'Would you like to hear me reading to
you?' Hermas agreed and heard 'great and wonderful things
which I cannot remember: for all the words were terrifying and
such as a man cannot bear'. But he did recall and quoted the final
sentences which were comforting.

> So when she had finished reading and rose from her chair,
> there came four young men and lifted the chair and
> departed towards the east. And she called me to her and
> touched my breast and said to me: 'Did my reading please
> you?' And I said to her: 'Lady, this last part pleases me, but
> the first was difficult and hard.' And she said to me: 'This
> last part is for the righteous, but the first is for the heathens

and the apostates.' While she was speaking with me, two men appeared and took her up by the arms and went away to the east, whither the chair had gone. But she went away cheerfully, and as she departed she said to me: 'Play the man, Hermas.'[1]

One notices that in this first vision, although the aged woman is clearly pictured as a venerable messenger of God, she is not identified by Hermas. His second vision takes place a year later. Hermas is again on the road to Cumae, and when he comes to the same place, he kneels and thanks God for his former vision.

> But after I rose from prayer, I saw before me the venerable lady whom I had seen the year before, walking and reading a little book, and she said to me: 'Can you take this message to the elect of God?' I said to her: 'Lady, I cannot remember so much; but give me the book to copy.' 'Take it', she said, 'and you shall give it back to me.' I took it, and copied it all, letter by letter, for I could not work out the division into syllables. So when I had finished the letters of the book, it was snatched from my hand; but I did not see by whom.

After fifteen days of prayer and fasting, he was able to interpret the writing. This allowed the Christians forgiveness for their sins up to that day, but required reform for the future. Hermas then had a revelation in a dream. A very beautiful young man said to him:

> 'Who do you think was that venerable lady, from whom you received the little book?' I said: 'The Sibyl'. 'You are misled,' he said; 'She is not.' 'Who is she then?' I said. 'The Church,' he said. I said to him: 'Why then is she old and venerable?' 'Because', he said, 'she was created the first of all things. For this reason she is old and venerable, and for her sake the world was established.'

This somewhat naïve narrative is curiously designed in one respect. Hermas was misled into identifying as the Sibyl the aged figure with the book whom he met on the road to Cumae; but also it is obvious that the author means to mislead his readers into the same misconception, until at the conclusion of the message the true identity of God's messenger is suddenly revealed. As we have seen, the picture of the Sibyl as aged was a popular legend. So also was her association with books of prophecies, and Cumae was her traditional home. No doubt a Christian would be familiar with all these ideas. But when it came to describing the Sibyl in action, either Hermas had no knowledge of the Vergilian picture, or else he felt that her prophetic frenzy was too unsuitable to apply to the Church. Instead she is represented as giving him a lecture from a chair like some contemporary teacher of philosophy. The only allusions made to the real identity of the subject are that symbolically the professorial chair is snow-white, a heavenly colour, and it and its occupant depart to the East, no doubt implying that the earthly origin of the Church was in Judaea.[2]

Why then did Hermas introduce this suggestion of the Sibyl at all, if it was to prove erroneous? There may be two possible motives, one literary and one theological. As a piece of literary technique Hermas may have felt some need to make his visions interesting. The device of hoodwinking the reader and then later revealing the true facts to him occurs in one branch of popular literature — the novel. There it is frequently employed to complicate the action and hold the reader in suspense. For instance in Apuleius' *Golden Ass* the hero describes how on returning to his lodging very drunk late at night he encounters three huge burglars whom he slays. Next day he is publicly tried for murder, and is about to be sentenced to execution when it is disclosed that his victims were only three bladders and the whole proceeding simply part of the Festival of Laughter (*Risus*). This deception is more elaborate and sophisticated than Hermas' device, but it is essentially the same technique. Although the *Golden Ass* was probably written some forty years after Hermas' *Shepherd*, its main theme and also the incidental episodes were modelled on earlier literature — the Greek novel with its complex conventions had probably already been evolved before the imperial age.[3]

Apart from the literary motive, Hermas may well have had another aim besides. It might seem remarkable that he would expect his Christian readers to accept initially the suggestion that the Cumaean Sibyl could be the mouthpiece of God's messages to believers. The Christian Fathers would not generally approve of any such view of the Sibyl and her function. At most, as we shall see, they regarded her as God's prophetess to the Greeks. But something may perhaps be learned from an opponent of Christianity. Celsus, writing about AD 160, tried to discredit the faith by calling attention to heresies and aberrations in it. One of these sects was the Sibyllistae, who apparently gave much credit to the authority of the prophetess. Celsus suggested ironically that the Christians would have done better to 'put forward the Sibyl as the child of God rather than Jesus, who led a most objectionable life and suffered a most contemptible death'. Celsus also accuses the Christians of interpolating 'many blasphemous things heedlessly' into the Sibylline Oracles.[4]

We owe the evidence for these attacks to Origen, who produced a detailed reply to Celsus about a century later. On the particular points he implied that Celsus' statements are in error. As for the Sibyllistae, Origen did not recognise their existence, and suggested that Celsus had mis-heard some statement on the subject. The alleged Christian interpolations he refused to accept on the ground that Celsus did not demonstrate the charge by citing earlier uninterpolated versions of the oracles. This second point is one which modern scholars can to some extent check independently. There are various passages in the extant *Oracula Sibyllina* which would now be accepted as Christian interpolations solely on the strength of their content, even though we do not possess earlier uninterpolated texts. Of course, as our collection dates from the end of the fifth century AD, it is impossible to prove that the Christian interpolators were already at work in the second century, as early as the time of Celsus. Some, at least, of the interpolations look likely to have been inserted much later. Yet on this argument one would be inclined to give Celsus the benefit of the doubt.[5] If so, one also may well ask whether Origen was justified in denying offhand by implication the existence of the Sibyllistae. Celsus, writing in Rome soon after the mid-second century AD may well have had evidence for the previous existence there of the Sibyllistae, while Origen in Caesarea writing shortly before AD 250 may have had no knowledge of them. Such a sect might have died out in the intervening century.

Certainly Hermas' introduction of the Church as a substitute for the Sibyl in his first two visions makes more sense, if one supposes that he was implicitly criticising some contemporary Christians who were excessively inclined to find God's messages in the oracles, and perhaps at times to help out the claim by producing Christianised versions. Here one may note the final word on the subject in Hermas' *Shepherd*. When the author asked why the Church appeared as 'aged and venerable', he was told that she was the first of created things. In other words, the Church was not created by Jesus in Palestine in the first century AD. In this respect the greater the antiquity, the greater the validity. It was often used as an argument for the higher authority of the Sibyl over other pagan prophets that she had prophesied in the earliest period of human history, even before Orpheus. But Hermas finally trumped this argument with the claim (which is also found elsewhere in the Christian Fathers), that the Church was the earliest of God's creations, before the world was made. After this statement it would be hard for any Christian to produce a Sibylline oracle as an alternative authority.[6]

There is only one passage elsewhere in the Christian Fathers where the Sibyl is used as a source of evangelical teaching in a way that implies her spiritual importance. Clement of Alexandria in the *Stromateis* quotes an apocryphical treatise — *The teaching proclaimed by Peter* (*Petrou Kerygma*). As Clement explains:

> God by giving the Prophets willed that the Jews should be saved, and similarly also when God had raised up from the Greeks the most esteemed who were of their native language as prophets, as they were able to receive the blessing from God, he distinguished them from the bulk of mankind. Paul the Apostle will reveal this in the *Teaching proclaimed by Peter*, when he says: 'Take also the Greek books, get to know from the Sibyl how she revealed one God and the things to come, and take and read Hystaspes and you will find written more conspicuously and more clearly the Son of God, and how many kings will make war on the Christ, hating him and those who bear his name, and their endurance and his appearing.[7]

The context of these words can only be conjectured, but it seems as though St Paul was represented as addressing a pagan audience and recommending them to read the oracles of the Sibyl and Hystaspes for the sake of their prophecies of the future, expressed in the terms of Christian apocalyptic visions. Hystaspes, who here, as in a few other places, is grouped with the Sibyl, was a legendary Persian king whose oracles had been originally concocted in the Hellenised regions of the Parthian empire. They were anti-Roman in feeling, but they spread westward into the Roman empire, where they, like the *Oracula Sibyllina*, became interpolated by Christians.

The composition of this apocryphal sermon of St Paul may have been influenced by his quotation from Aratus in his address to the Areiopagites. But here he goes much further by recommending the detailed reading of the Sibylline oracles and the book of Hystaspes. One need not suppose that this conveys any genuine evidence of St Paul's preaching, but it illustrates instead the high value which some early Christians were prepared to put on these pagan prophets. This attitude may belong to a preliminary stage in the complex process of establishing a selective relationship between Christian revelation and pagan literature.[8]

If we follow through the references to the Sibyl in the Christian Fathers, the next in date after the *Shepherd* of Hermas is Justin's *Apology* (soon after AD 150, perhaps 152/3). He discusses the resurrection of the dead and, after quoting references in the Gospels to Gehenna, mentions that Sibylla and Hystaspes foretold that there would be a destruction by fire of the mortal creation. This is the testimony of the Sibyl, which would be regularly cited by Christian writers over the centuries until the famous lines in the *Dies Irae*. It is interesting to notice how Justin, like the author of the *Teaching proclaimed by Peter*, grouped the Sibyl and Hystaspes together. But in this instance Justin need not have read an interpolated Christian version of either of these prophecies. The destruction of the world by fire occurs in the Jewish type of *Oracula Sibyllina*, and would probably have been familiar to Persian thought, from which indeed the Jews may have derived the idea.[9]

Elsewhere Justin refers again to Hystaspes and Sibylla together. He records how 'divine providence through the prophetic spirit' had warned mankind of the recompense for wicked deeds.

But by the activity of evil *daemones* death has been prescribed against those who read the books of Hystaspes or Sibylla or the prophets, in order that through fear they may turn aside men who were seizing the chance to obtain knowledge of the good, but might instead hold them enslaved to evil. But ultimately the *daemones* have not the strength to achieve this. For without fear we not only obtain these prophecies, but also, as you see, we bring them to your notice, knowing that they will appeal to all.

Here Justin was prepared to write of the same spirit of prophecy inspiring Hystaspes, Sibylla and the Old Testament prophets. His mention of the death penalty for reading these books has caused some trouble to those scholars who searched the legal texts for evidence of this offence. The nearest instance which they have found is a prohibition on all enquiry about the health of the emperor and the state of the commonwealth. But, as we have seen, as early as the principate of Augustus the inhabitants of Rome could be required to surrender their Sibylline books, and a similar requirement had been enforced by Tiberius. So there was probably even under Antoninus Pius in Rome at least a legal prohibition against possessing such oracular books, though as Justin implies, it may not have been enforced for many years, and whether the death penalty had actually been inflicted in such cases is very dubious. Still it was possible for Justin to regard this potential censorship as inspired by evil spirits for their wicked purpose to corrupt mankind.[10]

The later writers of apologies for Christianity occasionally cited Sibylline oracles as something which was familiar to their pagan readers and might prove some point with regard to their religious beliefs. For instance Athenagoras in an appeal addressed to Marcus Aurelius and Commodus (AD 177–80) cites examples of human beings regarded as divine. He begins with Semiramis, referring to Ctesias for the story of her life. Then he introduces the Sibyl as mentioned by Plato, and quotes the lines from Book 3 of the *Oracula Sibyllina* in which she describes Cronus, Titan and Iapetus as kings in the tenth generation after the Flood. Athenagoras follows with Heracles and Perseus, deified for strength, and Asclepius for skill, and ends with Antinous 'deified by the benevolence of your ancestors'. Apart from Ctesias, Sibylla is the only authority named here, and it is interesting that the six lines quoted from her are the first verbatim passage to appear in a Christian writer. The earlier references to Sibylline prophecies are without verbal quotation, and although it is possible to find passages referring, for instance, to the destruction of the world by fire in the surviving *Oracula Sibyllina*, one cannot prove that the earlier authors were actually referring to the same passages which we still possess. But here the extensive quotation points strongly to the belief that Athenagoras knew our *Oracula Sibyllina* Book 3, and regarded its prophecies as 'the Sibyl'.[11]

A remarkable contrast is provided by Tertullian's *Ad Nationes*, written some twenty years later (AD 197), soon after his conversion to Christianity. He gives a Latin paraphrase of the same passage in Book 3 but treats the Sibyl with bitter sarcasm. While he describes her as extant before all literature and 'the true prophetess of truth' (*veri vera vates*), he says the pagans have applied her name to the prophetess of demons. This is the way in which Christians would have described the Delphic Pythia, but it is not their usual view of the Sibyl. At this time Tertullian was still an orthodox Christian, but he was a man of such strong prejudices and violent impulses that we should probably discount his hostile attitude to the *Oracula Sibyllina* as a personal prejudice.[12]

His later life was to show that Tertullian was particularly susceptible to the influence of prophecy. For he deserted the orthodox church for the Montanists and ended by leading some splinter-group of his own. The Montanists deserve a brief digression on their own account, not because they show any sign of taking notice of Sibylline prophecies but because they present a remarkable parallel to it. The movement started in an out-of-the-way district in Phrygia, where its leaders were Montanus, Priscilla and Maximilla, who delivered a new prophetic revelation. Maximilla, the last of these to survive, behaved curiously like a Sibyl. She announced that the Lord had 'sent her to learn the knowledge of God as a founder of a sect to inform and interpret this time of trouble, and of a covenant and promise, under compulsion willy nilly'. She herself was to be a prophetess, but after her 'there would be no more, but the end of the world'. Accordingly she foretold that after her death there would be wars and confusions. To the satisfaction of the orthodox, this typically Sibylline prophecy was not fulfilled. Instead, as Eusebius records, this was an unusual interval of thirteen years of peace throughout the empire, and the Christians were also free for that time from persecution. This points conclusively to the supposition that the rise of the Montanists had occurred under Marcus Aurelius and the death of Maximilla had been followed by the period of tranquillity, which ran from the beginning of the sole reign of Commodus to about AD 193.[13]

The fact that the sect of the Montanists hailed from an out-of-the-way village in Phrygia reminds one of the similar place of origin attributed to Sibylla of Marpessus. It may be a mere coincidence, but to those who see something characteristic of Asia Minor in the form of Sibylline inspiration it may seem more like a recurrence of the same phenomenon. The content of Maximilla's prophecy, as reported by hostile orthodox Christians, is partly typical of apocalyptic revelation, but the reference to a covenant and a promise belong more to the co-founder of a religious sect. The one unusual feature which is especially reminiscent of the *Oracula Sibyllina* is the strong emphasis on the compulsion to prophesy, even against the diviner's will. The Sibyls in the corpus several times give expression to this feeling.[14]

It should be noted as remarkable that some ill-educated peasants in an obscure hamlet in Phrygia were able to start a movement which within a generation had reached Rome and exercised a significant influence on the religious life of its time. This was partly through the medium of transmission provided by the expanding Christian church. But also it would be true to say that this period from the time of Marcus Aurelius to that of Diocletian saw a great revival and development in the search for divine revelation in many forms. For instance, it was the time when under the guidance of the Julians, theurgy emerged as a form of cult and expressed itself in the Chaldaean Oracles. But this religious renaissance was not confined to new movements. The older institutions joined in the change of interest. For the first time we find that the long-established Apolline oracle-centres, especially in Asia Minor, are approached by a new type of enquirer. Enquiries about the nature of the gods and their functions, about the human soul and life after death are put to the priesthood and answered in discursive verses, which for the first time do not deal with questions of specific cult-practice but general problems of theology.[15]

It is possible that this developing attitude to the basic problems of theology and *Weltanschauung* can be held to some extent accountable for the changing treatment of the *Sibylline Oracles*, which both differs from earlier periods in Christian apologetics and also varies conspicuously from individual to individual among the Christian Fathers. Origen, as we have seen, never cites the Sibyl on his own account, and similarly his pupil, Eusebius, in his lengthy *Praeparatio Evangelii* only mentions her where references to her occur in quotations from Josephus, Clement of Alexandria and Tatian.[16] He never calls any special attention to her words. In contrast Clement of Alexandria himself quotes her quite often in all sorts of contexts, but it is noticeable that he does not treat her in any way markedly different from the numerous other Greek authors whom he quotes. He was prepared to believe that even pagans might be to some extent guided by the Spirit of God, and so was not inclined to accord any special merit to Sibylline prophecy.[17] But there is a further group of Christian authors who view the Sibyl quite differently. They treat the *Oracula Sibyllina* on much the same footing as the Hebrew prophets, regarding them as God's mouthpieces uttering his word to the Greeks. This high valuation of Sibylline prophecy harks back to the apocryphal teaching proclaimed by Peter. The earliest example in a formal evangelical work occurs in the *To Autolycus* by Saint Theophilus, bishop of Antioch in the last years of the second century AD. He expounds this view of Sibylline prophecy very elaborately and rather clumsily:

> The men of God, made bearers of the Holy Spirit and prophets, inspired by God himself and skilled, were made divinely taught and holy and righteous. Therefore also they were thought worthy to receive this reward, to become the instruments of God and to contain the wisdom from Him. By this wisdom they told of the creation of the world and all the rest, and foretold plagues and famines and wars. There were not one or two, but many in various times and occasions both among the Jews, and also Sibylla among the Greeks. They all uttered matter agreeable and in harmony with each other; the events that had happened before them and those in their time and those which are now being fulfilled. Therefore we are convinced about the future that it will be so, just as the early events have fitted with the prophecies.[18]

Theophilus modelled his own exposition on the Sibylline oracle known to him. This was evidently Book 3 in its original form. For he quotes from the lost beginning of the book the argument against polytheism that if the pagan gods were immortal and continued to propagate, the world would be crammed full of them. Also he began his narrative with the Creation, and, after citing the Sibyl on the Tower of Babel, later, when reverting to the attack on polytheism, he quotes from her, starting at the beginning, in two long extracts of 35 and 49 verses. Nothing like this elaborate use of the *Oracula Sibyllina* had previously occurred. Theophilus seems only to know Book 3 in its complete form, and evidently regarded it as divinely inspired and an ideal model for an evangelical tract. He was only the first of several writers to quote the Sibyl *in extenso*.[19]

The next was the author of the *Cohortatio ad Graecos* who passes under the name of Justin. Harnack has shown that it was probably written in the latter half of the third century before the Great Persecution under Diocletian. The writer quotes from *Oracula Sibyllina* Book 3 in its original form, and also Book 4; in addition he gives a prose paraphrase of what was probably the Christian interpolation in Book 8. He is even prepared to quote Orpheus *in extenso* to show that he too was an advocate of monotheism, not, as supposed, of polytheism. But he seems to have had a special interest in the Sibyl. He gives a long and detailed account of what he found about her on a visit to Cumae. Whether he had undertaken this journey because he was already inquisitive about her, or whether instead it served to rouse his interest, remains unexplained. He allowed himself to be guided by 'those who had received from their forefathers the ancestral traditions' as he solemnly introduces them to the reader, though elsewhere he simply calls them 'the guides'. They were no doubt pagans: in fact they may have been minor members of the staff of the temple of Apollo. But our author does not let that fact prevent him from reporting their descriptions of the site and accepting their explanation of the anomalies of Sibylline oracles. He, like other Christian Fathers, introduces the Sibyl to his readers as 'ancient and very old' and records her mention by Plato as part of her credentials. But also he accepted the implication of Plato's references, that the Sibyl, like other diviners, produced her prophecies in a state of trance, and when she emerged from this condition did not know what she had said. The pseudo-Justin wished to use this hypothesis as an explanation and excuse for the unmetrical and corrupt passages in the oracles, as he knew them. The Cumaean guides assured him that the Sibyl's words had been taken down from her mouth by ill-educated scribes whose errors the Sibyl was unable to correct through lack of recollection. Evidently to him the unliterary quality of the *Oracula Sibyllina* was a defect which he expected would put off his pagan readers. So it needed to be explained.[20]

The pseudo-Justin's defence of the Sibylline oracles is ingenious, but it partly fails because, like many modern scholars, he did not recognise the distinction between a clairvoyante and a medium and the corresponding difference between the Sibyl and the Pythia. The true explanation of the faults in metre and style in the *Oracula Sibyllina* is probably complex. On the one hand the authors (and most of the books had probably more than one author) were mostly not Greeks but Jews, and may have been writing in an acquired language. Even if they had spoken Greek from childhood, they probably had not received a normal and complete Hellenic education. So it was not to be expected that they could express themselves without error in quasi-epic diction and metre. But also another factor must be reckoned on. As we have seen, much points to the circulation of these oracles in lower circles than those concerned with high literature. Hence it is to be supposed that they were not copied by professional scribes but by all sorts of amateur writers who were not trained to read and write manuscripts correctly. One may recall Hermas' quaint account of his difficulties when faced with the task of reproducing the Church's little book.[21] The pseudo-Justin's apology for the literary deficiencies of Sibylline prophecy was to set a pattern for future writers.

There was a third Christian author who was to make even more extensive use of Sibylline oracles: Lactantius in his *Divinae Institutiones*, a massive work of Christian apologetics, written in Latin in seven books. A native of Africa, where he was converted to Christianity, he was summoned by Diocletian to Nicomedia to the post of professor of Latin rhetoric. There he began his great work before the Persecution and completed the first edition after he had fled to the West, probably to his native Africa. In the East he would have encountered the Sibylline oracles, in greater variety and extent than he could have known them before. The *Divinae Institutiones* show a close acquaintance with at least six books (3–8), and his references to them make it clear that he was not depending on some anthology but quoting direct from the texts. Again he derived from Varro the list of the ten Sibyls with some particulars about them. Probably in this instance there was some intermediate source. But Lactantius gave a canonical form to this traditional list which, as we have seen, was accepted from him both in Byzantine literature and by the Western Church. Unlike Theophilus and the pseudo-Justin, Lactantius does not quote long extracts from the *Oracula Sibyllina*. He mostly quotes only a line or two at a time, but in all, his citations run to hundreds of lines and are scattered throughout lengthy discussions of many different theological questions. More than any other Christian Father he gives the impression of having devoted scholarly time and effort to placing the Sibyls in their historical context and extracting the maximum of religious instruction from their message.[22]

It was a somewhat ironical situation that at the very period when Lactantius was striving earnestly to fit the *Oracula Sibyllina* into the work of Christian apologetics, the whole subject itself was undergoing a revolutionary change owing to the alteration of external circumstances. When he began to work on the *Divinae Institutiones*, Christianity was a minority religion still needing to justify its existence before an establishment which was about to turn on it in persecuting fury. His latest edition of the book was dedicated to Constantine as emperor of the West, who was soon to make Christianity the official religion of the whole Roman Empire. Hence it would not be necessary to write works convincing pagans of the need to treat Christianity seriously on the strength of supposed echoes of Christian teaching in pagan authors. The victory of Christianity would take almost a century to carry through to its conclusion, but already theology was turning its attention to the problems of formulating a detailed Creed and coping with those who objected to the rules and beliefs inherent in an established church.

Appropriately the last major statement on the Sibyl comes from the mouth of the first Christian emperor. Eusebius appended to his *Life of Constantine* a Greek translation of one of his Latin orations. This document has often been suspected as a later forgery, but recent opinion seems to agree on its authenticity and puts down its peculiarities partly to the clumsy work of the official translator and partly to the highly individual personality of the author. For it is no formal state document but an idiosyncratic statement of the emperor's feelings and attitude towards Christianity addressed to a congregation as a sermon. How far the content may have been derived from matter supplied by the emperor's advisers cannot be established. But he seems to have stamped his own personality on the resulting speech.[23]

Constantine introduces the Sibyl in this way:

It has occurred to me to mention the various evidences of Christ's divinity. The Erythraean Sibyl, who states that she was born in the sixth generation after the Flood, was a priestess of Apollo. Wearing the garland like the god whom she worshipped, and ministering the tripod round which the snake is coiled, she delivered Apolline oracles to those who enquired of her, through the foolishness of her parents who had devoted her to this service through which unseemly passions and nothing solemn arises as is shown by the legends about Daphne. She, then, within the *adyton*, carried away in that unreasonable superstition, and having become filled with a genuinely divine inspiration, prophesied in verse what would happen about God and clearly by the initial letters of the verses, which is called an acrostic, revealed the story of the coming of Jesus.[24]

Constantine proceeds to quote in full the 33 verses from *Oracula Sibyllina*, Book 8, which describe the Day of Judgement with an acrostic from the initials of the verses reading: 'Jesus Christ Son of God Saviour Cross'. He continues:

It was clearly from God that these things occurred to the virgin to prophesy. For my part I regard her as blessed, whom the Saviour selected as a prophetess of his forethought for us. But many men are unbelieving, and while they admit that the Erythraean Sibyl was born a diviner, suspect that someone of our religion with a share of poetic talent composed these verses.

But Constantine contradicts this insinuation, both praising the moral content of the poem and claiming that Cicero had known the passage and inserted a Latin translation of it in his writings; which fact proved that it was composed before Jesus' birth. This last extraordinary statement is evidently derived from an erroneous report of the passage in Cicero's *De Divinatione*, where he mentions the occurrence of acrostics in the Sibylline Books, but of course with no suggestion of these particular verses.[25] Constantine then leaves the subject of the Sibyl and takes as the other example of the prophecy of the Incarnation the *Fourth Eclogue* of Vergil, which he expounds in detail as based on a Cumaean oracle.

The whole passage is in marked contrast to the attitude of the Christian Fathers generally to the Sibyl. There is no suggestion that she was a counterpart in Greece to the Hebrew prophets. Instead she is an Apolline priestess, functioning like a Pythia, who, as it were, accidentally received a Christian inspiration. Why the emperor ascribes Book 8 to the Erythraean Sibyl is not explained: probably because she was the most famous. Again it is impossible to find a source for Constantine's statement that she claimed to be born in the sixth generation (or century?) after the Flood. One might argue on the basis of these two discrepancies that Constantine was quoting the passage from some version of Book 8 that differed considerably from what has reached us and in view of the fluid tradition of Sibylline prophecy this would not be an impossible supposition. But Constantine's scholarship is so slapdash, and his citations are so undependable, that it is better to suppose that these statements are the product of his own erratic composition. He evidently had in mind a stereotyped model of the pagan prophetess. For, similarly, when in a later letter to the eastern provinces he recalls the oracular responses from Apollo of Didyma, which had swayed Diocletian to initiate his great persecution, he writes of Apollo issuing 'his oracle from some cavern and darksome recess', and the priestess 'having let her hair fall down and driven by madness'. But there was no cavern at Didyma, and the description of it and the prophetess, like his account of the Sibyl, sounds rather to have been imagined by Constantine on the pattern of Vergil, *Aeneid* 6, which no doubt he had read.[26]

To have been quoted by an emperor in a public address was in one sense the high point of acceptance for Sibylline prophecy. But if Constantine conferred on the Sibyl a unique, if rather equivocal, accolade, he also by his general policy was removing the need for theologians in future to quote Sibylline oracles as authorities. When the sole emperor recognised Christianity as the state religion, Christian apologetics took on a new direction. Instead of being addressed to converting the educated pagan, it turned inwards on its own problems of defending itself against heresies and creating a formulation of catholic belief. The Sibyl had no contributions on these questions.

On one occasion something like the old function of the Sibyl could be revived. If the account of the trial of Artemius before Julian is correct, he appealed to the apostate emperor by the evidence of pagan prophecy. It is probably due to the influence of Constantine that he groups Vergil together with the Sibylline oracles as those who foretold the coming of Christ; but he lays most emphasis by quotation on a Christian figment of an Apolline response.[27] The Christian forgeries of Sibylline oracles or answers of Apollo were by this time the chief representations of prophecy to survive. They had won such general acceptance as almost to defeat their original purpose. So Sozomenus, the ecclesiastical historian, felt compelled to offer an explanation of how the Greeks had earlier remained unbelieving in the face of the Sibylline and other oracles, which had foretold the future events concerning Christ. He argues that only 'a few men of exceptional education knew these prophecies, which were for the most part metrical and expressed in a diction more elevated than one addressed to the common people'. Sozomenus saw the failure of the pagans to be converted by Sibylline oracles as due to their very limited circulation, because they were only intelligible to a special clientele. This explanation shows a strange misconception of the fact that Sibylline oracles were a popular literature circulating among the lower reading public. Actually Sozomenus only quotes one line from the corpus — 'O Blessed Cross on which God was stretched out' — which he mentions in connection with St Helena and the invention of the True Cross. One may, therefore, seriously doubt whether he had really read any text of the oracles. Probably he and other Christians of the period were simply acquainted with a number of stock quotations, which in practice came from the Christian interpolations or such passages as lent themselves readily to the same kind of interpretation.[28]

What strange and unfamiliar ground the *Oracula Sibyllina* could be to Byzantine scholars is shown by John the Lydian writing on the calendar early in the sixth century AD. He reproduces at length the conventional list of the ten Sibyls derived from Varro with interpolations from the pseudo-Justin and synchronisms with the Old Testament. For him the first Sibyl was the Chaldaean, who was also the Persian and the Hebrew, and for the identity of the Hebrew and Chaldaean he cites as an analogy Moses, described by Philo Judaeus as a Chaldaean. Then abruptly John interjects a personal aside:

A book of this Hebrew Sibyl I happened upon myself in Cyprus, in which she includes in her prophecies many also of Greek events. Among others about Homer, that God will raise up a certain wise man, who will chronicle the war of the heroes and eulogise the noblest of them. Also she foretells about Christ and the events after Christ's appearing; moreover, about the events till the consummation of time. Among these she prophesies some ill-omened utterances on the subject of Cyprus and Antioch: 'Miserable Antioch, they will no longer speak of you as a city, when by your wickedness you fall among spears' and following it: 'Woe, woe, unhappy Cyprus; a mighty wave will cover you and the sea rising in stormy days.'

There follows a quotation of the same line about the blessed cross which Sozomenus had quoted.[29]

The way in which John the Lydian treats the subject suggests that he was quite unused to reading actual manuscripts of Sibylline oracles and expected his readers to find the matter unfamiliar. This may show how little these texts may have circulated in literary society at the time. Also one may wonder how this particular manuscript fitted into our tradition. John does not explain why he identified it as the work of the Hebrew or Chaldaean Sibyl. None of the verses which he quotes occurs in *Oracula Sibyllina*, Book 3, whose prophetess describes herself as Babylonian. The references to Antioch and Cyprus are found in Book 4, and that to Antioch only is repeated in Book 13. The fourth book was probably written by a Jew soon after the fall of Jerusalem. It refers to *Nero Redivivus* and is anti- Apolline in sentiment, but contains nothing specially Christian, even in its account of the Day of Judgement. Book 13 was written in the reign of Gallienus or soon after. Apart from forecasts of the Roman emperors it contains some miscellaneous prophecies of doom, such as John quotes, but no specifically Christian oracles. The line about the cross, if John is really citing it from the same volume, occurs only in Book 6, the most explicitly Christian of the *Oracula Sibyllina*, but, as transmitted, it is very short and probably defective. The prophecies of Homer occur in Books 3 and 11. It is noticeable that John treats Homer with complete respect in the prophecy. This would fit with the reference in Book 11, but not at all with that in Book 3. So once more, if we try to connect this manuscript with our extant corpus, we are faced with a complete puzzle. None of the extant books contains in one volume the material which John quotes. If his report is correct, and there seems no justification in doubting it, it must have been a composite collection different from any now extant, and may be taken as an illustration of the confused materials out of which the anonymous editor behind the *Oracula Sibyllina* had to assemble his corpus.[30]

If we turn instead to the evidence for Sibylline oracles in the West, we find a quite different picture, but also a changed situation from that under the earlier Christian Fathers. With the founding of Constantinople and the continued residence of the emperor in the East, the distinction between the two halves of the empire began to develop. Hermas, the first Christian Father to mention the Sibyl, had written about her in Greek, even when resident in Rome.[31] But by the late fourth century, Latin was entirely dominant as the language of the western Empire. This meant that the circulation of the original Greek texts of the Sibylline Oracles would diminish. They would cease to be intelligible to the lower classes, and they had not the same importance as before for scholars. Augustine supplies our best example. In the vast collection of his writings the Sibyl plays only a small part, and not always much to her credit. For instance in the treatise *Against Faustus* the Sibyl finds herself lumped together in rather miscellaneous company:

> The Sibyl, or Sibyls, and Orpheus and I know not what Hermes and any other prophets or preachers (*theologi*) or wise men or philosophers of the gentiles are alleged to have foretold or told the truth about the Son of God and God the Father. This is of some value towards refuting the emptiness of the pagans, but none towards conveying their authority. For we have shown that they do not worship the god, whom they would not pass over in silence, and to some extent they have dared to teach their fellow gentiles that idols and demons should be worshipped or to some extent have not dared to forbid such worship.

This view of the Sibyl goes even further than Constantine in regarding her as merely an occasional or unintentional mouthpiece of God. Elsewhere Augustine can use the Sibyl's oracles as an argument against paganism, but with a noticeable lack of precise quotation.[32]

The fact was that Augustine, who read few Greek authors, had very limited acquaintance with Sibylline oracles, as he reveals in the *De Civitate Dei*. There, in his historical survey, at the reign of Romulus in Rome and Ahaz and Hezekiah in Judaea, the Sibyl of Erythrae was said by some to have uttered her prophecies. This Sibyl's writings about Christ Augustine had previously only known in an anonymous Latin verse translation, which he describes as badly composed. However, when he was discussing Christ with 'the proconsul of Africa, Fabianus, a man of fluent eloquence and much learning, he produced a volume in Greek, which he said was the poems of the Erythraean Sibyl'. He showed Augustine a passage containing an acrostic, which was evidently the favourite Christian interpolation, which Constantine had earlier quoted. Augustine goes to the trouble of reproducing this extract in Latin verse with a similar acrostic. Then he passes judgement:

> this Sibyl, whether Erythraean or, as some prefer to believe, Cumaean, has nothing in her whole poem (of which this is a tiny extract), which is connected with the worship of false or fictitious deities. On the contrary she even speaks against them and their worshippers. Therefore it seems that she ought to be reckoned in the number of those who belong to the city of God.

Accordingly Augustine proceeds to produce a prose paraphrase, based on Lactantius' quotations, of what he regards as the teaching of the Sibyl.[33]

This final verdict of St Augustine in the Sibyl's favour must have gone far to guarantee her credentials in the West. The tradition there stems from him and from Lactantius and depended on Latin verse translations and prose paraphrases.[34] Also the West could spin its own legends about the Sibyls throughout the Middle Ages. But the literary tradition of the Sibyls was only part of the medieval heritage. From the thirteenth century they became a favourite subject in religious sculpture and later were even more frequently portrayed by the painters of the early Renaissance. This was something which, so far as we know, had virtually no counterpart in the Greco-Roman world, where the Sibyl was only very rarely represented in art. The climax was to come on the ceiling of the Sistine Chapel, where Michelangelo was to paint five of the Sibyls in company with seven of the Old Testament prophets. This was their great apotheosis.

Notes

1. Hermas, *Pastor*, visions I and II. The old manuscripts read εἰς κώμας at I, 1.3, but the usual emendation εἰς Κούμας seems necessary. A. Harnack, *Geschichte der altchristlichen Literatur bis Eusebius* 3 vols (1893–1904) II, 1.257ff, dated this part of the *Shepherd* to *c.* AD 110, and supposed that the remainder was appended and developed to *c.* AD 140.

2. Hermas may have based his picture of the Sibyl in action on a non-literary local tradition. A century later at Cumae the author of the *Cohortatio ad Graecos* was told that she sat on a chair on a high platform to prophesy. Cf. Ch. 4, p. 84.

3. Apuleius, *Golden Ass* 2.32–3.9. I have chosen this example because

in it Lucius, like Hermas, narrates his misunderstanding in the first person. In Greek novels it was usually the heroine whose apparent murder was described in the third person, and then explained away: e.g. Heliodorus, *Aethiopica* 1.29–2.6; Achilles Tatius, 3.15–18.

4. Origen, *Cels.* 5.61.625; 7.53.732; 7.56.734. For Celsus' dates, see H. Chadwick, *Origen: Contra Celsum* (1953), XXIV. As Chadwick points out (p. 312 n. 3), Origen 'did not regard the Sibylline Oracles with respect: he never quotes from them in his own works'.

5. Of the *Oracula Sibyllina*, Book 3, the most often quoted by Christian authors, actually contains no obvious Christian interpolations. 3.776 with the MSS reading υἱόν would appear to have a Christian meaning, but it is probably not a deliberate Christian interpolation, rather an accidental corruption by a Christian scribe. Book 5 is interpolated: obviously at lines 256–9, and, Geffcken believes (*Komposition und Entstehungszeit der Oracula Sibyllina* (1902) 26ff), elsewhere. Book 6 is brief and probably a mere fragment. It is completely Christian and dated by Geffcken (op. cit., p. 32) to the second century. Book 7 is very fragmentary: the earlier parts are pagan and could be pre-Christian, but the ending is gnostic. Book 8 is based on a pagan Sibylline oracle, but was assembled under Marcus Aurelius, probably by a Jew. It foretells the end of the world in AD 195, but from l. 217 to the end it is a Christian *réchauffé*, beginning with the famous acrostic known to Lactantius, Constantine and Augustine. Books 1 and 2 were originally a Jewish version produced in Asia Minor, probably in the second century AD, but l.319 to the end is again a Christian *réchauffé*. Books 11 to 14 were produced after AD 200 and so are irrelevant to the state of affairs in Celsus' day. Harnack (*supra.* n. 1), II.1. 581–9, examines the material in detail, and comes to the negative conclusion that nothing can be shown to be Christian from the time before Irenaeus, and he is obviously inclined to argue for the third century as the most likely period for interpolation. This would make Origen's implied contradiction more difficult to justify. For a later rebuttal of Christian forgery rather than interpolation, see Lactant. *Div. Inst.* 4.15–26.

6. One may note the lists of Sibyls produced by Varro and Pausanias, with the deliberate effort to establish the earliest. Clement of Alexandria (*Strom.* 1.21. 384P) when arguing for the superior antiquity of Moses over the Greek gods, prophets and poets, cites the Sibyl as earlier than Orpheus. In many places the Sibyl is dated before the Trojan War, with an implied advantage over Homer. Tatian (*Ad Gr.* 41) states that Moses is older than Homer, and also than a long list of poets and prophets including the Sibyl. For the Church as the first creation, see 2 *Clement* 14.1–2. Clement of Alexandria (*Protr.* 9.69P; *Strom.* 4.8.593P) distinguishes between the earthly church and the heavenly church: the former is just an image of the latter.

7. Clem. Al. *Strom.* 6.5.761P. On the *Kerygma Petrou* see Harnack (*supra* n. 1), I, 129; II, 1.492: it was probably derived from a lost *Acta Pauli* and produced AD *c.* 100–40. On Hystaspes, H. Windisch, *Die Orakel des Hystaspes* (1929).

8. For illustrations of the easy use of pagan analogies and legends, see 1 *Clement* (*c.* AD 95), which compares kings who sacrificed themselves

at the command of oracles to avert plague with Christian martyrs, and tells the story of the Phoenix to illustrate the resurrection of the dead.

9. Justin, *Apol.* 1.20. *Or. Sib.* 3.52ff.; 4.17. Justin goes on to refer to the Stoic theory of *ekpyrōsis*.

10. Justin, *Apol.* 1.44. Windisch (*supra* n. 7), 32. Augustus and Tiberius, *supra* pp. 142 and 143. Paulus, *Sent.* 5.29.3.

11. Athenagoras, *Leg. pro Christ.* 30. *Or. Sib.* 3.108–13. Cf. Melito, *Apol.* 4 (extant in Syriac) apparently referring to *Or. Sib.* 3.722.

12. Tert. *Ad Nat.* 2.13, referring to *Or. Sib.* 3.108ff; Tert. *Apol.* 19.10.

13. Epiph. *Adv. Haeres.* 48.2; 13. Euseb. *Hist. Eccl.* 5.14–20. Harnack (*supra* n. 1), II, 1, 365.

14. For compulsion to prophesy, see, for instance, *Or. Sib.* 2.1–5; 3.1–7; 295–300; 489–91; 698–701.

15. Chaldaean Oracles, H. Lewy, *Chaldaean oracles and theurgy* (2nd edn, 1978). Flowering of Apolline oracle-centres, H.W. Parke, *The oracles of Apollo in Asia Minor* (1985), 72ff; 146ff.

16. Euseb. *Praep. Evang.* 9.416D; 10.495C; 13.678D; 681D.

17. For instance, Clem. Al. *Protr.* 2.24P (*Or. Sib.* fr. 1.23–5; 27–30); 4.54P (*Or. Sib.* 4.7); *Paed.* 3.3.261P (*Or. Sib.* 4.155); *Strom.* 3.3.517P (*Or. Sib.* fr. 1.1); 5.14.714P (*Or. Sib.* fr. 1.10–13).

18. Theoph. *Ad Autol.* 2.9.

19. Theoph. *Ad Autol.* 2.36. On Theophilus see Harnack (*supra* n. 1), I, 496–502. On later use of Sibyls, B. Thompson, *The Review of Religion* 6 (1952), 115–36.

20. Harnack (*supra* n. 1), II, 1.515ff. *Cohortatio ad Graecos*, 16; 37–8 (Sibyl); 15 (Orpheus).

21. Hermas, *supra* p. 153.

22. On Lactantius and the Sibylline Oracles, see R. Pichon, *Lactance. Étude sur le mouvement philosophique et réligieux sous le règne de Constantin* (1901), 209–13; R.M. Ogilvie, *The library of Lactantius* (1978), 28–33.

23. Constantine, *Ad Sanctum Coetum*. Harnack (*supra* n. 1), I, 762, no. 14. T.D. Barnes, *Constantine and Eusebius* (1981), 73ff.

24. Constantine, *Ad Sanctum Coetum* 19 (*Or. Sib.* 8.217;243).

25. Cic. *Div.* 2.54.112 (cf. *supra* p. 139). Lactantius refers to this passage several times (*Div. Inst.* 7.16.11; 19.9; 20.3), and distinguishes the Sibyl of Book 8 from the Erythraean Sibyl of Book 3. In *Div. Inst.* 4.15.26 he mildly rebuts the view that the Sibylline oracles are forgeries by referring to Cicero, Varro and the other ancient authors who mention the Erythraean and the rest of the Sibyls. Constantine might have picked up suggestions from Lactantius whom he had made the tutor of his son, Crispus (Jerome, *Chron.* 230 c.; *De Viris Illustribus* 20). But Lactantius would never have produced such wild statements.

26. Eusebius, *VC* 2.50. Constantine's exposition of the *Fourth Eclogue* shows his familiarity with Vergil. He is the first to use that poem as a Christian prophecy. For Augustine later, cf. *infra* pp. 169–70.

27. Philostorgius, *Artemii Passio* 27; 46. For the Apolline oracle, cf. also G. Wolff, *Porphyrii de Philosophia ex Oraculis Haurienda Librorum Reliquiae* (1856), 235.

28. Sozomenus, *Ecclesiastical history* 1.1.6; 2.1.10 (*Or. Sib.* 6.26).

29. Joannes Lydus, *De Mensibus* 4.47.

30. Antioch, *Or. Sib.* 4.140–1; 13, 125–6. Cyprus, *Or. Sib.* 4.143–4. The Cross, *Or. Sib.* 6.24. Homer, *Or. Sib.* 3.419ff; 11.163ff.

31. Hermas, *supra* pp. 152–6.

32. Augustine, *Contra Faustum* 12.15; *De Consensu Evangelistarum* 1.49–50.

33. Augustine, *De Civ. D.* 18.23, where he also parenthetically mentions Varro's statement that there were more Sibyls than one, and an unspecified tradition (*nonnulli*) that the Erythraean Sibyl lived at the time of the Trojan War. This could all be derived from Lactantius.

34. See, for instance, B. Bischoff, *Mittelalterliche Studien I* (1966), 150–71.

Appendix I
The *Theologoi*

It is worth while to devote an appendix to an examination of the *theologoi*, the group of poets whose works in epic verse originated in the archaic period and contained theogonies, oracles and other religious subjects.[1] They were contemporary approximately with the production of the earliest Sibylline oracles and covered much the same field. So the study of the traditions about them provides analogies for the legends of the Sibyls, just as the Sibyls provide illustrations of a similar phenomenon. At the risk of arguing in a circle each can be used to explain the other.

Epimenides is the most important instance.[2] He is the only one of the *theologoi* with a serious claim to be a historic character. His very normal Greek name, containing no significant meaning, of itself suggests that he was not an imaginary figure. The account of this religious personage, who was fetched from Crete to purify Athens from a plague in the pre-Solonian period, is likely to be founded on fact. The conventional date (46th Olympiad, 596–593 BC) is probably based on calculation rather than a record and even the connection with the Cylonian blood-guilt may be a later construction for the purposes of propaganda. But the fact of the purification can be taken as authentic. Crete had a traditional expertise in purificatory rituals, and Epimenides is represented as a man in late life of high reputation for his relation with the gods.[3]

By the time of the foundation of the Museum in Alexandria and later, there were extant various works in prose and verse attributed to Epimenides. Unfortunately the lists of these, particularly in Diogenes Laertius and the *Suda*, have been garbled in transmission. For our purpose the prose works — for instance, a history of Crete and a work on purifications — may be disregarded as late and pseudonymous. The verses are variously called *Oracles, Theogony,* or *Purifications.* The problem is whether these should be treated as two or three separate productions, or whether they formed a single composition of rather miscellaneous content. The *Oracula Sibyllina* show how it was quite possible to combine a theogony with a body of prophecies. But in this instance we must allow for Epimenides' oracles as having a peculiar character. In the earliest extant reference to his poetry Aristotle remarks that 'he did not produce divinations about future events, but about past events which were obscure.' As with so many of Aristotle's illustrative examples, when we have no independent evidence, his exact meaning is not clear. The best interpretation is that Epimenides described events from history or legend, and applied them to explain subsequent disasters. The event would be divined as causing the wrath of some god, which could then be used as the explanation for the later trouble. Such a work might be called *Oracles.*[4]

One may offer here a conjectural illustration of the type of material which Epimenides' work might have contained. In 480 BC the Cretans jointly consulted the Delphic oracle on the question of whether to help in the defence of Greece against the Persians. The Pythia rejected the proposal in a scornful reply in iambic verse, in which she reminded the Cretans of their sufferings due to the wrath of King Minos. They had failed to avenge effectively his murder in Sicily and, to make matters worse, had been prepared to join the other Greeks in avenging Menelaus in the Trojan War. Herodotus, in explaining the oracle, attributed to the wrath of Minos two devastations of Crete by famine. The Delphic authorities evidently knew of this complicated Cretan tradition and could count on the Cretans to accept the plausibility of this interpretation. I would suggest that it was known to appear in Epimenides' *Oracles,* where it would have been highly appropriate for him to have warned his fellow-countrymen of such heroic wrath as a dreadful example. Also in view of Epimenides' relations with Delphi the response would have a peculiar irony.[5]

Also if the accounts of divine vengeance were accompanied with advice on how such wrath might have been previously averted or might be forestalled for the future, the work might also be described as *Purifications.* So while I recognise that the point cannot be proved, I would believe that Epimenides' verses circulated as a book or books, forming one corpus.

If this is accepted, the further problem remains about the

authenticity of Epimenides' oracles. This resembles the problem about Sibylla of Marpessus. It would be possible to accept that Epimenides himself was a historic character, a religious expert who purified Athens towards the end of the seventh century BC but who had not produced any written works. Then, as it would be supposed, at some later date — M.L. West suggests the late fifth century — a forger wrote the pseudonymous poems. But I agree with Jacoby in believing that a work of this kind is most unlikely to have originated after the archaic period. That it was actually produced by Epimenides in the late seventh century cannot be proved, but I would prefer to believe that he acquired an international reputation not only by some successful purifications, but also by expounding his appropriate interpretation of Greek legends in these terms. The Sibylline oracles show how a work of this sort might have continued to circulate through the hands of *chrēsmologoi*, and in its progress receive occasional interpolations and alterations to fit the run of events. Hence it would not be surprising if by the Hellenistic period the *Oracles* of Epimenides contained a prophecy of the Persian wars, and possibly also the warning to the Athenians about the dangers to them latent in Munichia.[6]

In any case, if we take it that there were oracles of Epimenides circulating like the oracles of Sibylla, the parallel between the legends current about the two are worth emphasising. First of all there is Epimenides' connection with the nymphs. According to one legend he was the son of a nymph (Blasta) and a mortal man, for whom various names were given.[7] It is never stated that Epimenides acquired his inspiration from the nymphs, but it seems to be implied that it came to him after he had had his famous sleep of fifty-seven years in the cave. Even the cave is not described as belonging to the nymphs, but Theopompus is cited for the legend that, when Epimenides was fitting out a sanctuary for the nymphs, a voice from heaven burst out crying: 'Epimenides, not sacred to the nymphs, but to Zeus.' This seems to fit in his legend as an episode after his sleep. The cave was not till then recognised as sacred, but Epimenides afterwards is about to dedicate it to the nymphs, when Zeus, the great god of Crete, asserts his superior claim.[8] Also the Hellenistic writer, Demetrius of Magnesia, told that 'he obtained from the nymphs a kind of eatable which he kept in a cow's hoof; when he partook of it in small amounts, he never evacuated his bowels, nor was he seen ever to eat.' This is an old folk-tale motif associated with shamans. But the point to emphasise here again is Epimenides' indebtedness to the nymphs.[9]

In contrast he is not originally associated with Apollo. In fact one of the few verbatim quotations from his poem shows him going out of his way to contradict strongly a favourite Delphic tradition — that the *omphalos* was the mid-point of the earth. 'There is no middle navel of the earth or of the sea, and, if there is, it is revealed to the gods, but not manifested to mortals.' So, like Sibylla, Epimenides was linked to the nymphs and originally hostile to Apollo. But also like Sibylla, no doubt Apolline tradition managed later to enmesh him in its toils. One of the versions of his mission to Athens alleged that he had been invited in fulfilment of a Delphic response, but as this is joined with the statement that he was escorted from Crete by Nicias, the son of Niceratus, it is probably to be discounted as a late fifth-century elaboration.[10]

As a final point of resemblance to Sibylla, one may note Epimenides' exceptional length of life. The simplest version credited him with 157 years, made up of fifty-seven years sleeping in the cave and a century of normal existence. The Cretans, however, were said to tell that he lived three centuries less a year. While the Sibyl's longevity appears to have been meant partly at least to give her the authority of high antiquity, Epimenides' longevity seems simply to serve to keep up the picture of an exceptional personage and, in so far as it is made up of an addition of his years of sleep, to answer the obvious question whether that period had counted towards his age.[11]

With Epimenides, as with Sibylla, the problem remains how far the legendary items are based on passages in his works. If we accept the rather vague statements of Maximus of Tyre, Epimenides told how in his dream in a cave he 'had met gods and the words of the gods and Truth and Justice' and claimed that this was the source of his knowledge. Here scholars usually cite the most famous line of his verse, the one quoted by St Paul: 'Cretans, always liars, evil beasts, workless bellies'. The generally accepted explanation is based on the fact that it is clearly derived from Hesiod's account of the speech addressed to him by the Muses, when they called him to be a poet. Hence it is supposed that in his vision some deity called to Epimenides, prefacing his summons with this even more scornful address. This is very plausible, and, in default of any precise indication of its context, it would serve to explain the occurrence of this derisory description of the prophet's fellow-countrymen. Actually, I have at times wondered whether, on the analogy of the *Oracula Sibyllina*, it could have been the initial opening of the work. It would not be unlikely that Epimenides, who could dismiss the legend of the Delphic *Omphalos* with abrupt contempt, should assume a high-and-mighty attitude to his audience. Also it is perhaps a little more easy to understand how the line would acquire popular currency, as it evidently had done already by the time of Callimachus. The first verse of a poem often catches the public fancy where the rest is forgotten. At any rate, wherever it occurred, it can be taken as some indication of the manner in which the *theologos* could set himself apart from the rest of mankind.[12]

There are no quotations from Epimenides which show him applying his divination to particular events. References to Minos, Munichia or the Persian wars have to be read into his works by conjecture. The reverse is true of Musaeus.[13] He is an entirely unconvincing person historically, but there are actually quotations from his oracles. The first reference to him in this connection occurs in Herodotus, when describing how the Pisistratidae had gone up to the court of Xerxes at Susa accompanied by 'Onomacritus, an Athenian, who was a *chrēs-mologos* and editor (*diathetēs*) of the oracles of Musaeus'. As Herodotus explains, Onomacritus had been earlier much favoured by Hipparchus, but when the lyric poet, Lasus of Hermione, caught him in the act of interpolating into the oracles of Musaeus a prophecy of the disappearance into the sea of the islands lying off Lemnos, Hipparchus had expelled him from Athens. Evidently the breach between the Pisistratidae and Onomacritus was healed when Hippias was driven into exile, and at the court of Xerxes he is pictured as suppressing any prophecies predicting a Persian defeat, but producing oracles about their successes; particularly that a Persian was fated to bridge the Hellespont. Herodotus leaves it vague whether these particular oracles were to be attributed to Musaeus, but evidently he knew a collection under that name. For when later he cites passages from Bacis foretelling the battles of Salamis and Plataea, he mentions on each occasion that there were similar prophecies by Musaeus.[14]

The clear implication of Herodotus' account is that there were oracles of Musaeus already extant before the time of the Pisistratidae and that, when the family had employed Onomacritus to collect and arrange them, he took advantage of the opportunity to improve them by interpolations. This is consistent with Herodotus' earlier statement that the Pisistratidae had kept a collection of oracles on the Acropolis, which was seized and removed by King Cleomenes when he drove them into exile. Pisistratus had traditionally been nicknamed Bacis; presumably because of some habit of quoting oracles, and Hippias was credited with being well versed in the subject.[15] Later writers, perhaps building on Herodotus' reference, were inclined to deny the authenticity of Musaeus' works and attributed them to Onomacritus. For instance, Pausanias, who claimed to have read the oracles of Musaeus, states in one place his personal view, that the only genuine poem of Musaeus was a hymn to Demeter composed for the Lycomidae, and elsewhere he regularly cites under the name of Onomacritus a *Theogony* which otherwise would have been assigned to Musaeus.[16] But in the one passage where he explicitly cites 'from the oracles of Musaeus', he does not mention Onomacritus or suggest any doubts about authorship. This is the passage discussed elsewhere for its quotation of a Sibylline oracle which Pausanias interpreted as foretelling the battle of Aegispotami. The quotation from Musaeus runs: 'Also on the Athenians comes a savage down-pour by the wickedness of leaders. But there shall be some consolation for defeat: they shall not evade the city, but shall pay the penalty.'[17] This is very similar to the lines of the Sibyl, except that there is no explicit indication that the defeat struck the Athenian fleet, and Musaeus is even more specific than Sibylla about the responsibility of the leaders and the vengeance to fall on them. Without more extensive quotation of the context it is impossible to decide whether it was composed with a positive intention of suggesting the circumstances of Aegispotami. Sophocles called Musaeus a *chrēsmologos*, and Aristophanes mentioned him as one who revealed cures for diseases and oracles. So prophecies under his name were circulating during the Peloponnesian War, and it would be in the interest of the oracle-mongers that they were brought up to date by identifying or inserting references to contemporary battles.[18]

If we turn from his alleged works to the prophet himself, the traditions about Musaeus show a rather awkward combination of different elements. On one side he is linked with Orpheus, the Muses and Thrace; on the other with Athens and the Eleusinian mysteries. In neither direction has he any association with nymphs (though he may have been inspired by the Muses); also he is not connected with Apollo. This is not surprising, as his origin no doubt lay outside Apolline circles and Onomacritus,

under the patronage of the Pisistratidae, would have had every
reason to shun links with Delphi. The miraculous element in his
legend which remains unexplained is that he is frequently
described as a son of the Moon. Presumably this belongs to the
oldest legend about him. When alternative Attic genealogies were
invented to connect him with Eleusis, the Moon was dropped
from the legend, or became 'a woman, Selene'. It may have been
under the influence of Onomacritus that Musaeus became
Athenian, and he also may have fitted out his works with a
theogony, as the proper accompaniment of a collection of oracles.
But the oracles themselves appear to have circulated separately,
as in Herodotus, Aristophanes and Pausanias. Also Musaeus
continued in Orphic circles to be recognised not as a prophet, but
simply as the ideal pupil of his master, Orpheus. His functions as
theologos and prophet tended to fall apart. In the latter aspect he
represents an attempt by the authorities of Athens to secure from
abroad someone who could provide a local corpus of oracles.[19]

If Musaeus was more *theologos* than prophet, there was another
contemporary author whose works are mainly known for oracles
rather than theology. This is Bacis, who is regularly mentioned in
conjunction with Sibylla by Aristophanes, Plato and Aristotle,
and then in imitation of them by later writers. Like Sibylla he
started as one person, born in a village attached to a larger town
in Boeotia, but by the Hellenistic period he had split into three
individuals. As Pausanias explains, his oracles were still in
circulation in the later second century AD.[20] None of our ancient
authorities attempts to date Bacis. The only evidence in them is
that Pausanias believed that he foretold the end of the Second
Messenian War, and that Euclus the Cyprian wrote before him,
while Euclus had prophesied that Homer would be born in the
Cyprian Salamis.[21] The earliest author to name Bacis is
Herodotus, who quotes him for prophecies of the Persian War. So
it might be possible to date his origin in actuality to the early fifth
century. But, as we have seen, there was a tradition that
Pisistratus had been nicknamed Bacis, and, if this is true, it
implies that the prophet was already familiarly known by the
mid-sixth century or not much later.[22] Bacis also has no tradition
of his parentage, but that he was inspired by the nymphs is more
positively evidenced than for any other prophet. Pausanias twice
mentions the legend, and probably took it from a statement in
Bacis' own poetry. For Aristophanes in the *Peace* makes the
chrēsmologos, Hierocles, quote: 'If indeed the goddess nymphs did

not deceive Bacis.' The line probably was used in his own oracle in the third person to introduce some surprising prophecy. Here, as elsewhere, Aristophanes concocted the oracles which he put into the mouth of a *chrēsmologos* out of a mixture of authentic verses or phrases and his own ludicrous parodies.[23]

Actually there is some limited but very convincing evidence that there was a cult of the nymphs associated with divination in archaic Boeotia, though it has no explicit connection with Bacis himself. Before the battle of Plataea, Delphi, when consulted by the Athenians, had prescribed a vow to the Sphragitid nymphs among other deities as a pledge of victory, and the tribe Aeantis performed the appropriate sacrifice annually at the state's expense in later years. In explaining this response, Plutarch records that there was 'a cave sacred to these nymphs on one of the peaks of Cithaeron facing the summer sunset [northwest]; in it there was also formerly, as they say, an oracle-centre, and many of the local inhabitants used to become possessed, whom they called "nympholepts"'. Pausanias also knew of the cave and its tradition of an ancient cult of divination. So though neither author mentions Bacis in this connection, we can at least assume that in the archaic period there had been an actual shrine of prophetic nymphs on Cithaeron, which would make the notion of their inspiration completely plausible to Boeotians.[24]

We have suggested that Sibylla of Marpessus, claiming to be the daughter of a nymph, had a similar source of inspiration. Also she has clear evidence for an earlier origin, which indicates at least the possibility that Bacis was deliberately modelled on her. Hesiod by his parentage reminds one of the links between the Aeolian towns of Asia Minor and inland Boeotia. So if the tradition is correct that Bacis was supposed to hail from Eleon in the territory of Tanagra, there is no difficulty in supposing that suggestions for such a prophetic figure might have reached there from the Troad, and, if so, would have fallen on fertile soil.[25]

Incidentally it is curious to note that this out-of-the-way village appears again in the sixth century in connection with other divination. Herodotus in his detailed account of the complex adventures of Dorieus records how, after the failure of his colonising attempt in North Africa, he was advised by 'Antichares, a man of Eleon, in accordance with the oracles of Laius to found Heraclea in Sicily'.[26] These oracles of Laius do not occur elsewhere in literature, but presumably it is implied that Antichares was a *chrēsmologos*, who claimed to possess a collection which had belonged to the Theban king of that name. In itself there is no immediate connection between this and the oracle of Bacis, but it is strange to find them both associated with this unimportant place. If Antichares was still active in 510 BC, when he met Dorieus, he could possibly, as a much younger man, have produced or circulated the oracles of Bacis in time for Pisistratus to acquire his nickname from them before his death in 526 BC.

If these oracles were produced in the latter half of the sixth century, we have no clue of their actual contents. For the earliest prophecies extant deal with the invasion of Xerxes. One quotation warning to 'keep goats away from Euboea, when the barbarian speaker casts his yoke of papyrus into the sea' is connected by Herodotus with an episode after the battle of Artemisium, but could be regarded as vaguer and more general in reference. But the prophecy of Salamis is highly specific, and is quoted by Herodotus as his example of a perfect forecast:

> But when they bridge with ships between the sacred beach of Artemis of the golden bow and Cynosura on the shore, after with mad expectation they have sacked wealthy Athens, holy Justice will quench powerful Pride, the son of Violence, in his terrible rage when he looks to overthrow everything. For blade will meet blade, and Ares will stain the sea red with blood. Then a day of freedom for Hellas is brought on by Zeus, the far-seeing, and sovereign Victory.

Herodotus' famous comment is: 'When Bacis speaks so clearly about these events, I would not dare to express a contradiction on the subject of oracles, nor would I accept it from others.' He evidently had this oracle in mind earlier when writing his account of the battle of Salamis. For he put in references to Cynosura and Munichia ('the beach of Artemis') in a proper way to emphasise the fulfilment of the forecast. Again he introduces his description of the battle of Plataea by refuting an anonymous oracle, which he alleges the Persian commander had quoted, and by citing instead some lines of Bacis: '. . . the meeting of the Greeks at the Thermodon and the leafy-fringed Asopus, by which many of the bow-bearing Medes shall fall beyond their lot and drown, when the fatal day arrives'. This time he contents himself with explaining the geographical reference to the river Thermodon.[27]

Evidently Bacis' prophecies of Xerxes' expedition were a conspicuous feature of his oracles, and this would be explained by two alternative interpretations of the legendary tradition. The Boeotians might be expected to have had a great interest in the war, which altered the history of their country so drastically. Here it is worth noting that while the prophecy about Artemisium is vaguely ambiguous and that about Plataea mentions the Persians' untimely losses in rather general terms, the forecast of Salamis is a highly moralising statement. Not only is the victory greeted as the cause of Greek freedom, but the Persian aggression is described with all the terminology appropriate to a villain in Attic tragedy. This could be accounted for by either of two explanations. After the failure of their Medism the Boeotians might have wished to circulate oracles in the name of a native prophet which showed enthusiasm for Hellenic freedom and condemnation of Persian aggression. Alternatively, one must note that by the Hellenistic period at least there was an accepted tradition of an Athenian Bacis.[28] How this was made to square with the Boeotian tradition is not explained. Presumably the corpus of Bacis' oracles did not contain precise statements about his parentage and native locality: nothing of the sort is ever quoted. So it would be quite possible for a *chrēsmologos* in Athens to fake a new legend that the prophet whom he quoted was Athenian. The obvious date for such a creation would be at any time after the battle of Coronea had broken Athens' link with Boeotia (447 BC). It must have come into its own during the Peloponnesian War. Aristophanes is very contemptuous of oracle-mongers, but it is clear by the *empressement* with which Cleon names Bacis as the author of his oracles that at this time he had the greatest reputation in Athens. Sibylla, as we saw, had lately arrived, but was not so strongly established. The passages where Bacis is mentioned contain no reference to his origin so it would be possible to treat him throughout as an Athenian.

That a native Boeotian tradition of Bacis persisted independently into the fourth century is proved by the emergence of a final, third, manifestation under this name. He was an Arcadian from Caphye and was also called either Cydas or Aletes, according to Philetas of Ephesus, presumably a Hellenistic writer, who also produced a list of three different Sibyls.[29] Cydas sounds a real personal name; Aletes ('Wanderer'), like Phyto as the name of the Samian Sibyl, suggests a wandering diviner. But the historic occasion for the invention of this figure is clear. When in 370 BC Epaminondas re-founded Messene, a great effort was made to provide the revived state with a mythological background to support its morale against its great enemy, Sparta. As part of this process Thebes lent the support of her native soothsayer. Pausanias states that

> what particularly induced Epaminondas to the settling of the Messenians was the oracle of Bacis. For he, inspired by the nymphs, among the prophecies about the Greeks foretold: 'And then indeed the fair flower of Sparta shall be destroyed, and Messene shall be inhabited again for all time.'[30]

Besides this obvious forecast Pausanias claimed to have detected elsewhere in Bacis' oracles a prophecy of the fall of Eira — traditionally the last episode of the Second Messenian War. Earlier Pausanias had described how the final stand of the Messenians had been plagued by thunderbolts and rainstorms. Here he quotes as a forecast the fragmentary sentence: 'Who from Messene, when it was subdued by rattle of thunder and springs of water'.

These quotations show that in the corpus of Bacis' oracles circulating in Pausanias' day there was a section dealing with the fate of Messenia. This will have led Hellenistic scholarship to distinguish a local Arcadian diviner from the others of the same name.[31]

We have seen passages appropriate to the Athenian and the Arcadian Bacis. Pausanias also quotes a curious passage which could only have had significance for Thebans and Phocians. It is not a prophecy of Sibylline type but is instead an *aition*, such as might have been enshrined as a response in a legend of the consultation of the Delphic oracle:

> But whenever a man of Tithorea shall pour appeasing offerings to Amphion and Zethus in prayerful libations, while the famous bull is being charmed by the might of the sun, then be on your guard for no small evil coming on the city. For the crops wither away in it, when they have shared out the earth and are carrying it to the monument of Phocus.[32]

Pausanias explains that Amphion and Zethus have a common grave — a small earth mound just north of the Cadmeia. In April each year (when the sun was in Taurus) the Thebans set a guard on the site to prevent the Phocians from stealing soil from the grave and carrying it to Tithorea, where there was a common tomb of Phocus and Antiope. The connection between the two burial places was that Antiope, the mother of Amphion and Zethus, had married Phocus as her second husband and was buried with him. Pausanias narrates the legend of how she came to wed the eponym of the Phocians. He also refers again to the whole subject and the oracle of Bacis when in his itinerary he comes to describe Tithorea. He treats the ritual of the guard at Thebes as if it was a traditional practice still maintained in his day, but evidently regards Tithorea as fallen on evil times, though he remarks that it had the building of a theatre and an enclosure of an older market-place, seeming to imply that both were out of use.

The theological thought behind this oracle is typical of the archaic period. A hero's grave, particularly that of some royal founder, was believed to possess great potency for good or ill towards the land where it was situated. Failure to guard the tomb of Amphion and Zethus from the incursion of neighbours would rouse the heroes' wrath, which could manifest itself in a blight on the crops. On the other hand, by making appeasing offerings to the heroes and carrying off some of the soil where they lay, the Phocians could transfer some of their potency for good from Thebes to Phocis.

The practice, then, might have originated in the archaic period, but this dating must be qualified by another consideration. The raid from Tithorea to Thebes is not a matter of border warfare. Tithorea lay far up the valley of the Cephisus, and was evidently made the base of the attack as the capital of Phocis; a point which is also emphasised by the fact that the earth was carried to the grave of Phocus, the eponymous hero. It is not till the sixth century that we hear of the Phocians taking combined military action in their wars with the Thessalians. Also towards the end of the century they produced a federal coinage. The temple of Apollo of Abae was their common sanctuary, and Tithorea, or the archaic town on its site, may well have been the federal centre. For Pausanias believed that it was the same place as Neon, which Herodotus mentioned as though it was the chief place at the time of Xerxes' invasion. So the *aition* in this form is not likely to have been invented before the mid-sixth century at the earliest.[33]

The style and diction of the oracle are near enough to epic to be datable to the late sixth century, but one feature suggests a much later date: that is the definition of the time of year by reference to the sun in a constellation. The systematic naming of the constellations was not established before Eudoxus of Cnidus (*c.* 390–*c.* 340 BC), who is the first author cited for Taurus.[34] Hence even if the ritual custom had been started earlier, it is more likely that the passage in this form was not inserted in the oracles of Bacis before the mid-fourth century. That was of course a time of bitter hostility between Phocis and Thebes, when it may have been appropriate to invent or revive this legendary motive. If the guard on the tomb was still mounted by the Thebans in Pausanias' day, it is hard to believe that by then the Phocians of Tithorea posed a serious threat to their security. The custom may have been, as Schachter suggests, an archaising ceremony.

Unlike the other *theologoi* Bacis has no tradition of having produced a theogony. Perhaps with the previous existence of the examplary *Theogony* of Hesiod of Ascra, no other Boeotian poet would attempt such a subject. The other activity attributed to Epimenides and Musaeus, of founding religious ceremonial, particularly purificatory, is not recorded of Sibylla, but is assigned to Bacis in one legendary allusion. Theopompus wrote that, when the Spartan women had been driven mad, Bacis (probably the Arcadian) purified them, when he had been assigned to the duty by Apollo. The source of madness is not explained. If it was Bacchic it would suggest that the story was imitated from the myth about Melampus and the women of Argos. It is typical, as we have seen, that by the fourth century the religious activities of the *theologoi* should be attributed to the good offices of Apollo.[35]

This survey shows how the legendary traditions about the *theologoi* whom I have chosen to examine have much in common. Also, though Musaeus certainly, and Bacis probably, were assigned to the mythological past, they both, and Epimenides, really are literary phenomena of the Archaic period. Musaeus' and Bacis' works are pseudonymous; Epimenides is probably authentic. None of them was originally an agent of Apollo. Epimenides and Bacis, like Sibylla, were inspired by the nymphs, and even Musaeus was probably inspired by the Muses who could be regarded as a kind of specialised nymphs. Epimenides and Musaeus produced theogonies as part of their inspired writing; and so also, as we have suggested, may the Sibyl. Epimenides' oracles had a special function connected with his purifications and the manifestations of divine wrath. Musaeus and Bacis tended to prophesy war and the outcome of battle. All these were and remained favourite Sibylline subjects. Some of Musaeus' works may have been read in Orphic circles by religious initiates, but the oracles of the *theologoi* and Sibylla were mostly circulated to a general public by *chrēsmologoi*, and this term was even applied to the prophets themselves.

Notes

1. I have used the term *theologoi* as a convenient designation for this group of writers and their works, whether pseudonymous or not. Cf. August. *De Civ. D.* 18.14. E. Rohde, *Psyche: Seelencult und Unsterblichkeitsglaube der Griechen* (2nd edn, 1898), 292ff, was the first to produce a beautiful characterisation of them, somewhat marred by treating Sibyls and Bacides as types, not individuals.

2. The best collection of material and discussion is Jacoby, *F. Gr. Hist.* 457. For a recent view, M.L. West, *The Orphic poems* (1983), 47–53.

3. The purification of Athens, Arist. *Ath. Pol.* 2.1; Plut. *Sol.* 12.7; Diog. Laert. 1.110; *Suda*, Epimenides. Diogenes and the *Suda* give the date; Pl. *Leg.* 1.642D says 'ten years before the Persian wars'. Crete and purification, e.g. Paus. 10.7.2; Parke and Wormell, *DO* II, no. 339.

4. Arist. *Rhet.* 3.17. 1418a21.

5. Hdt. 7.169 (Parke and Wormell *DO* II, no. 93). It is possible that Herodotus is using as his immediate source Charon of Lampsacus' *Cretica* (*F. Gr. Hist.* 262, t.1), which was no doubt based partly on Epimenides. As Jacoby rejects the evidence that Charon wrote before Herodotus, this hypothesis is not open to him. For Epimenides and Delphi, cf. *infra* p. 177.

6. West (*supra* n. 2), 51. The Persian Wars, Pl. *Leg.* 1.642D. Munichia, Plut. *Sol.* 12.10. See further Jacoby's commentary.

7. Son of Nymph, Plut. *Sol.* 12.7; *Suda*, Epimenides, where his mother is named, but not described as a nymph. A major problem is that Aelian, *NA* 12.7 (*F. Gr. Hist.* 457 f 3) ascribes the following verse to Epimenides: 'I am the offspring of the fair-haired Moon.' The traditional corpus of the Sibyl could contain contradictory accounts of the author's identity (Paus. 10.12.2), but it seems preferable to suppose that Aelian, not the most accurate of writers, may have quoted Musaeus in mistake for Epimenides. For Musaeus, the parentage of the Moon is frequently alleged. If Aelian is correct, some *chrēsmologos* must have wilfully introduced an imitation of Musaeus into the Epimenidean corpus.

8. Diog. Laert. 1.115 (Theopompus, *F. Gr. Hist.* 111 f 69). Late writers tend to mention either the Idaean (Diog. Laert. 7.3) or the Dictaean (Max. Tyr. 10, p. 110) cave in connection with Epimenides. But this is just the error of substituting the famous for the unknown. The point of the original legend was that Epimenides was a simple peasant going to take a siesta in what he supposed was an ordinary cave.

9. Demetrius *ap.* Diog. Laert. 1.114. Plut. *Mor.* 157D. See Jacoby's commentary for further references.

10. Plut. *Mor.* 409E (*F. Gr. Hist.* 457 f 6) on the Omphalos. The Delphic oracle and the purification of Athens, Diog. Laert. 1.110. I would not now propose the harmonisation attempted in Parke and Wormell, *DO* I, 111. For the late origin of Nicias' family, J.K. Davies, *Athenian propertied families* (1971), 403.

11. Diog. Laert. 1.111. *Suda*, Epimenides, does not give a precise age, but if γέγονε refers to this acme in the 30th Olympiad, not his birth, no doubt he was supposed to be at least a centenarian.

12. Max. Tyr. 10. p. 110; 38 p. 439. St Paul, *Ep. Tit.* 1.12. Hes. *Theog.* 26ff. Callim. *Jov.* 8 and perhaps an allusion in Aratus, *Phaen.* 30. For the myth said to be the origin of the accusation of mendacity against the Cretans, Athenodorus of Eretria *ap.* Phot. *Bibl.* 190 (Müller, *Fragmenta Historicorum Graecorum* IV, p. 345). I have left out of discussion the large body of material connecting Epimenides with Sparta and Argos. Both cities had strong links with Crete.

13. The best collection of material is in H. Diels and W. Kranz, *Die Fragmente der Vorsokratiker* (6th edn, 1951), no. 2.

14. Hdt. 8.6.3–5 (at Susa); 8.96.2 (Salamis); 9.43.2 (Plataea).

15. The Pisistratid collection of oracles, Hdt. 5.90.2. Hippias' skill in the subject, Hdt. 5.93.2. Pisistratus' nickname, *Suda*, B47; Sch. Ar. *Pax.* 1071: also cf. Hdt. 1.62.4 (Amphilytus).

16. Paus. 1.22.7 (the hymn to Demeter). Onomacritus, Paus. *loc. cit.* this note; 8.31.3; 8.37.5; 9.35.5.

17. Paus. 10.9.11. For the Sibylline oracle, cf. *supra* p. 100.

18. Ar. *Ran.* 1033, with Schol.; Soph. fr. 1116.

19. Musaeus and Orpheus, Plat. *Prot.* 316D; *Rep.* 2.363C. Aristoxenus *ap.* Harp. Musaeus, for his connections with Thrace and Athens. His two Attic genealogies, *Suda*, Musaeus; Andron, *F. Gr. Hist.* 10 f 13 (Sch. Soph. *OC.* 1053). His mother the Moon, Hermesianax, *Leontion* 15 (Ath. 13.597D); Philochorus, *F. Gr. Hist.* 328 f. 208 (Sch. Ar. *Ran.* 1033). See also Servius, *Verg. Aen.* 6.60. The *Suda, loc. cit.* this note, converts his mother into Σελήνης γυναικός. A. Hendricks, *ZPE* 58 (1985), 1–8 discusses a new fragment of Philodamus with a quotation of Musaeus, stating that he was the son of Pandia, daughter of Zeus and Semele.

20. For collections of material and discussion see Kern, *RE* 2 (1896) col. 2801; I. Trencsényi-Waldapfel, *Untersuchungen zur Religionsgeschichte* (1966), 232–50. Ar. *Eq.* 61; 1003; *Pax* 1070ff; 1095; 1116; 1119; *Av.* 962. Pl. *Theag.* 124D. Arist. *Probl.* 30, 954a36, where the plurals are best taken as generalising rather than referring specifically to the existence of more than one Sibylla and Bacis. Cf. Plut. *Mor.* 399A. For other late instances of the two in conjunction, Cic. *Div.* 1.18.34 (also with Epimenides); Plut. *Mor.* 243 B; Dio Chrys. 35.2; Aristid. *Or.* 45.12; Lucian, *De Mort. Pereg.* 29–30; Paus. 10.12.11.

21. Bacis and the Second Messenian War, Paus. 4.27.4; cf. *infra* p. 184. Bacis and Euclus of Cyprus, Paus. 10.14.6; 24.3.

22. Hdt. 8.20.1, etc. Cf. *infra* pp. 182–3. Pisistratus' nickname, *supra* n. 15.

23. Paus. 4.27.4; 10.12.11. Ar. *Pax* 1070. I believe that the following

line is a parody attached to it by Aristophanes.

24. The annual sacrifice of the tribe Aeantis; Cleidemus, *F. Gr. Hist.* 323 f 22 (Plut. *Aristid.* 19.6; 628F). The Delphic response, Parke and Wormell, *DO* II, no. 102 (Plut. *Aristid.* 11.3). Paus. 10.3.9.

25. Hes. *Op.* 636, from Cyme to Ascra. Bacis from Eleon, Philetas of Ephesus *ap.* Sch. Ar. *Pax* 1071; Ael. *VH*, 12.35.

26. Antichares of Eleon, Hdt. 5.43.

27. After Artemisium, Hdt. 8.20.1; Salamis, 8.77.1 (cf. 8.76.1; 8.96.2); Plataea, 9.43. For Bacis and the Persian wars, Paus. 10.14.6. Also see the discussion of the Sibylline oracle about Chaeronea as probably borrowed from an oracle of Bacis on Plataea, *supra* pp. 119–20. The scholiast on Ar. *Av.* 978 believed that αἰετος ἐν νεφέλῃσι was to be found in Bacis.

28. The Athenian Bacis, Philetas of Ephesus, *ap.* Sch. Ar. *Pax* 1071; Clem. Al. *Strom.* 1.21.398P; Ael. *VH* 1235. It is worth noting that Plato, in the *Theages* 1240, distinguishes Amphilytus from Bacis and Sibylla by the epithet 'native' (ἡμεδαπός). This seems to show ignorance or disregard of the legend of an Athenian Bacis. But it also clashes with Hdt. 1.62.4, where Amphilytus is described as Acarnanian — a favourite source of diviners.

29. Philetas of Ephesus, *loc. cit.*, n. 28.

30. Paus. 10.27.4. For other instances of Messenian myths created at this time with backing from Thebes, Parke and Wormell, *DO* I, 268ff.

31. Paus. *loc. cit.*, n. 30. For the fall of Eira, *Paus.* 4.21.7.

32. Paus. 9.17.5–6; cf. 10.32.8–11. For a discussion of the grave of Zethus and Amphion (elsewhere usually called the Amphaion) with references, A. Schachter, *Cults of Boeotia* vol. 1 (1981), 28–9.

33. For the Phocian federation, B.V. Head, *Historia Numorum* (2nd edn, 1911) 338. For the various traditions about the grove of Phocus, representing no doubt rival claims to be the centre of the federation, Eitrem, *RE* 20, 1 (1941), col. 497.

34. Taurus, as constellation, Eudoxus *ap.* Hipparch. 1.2.10. The systematic naming of the constellations, I. Bulmer Thomas, *CQ* 34 (1984), 108.

35. Theopompus, *F. Gr. Hist.* 115 f 77. Melampus, e.g. Bacchyl. 10.44; Hdt. 9.34.

Appendix II
The *Libri Sibyllini*

We have already discussed the legend of the Sibyl who sold her books to King Tarquin, because it forms part of the traditional story of the Sibyls. But that folk-tale cannot be accepted literally. It served as a picturesque way of accounting for the historic fact that the Roman state possessed books of prophecies in Greek verse, which were treated with great reverence. According to the Roman annals they were consulted on numerous occasions starting soon after the fall of the monarchy, and there is every reason therefore to believe that they had been received first by one of the kings. As their authorship was attributed to a Sibyl, it was to be expected that legend would represent her as conveying them in person. The association with Cumae does not appear in the earlier annalists, though traces of it can be found in an alleged Sibylline oracle probably produced at the end of the third century BC. As Cumae was the only city in Italy credited with possessing a Sibyl, the connection was obviously to be inferred, whether or not it had any actual evidence to support it. But it need not be supposed that the king of Rome obtained the books officially from the cult-centre in Cumae: Magna Graecia, like Greece, may well have had its *chrēsmologoi* who were travelling about equipped with copies of oracles. The parallel has often been noticed between the Pisistratidae with their collection of prophecies on the Acropolis and the Tarquins with the *Libri Sibyllini* on the Capitol. Similarly, the Tarquins may have had their equivalent to Onomacritus.[1]

Various features in the institution of the Sibylline books under the Republic can plausibly be supposed to date from the Regal period. The place of custody on the Capitol in the precinct of the temple of Juppiter Optimus Maximus suits with the building period of the late sixth century. Their guardians, originally a duumvirate nominated by the king, fit with other pairs of officials, such as the *duumviri perduellionis*, functioning under the early Republic but dating as institutions from before the fall of the monarchy. The only recorded duumvir of the regal period is a legendary figure — Marcus Acilius, or Atilius, one of the first pair. He was guilty of secretly copying some of the text, and suffered the extreme penalty. This was traditionally the same as for parricide — to be sewn up in a sack and thrown into the sea. The Acilii and Atilii were plebeian *gentes* in historic times, and therefore are most unlikely to have held high office under the kings. But the penalty with its primitive avoidance of ritual pollution was a cautionary tale invented in early times. In 348 the number of the college was raised from two to ten, divided equally between patricians and plebeians.[2]

The numerous records of particular consultations of the Sibylline books tend to fall into certain standard patterns, but are not on that account to be treated as unhistoric. Roman ritual was inclined to be stereotyped in form. Generally the purpose of consultation was to strengthen or re-establish the *pax deorum*. Hence the first step was the report of some breach of the *pax*. This might take the form of a public disaster, such as a famine or a pestilence, or else the occurrence of some prodigy or series of prodigies. On the report of such signs of divine displeasure the *pontifex maximus* and his college were empowered to take immediate steps as reckoned appropriate. For instance, if it had 'rained with stones', a 'nine-day ritual' (*novendiale sacrum*) was recognised as the proper remedy (*procuratio*). But if a succession of prodigies had occurred, or one of peculiar horror, such as the birth of a hermaphrodite, the report of such events would induce the Senate to instruct the keepers of the Sibylline books (the duumvirs and later the decemvirs) to approach them.[3]

The precise method of approach employed is never described. For instance, did the duumvirs read through the books till they came on a significant passage or were they supposed to have an index? Alternatively, did they employ some method like the *sortes vergilianae*, unrolling the books at random and lighting on a particular passage?[4] Usually the Senate was informed of the result and approved the proper action. At other times the original *senatus consultum* had already empowered the appropriate magistrates in advance to act in accordance with the decemvirs' findings.

The prescription from the Sibylline books could take either of two forms or sometimes both. The decemvirs might advise some immediate ceremonies meant to avert the danger to the state, or they might instead recommend the creation of some permanent institution — the erection of a temple or the establishment of a periodic festival with the same purpose. Our records of consultations in the large majority of instances make no attempt to reproduce the text of the oracle: they simply report the practical conclusions which the decemvirs recommended on the basis of their inspection of the books. So it is impossible to apply any critical analysis to the Sibyl's words. At most one can draw some deduction from the kind of recommendation which the decemvirs gave. These appear to fall into certain patterns. But the problem constantly arises of how far the records of the decemvirs' reports are modified by extraneous factors in the transmission of our evidence.

For instance, it is notable how often the early instances of Sibylline consultations result in the building of temples to deities not previously worshipped, while this form of prescription is only very sporadic in later times.[5] Obviously there was more scope for the introduction of new deities and therefore the dedication of more temples in the earlier stages of republican history. But the reason why they form so large a proportion of recorded consultations in the fifth century is because the annual records of the *pontifices* (the *Annales Maximi*) were evidently not extant for that period, if they had ever existed. It is not surprising, however, if the temples themselves preserved among their documents the record of why they were vowed and when consecrated. This is the explanation of the preservation of the records of these early consultations of the *Libri Sibyllini*. In fact the alleged consultations not connected with temples are all to be accounted spurious. One group of these is concerned with the *Ludi Saeculares*, 509 or 504 and 456 or 449 BC. The true fact appears to be that this festival was first celebrated in 249 BC. But as it was linked with the concept of a recurrence every *saeculum*, it was only to be expected that attempts would be made to trace it back to earlier legendary celebrations. This would originally have led to examples every century. But Augustus added confusion by insisting on holding a celebration on the tenth anniversary of his principate (17 BC), and for this purpose devising a *saeculum* of 110 years, which then suggested a different pattern for previous celebrations. In any case all the alleged consultations of the *Libri Sibyllini* connected with secular games before the third century BC are to be expunged.[6]

Of the remaining accounts of consultations in the fifth century by the duumvirs, one is an obvious fiction, but is significant as illustrating the wrong picture of the Sibylline books and their function which was accepted by the later annalists. The year 461 BC begins with a series of ominous prodigies like those reported in the late third and second centuries: the heavens blaze, there is a vast earthquake, an ox speaks, and it rains flesh, which birds snatch as it falls, and when it reaches the ground, it does not decay. The books are consulted, but instead of providing a ritual for 'procuring' the omens, they utter a prophetic warning. 'Dangers were foretold from a coming together of foreigners, lest there should be an attack on the high places of the city and slaughter thereafter. Among other things a warning was given that they should abstain from seditions.' These phrases are evidently meant to suggest the actual words of the Sibylline oracle. The use of vague paraphrases, such as 'foreigners' and 'high places of the city', reproduces the traditionally obscure wording of such prophecies. It is impossible to decide whether a Greek text actually lay behind the words or more probably it was just part of the fictitious dressing up of the story. Evidently, as Dionysius shows, this oracle was meant to be understood as a forecast of the seizure of the Capitol by Appius Herdonius in the following year. But Livy, who is much more interested in the Struggle of the Orders, links the warning against seditions with the dispute over the *Lex Terentilia* and the trial of Caeso Quinctius. When next year he comes to the coup of Appius Herdonius, unlike Dionysius he does not put in any reminder to the reader that the event had been foretold by the Sibyl. The whole episode is to be taken as legendary, and the consultation of the books as a fiction meant to emphasise the significance of the catastrophe. It must not be taken as evidence that the Sibylline books really contained such prophecies.[7]

Besides the foundation of new temples the Sibylline books are credited with the introduction of new forms of ritual of an especially Hellenic style. The chief example was the *lectisternium*, an imitation of a Greek *theoxenia*. This is first recorded in 399 BC as a result of a consultation of the Sibylline books on the occasion of a pestilence. Six deities were honoured: Apollo and Leto, Hercules and Diana, Mercury and Neptune. Their statues were grouped in pairs on three couches, and feasts were laid before them. The choice of Apollo to head the list can be explained because of his power to avert plague, which had been recognised by the establishment of his temple in 433 BC, also on Sibylline instructions. Apollo had brought Diana (Artemis) and Leto with him as a traditional triad. The cult of Mercury may have been introduced by Sibylline instructions, and possibly that of Hercules. Certainly later it was believed that the temple of Hercules Custos had been founded on that authority. Neptune is somewhat strange in this ceremony, though he pairs with Mercury as a protector of trade by sea. He is evidently Poseidon and not the old Italian god of water.[8]

This ritual of *lectisternium* became an established Roman practice as a means of averting plague. Another occasion unrecorded must have occurred within the next thirty years, for in 365 BC Livy mentions the third *lectisternium*. It is not explicitly stated that the books had been consulted in this instance. So possibly one is to assume that the precedent had been set, and that therefore the *pontifices* acted on their own authority. But in 348 BC, probably the next occasion, a pestilence is followed by a consultation of the Sibylline books, which prescribe again a *lectisternium*. The next pestilence is in 295 BC, when the books were again approached, but Livy fails to mention what ritual was prescribed. Apparently the cure was ineffective, as the pestilence continued into a third year. So in 293 BC the Sibylline books were again consulted and this time a new remedy was found, that Aesculapius should be fetched from Epidaurus. It was the same centre from which the god had been fetched to Athens in 420/19. The operation took some time to arrange, but the temple on the Tiber island was dedicated on 1 January 291. Yet even the presence of Aesculapius could not completely protect the city from pestilence. In 273 BC a recurrence occasioned a further consultation, and for the first time the books were cited as giving a reason for divine displeasure: that 'many individuals had seized numerous sacred sanctuaries and were holding them as private property'.[9]

It is part of the defective character of our sources for this period that no more is told on the subject. In fact few consultations by the decemvirs are recorded for the seventy years which are missing owing to the loss of Livy's second decade. But we can perhaps deduce a certain development in the use of the Sibylline books, particularly in reference to recurrences of pestilence. In 433 a temple was vowed to Apollo Medicus. There was probably already some cult of Apollo in Rome at an altar. The Sibylline books had previously been found to advise the foundation of a temple to a Greek deity. In 399 a novel Greek ritual, the *lectisternium*, is performed for the first time. This became a recognised response to an outbreak of plague, but when in 293 this had not proved sufficient, the books were found to recommend the introduction of a new deity of healing — Aesculapius — brought all the way from Greece. Then in 273 BC on a recurrence of pestilence the Sibylline books are for the first time used for the somewhat new purpose of specifying a particular type of offence which has occasioned the wrath of the gods. We shall see in the same way a similar crescendo in the use of the *Libri Sibyllini* during the continued strain of the Hannibalic War.[10]

Of the three consultations of which record survives from the lost period of Livy's second decade, two instances are peculiar. The dedication of a temple to Flora and the establishment of games in her honour in 238 BC could be treated as a typical prescription of the Sibyl. Flora was an old Italic deity, with a minor *flamen*, but the games were a thoroughly Hellenic feature. Much stranger were the *Ludi Saeculares* first celebrated in 249 BC. The concept of a *saeculum* as an epoch in world history was not familiar to the Greeks but was typical of Etruscan theology. The worship of Dis and Persephone at an underground altar which was buried at the conclusion of the rites could be paralleled from examples in Magna Graecia, but also would probably fit well enough with Etruria. It is the first instance of a prescript of a Sibylline oracle which can be used to support to some extent the theory that the *Libri Sibyllini* came from Etruria rather than from Cumae. But of course we are handicapped by the question, how far can we trust the decemvirs to have actually read in the books the prescript which they reported to the Senate? It would not be surprising if the longer the practice of consulting the books had continued, the more the priests would tend to move from a strictly limited performance of their function.[11]

The other example from 228 BC raises this problem more acutely. In accordance with the Sibylline books a pair of Gauls and a pair of Greeks, one man and one woman of each, were buried alive in the Forum Boarium within the city. Our ancient sources are shocked at the ceremony, which they regard as completely unhellenic and barbarous. The explanation which they offer is that a prophecy had come to the Romans that Greeks and Gauls would occupy their city; so the Romans by burying members of these peoples within their walls had nullified the prophecy by fulfilling it literally. The motif that the dead are occupying the land where their bodies lie was quite traditional in Greek, but is not typically Roman. Again the theory that a forecast might be evaded by some alternative method of accomplishment is quite Hellenic. So though it is impossible to prove that this was not the motive behind the Roman ritual, it is not very convincing, and it is more likely that we should discount this explanation as a later misguided interpretation produced by Greek scholars.[12]

The fact seems to be that the original sources did not specify what occasioned the consultation of the books, but that it was much more likely to have been some prodigy. Hoffman has argued that it was a case of unchastity brought against a Vestal Virgin, because this was apparently the occasion for the repetition of the ritual in 216 and again in 114 BC. This may possibly be correct. The proper penalty for a Vestal Virgin who had broken her vows was to be buried alive. So some kind of connection seems to be indicated. If so, the question still remains why, if a Vestal had offended, the ritual should not be confined to punishing her, but should be extended to these foreigners. Hoffman refused to believe that this prescription occurred in a collection of Greek oracles, but used it as an argument instead that the *Libri Sibyllini* were Etruscan in origin. He maintained that the savagery of the penalty would be appropriate to the Etruscans, and that the Greeks and Gauls would be regarded by them as their natural enemies. But this argument turns on the belief that the decemvirs in the latter half of the third century gave an approximately sincere reading of the books; which is at best a doubtful proposition.[13]

The most that a modern scholar can do is to conjecture what were the motives behind the ritual. If it was linked with the shocking occasion of the pollution of the state by one of its priestesses, the intention may have been to rid the community of this pollution by providing scapegoats. The choice of foreigners as *pharmakoi* can be supported by analogies from Ionian cities. Probably such victims were originally done to death, though in historic times they may merely have been expelled. But in this instance the traditional Italic penalty for the Vestal Virgin may also have seemed appropriate for the surrogates, who were to carry with them the same defilement. This is probably all that can be proposed as a positive explanation of an extraordinary event: negatively it does not provide evidence that the Sibylline books contained either Etruscan elements or forecasts of the future.[14]

With the Hannibalic War and the third decade of Livy's history we encounter horrendous events (which called for much ritual of appeasement) and a narrative which records in detail the occasions and the ceremonies. Already in 218 BC, before any of the disastrous defeats, Livy pictures the plebs as alarmed at a variety of prodigies which are 'procured' by a whole range of different ceremonies: for example, the usual *novendiale sacrum* for a 'rain of stones'; a lustration of the city, one gift of gold to Juno at the site of one prodigy and a *lectisternium* at the site of another. These were all conventional types of ritual already, though sometimes offered to unusual deities: e.g. a *lectisternium* to Youth (*Juventus*). The only novel procedure was that the praetor was ordered to make vows to be fulfilled if ten years later the state was in the same condition — a very Roman type of bargain with the gods. The length and complexity of the list might simply be ascribed to the availability of a much more detailed source, but it does rather suggest that the *pontifices* and the decemvirs at the beginning of the war were already prepared to make an unusual effort to guarantee the *pax deorum*. If so, as in many other directions, the Roman authorities had not foreseen in 218 BC to what lengths they would be driven later.[15]

In 217 BC, after Hannibal's crossing of the Alps and the battle of the Trebia, Livy records a long list of major prodigies and also some minor ones to which he says credence was given on their account. When the consul consulted the Senate, it decreed offerings of full-grown and suckling victims and a *supplicatio* for three days. This expiation was evidently on the Senate's own responsibility, but they also decreed that after the decemvirs had consulted the books, the will of the gods as indicated in the oracles should be fulfilled. The acts recorded are not unusual: gifts to the Capitoline triad and Juno of the Aventine and Juno Sospita. The matrons were to make a collection for Juno of the Aventine and the slave-women for their special deity, Feronia. Such collections were a known Greek rite: so the idea, if new, could have come from a Greek oracle. A special sacrifice was to be conducted by the decemvirs at Ardea, and the next December the *Saturnalia* at Rome was to be the occasion of a special *lectisternium* and public feast, which was to be repeated annually.[16]

Only a few months later, after the disaster of Lake Trasimene, the dictator, Fabius Maximus, induced the Senate on this account to order a second consultation of the books — previously unparalleled in one year. The decemvirs also exceptionally gave a reason for the failure of the previous ritual to achieve its results. They declared that the vow to Mars for the sake of the war had not been correctly performed and must be repeated on a larger scale. Great games were to be vowed to Juppiter and temples to Venus of Eryx and to *Mens*, and a *supplicatio* and a *lectisternium* were to be held. So far the prescriptions were on an enhanced scale but not without precedent. It was seventy-five years since the books had required the dedication of a temple. But the final requirement of the decemvirs — that a 'consecrated spring' (*ver sacrum*) should be vowed — was unique to the Sibylline books so far as our records go. It appears to be a revival of an old Italic custom: the produce of one spring was to be dedicated to the gods. Originally this should have included the human offspring who would be sent away to settle elsewhere, but on this occasion the vow was confined to the young of cattle, sheep and goats which were born five years later. They were vowed to Juppiter if the state had survived the war as wished by that date. This could be regarded as a greatly enhanced version of the vow which the praetor had made in 218 BC, but it was so exceptional that it was decided that the procedure should be embodied in legislation and passed formally as a law of the people.[17]

If one asks how far these prescriptions can plausibly be attributed to the oracles of a Sibyl, of the two deities to receive temples, Aphrodite of Eryx might have appeared somewhere in Greek writings of the late sixth century, but one may wonder whether it was rather suggested to the decemvirs as the scene of the last stages of the First Punic War. *Mens* was a thoroughly Roman concept as a deity and cannot be imagined in a Sibylline oracle. As for the *ver sacrum*, in the form as drafted for Roman legislation, it appears very Italic in character, but actually Greek legend had tales of peoples who were 'tithed' in dedication to Apollo.[18]

In the following year (216 BC), before the legions went out, prodigies were reported and were 'procured' in accordance with the books, though no details are recorded. But the disaster of Cannae which followed overshadowed all other considerations. The ominous situation was made worse by the report of the violation of a Vestal Virgin's chastity. The books were approached again and the double sacrifice of Gauls and Greeks as in 228 BC was repeated. But it appears as if the magistrates felt that none of the traditional methods of consulting the gods was adequate. Instead Quintus Fabius Pictor was sent to Delphi to consult the

Pythian Apollo, 'by what prayers and supplications the gods would be appeased, and what was to be the end to such great disasters'. No doubt we owe to Fabius Pictor's own *Annals* the account of his visit to Delphi. It is the first instance of an enquiry there by the Roman state which can be regarded as fully authenticated.[19]

The feeling that the Sibylline books were not adequate to the emergency, or at least would usefully be supplemented by another oracle, was shown again in 213 BC. The praetor, M. Aemilius, was instructed by the senate to hold an investigation (*conquisitio*) for prophetic books. Presumably he ordered by edict those who had such documents to submit them to his inspection. The original purpose may simply have been to put a check on the circulation of unofficial prophecies, such as tended to emerge in times of anxiety. Anyway, in the proceedings there came into his hands two volumes of a prophet, Marcius, which he handed on to Sulla, the praetor of the following year (212 BC). The one volume contained verses which in proper oracular language forecast all too obviously the battle of Cannae. The sons of Troy were warned to avoid the river in the plains of Diomedes, and so forth. The second poem contained a prescription for future success in the war: that the praetor was to preside over annual games in honour of Apollo and the decemvirs were to offer sacrifices. A day was devoted to 'expiating' the poem, and on the following day the Senate authorised the decemvirs to consult the books on the subject. The inspection evidently was favourable, for the necessary legislation to establish Apolline games and a sacrifice was passed.[20]

The whole business can only be described as a put-up job. The oracles of Marcius were a forgery, produced after Cannae. In a manner perhaps suggested by the technique of contemporary Greek Sibylline oracles, the first poem with its transparently obvious forecast of that disaster was intended to provide credit for the prescriptions of the second poem. It is even possible that the investigation for oracles in 213 BC was ordered with the deliberate intention of providing the occasion for discovering the words of Marcius. The *Ludi Apollinares* contained nothing very extraordinary: sacrifices to Apollo in Greek ritual and a collection (*agermos*). It could perfectly well have been initiated after a normal consultation of the Sibylline books by the decemvirs. But some guiding body in the Senate appears to have felt that there needed to be something to enhance the impact of the occasion on the populace. So Marcius was produced with an explicit promise that his prescription of the *Ludi Apollinares* would drive the enemy from the plains.

Nothing of this sort is recorded for several years, until in 207 BC Livy lists a number of prodigies with appropriate 'procurations', which were followed by a more horrible omen — the birth of a hermaphrodite at Frusino. The correct way to dispose of it was determined by fetching the *haruspices* from Etruria. As an atonement a hymn written by Livius Andronicus was sung by a choir of virgins. When the temple of Juno on the Aventine was struck by lightning the *haruspices* were again consulted on what was their special field — such manifestations of thunderbolts; and the matrons were required to provide an appeasing collection. Throughout this detailed passage there is no explicit mention of the Sibylline books. The earlier procurations were by decree of the *pontifices* and the decemvirs were concerned in some of the later ritual. Probably one should assume that the books were consulted in the normal way, but that Livy for the sake of variety had left out this conventional feature while laying stress on the more unusual happenings. This supposition is almost forced on us by the fact that for the first time the prodigy and its proper procuration are precisely illustrated by the verbatim text of what is described as a Sibylline oracle.[21]

Phlegon of Tralles during Hadrian's reign in his book, *Concerning marvels*, records among a list of hermaphrodites the birth of one in Rome in 125 BC. The decemvirs, on consulting the books, produced a prophecy which he quotes at length. As preserved it contains 70 hexameters, but there are three lacunae, and some 30 lines are missing at the end. Diels has shown that this is really the text of two poems elaborately composed in acrostics: the initials of the verses correspond to the first line or lines of the poems. But though the first oracle begins by foretelling the birth of a hermaphrodite, the rest of the prophecy clearly does not fit with 125 BC. Rome is evidently engaged in a serious war and is depending on help from Greece. As Diels proposed, the best explanation is that, while Phlegon found his text in some source for the events of 125 BC, the original oracles had been produced in the latter years of the Second Punic War, when similar unnatural births had given occasion for consultations of the Sibylline books with these results. The poems were evidently intended to pass as the actual words of the Sibyl, and the use of acrostics in this way was regarded by Cicero as one of the features of authentic oracles. Also in a passage impaired by a lacuna the Sibyl is made to refer in prophetic forecast to the founding of Cumae by a conquering expedition from the offshore islands and the establishment there of a temple and cult-statue of Hera. This must be part of the effort to give plausibility to the forgery by showing the Sibyl of Cumae foretelling known historic events as well as the future fate of Rome. The stress on the cult of Hera may simply be determined by the fact that the Sibyl was about to prescribe sacrifices to Juno. But as evidently the author had a correct tradition of the original starting-point of the expedition, so he might also have known of some tradition too of a connection between the Sibyl and the cult of Hera at Cumae. One may recall that after Cannae, Cumae had become an important base in thwarting Hannibal's attempts to reach the Campanian coast. So perhaps for the first time high-ranking Romans must have been in constant touch with citizens of Cumae.[22]

There can be only one explanation for the production of this elaborate forgery: it must have been intended to publish this text, instead of following the usual practice of the decemvirs — to announce to the Senate what ritual the Sibyl prescribed but without quoting her actual words. This change of practice must have been brought about by the need to satisfy the anxieties of the public by showing that the prodigy had been foreseen and its proper procuration already prescribed. Under the continuing strain of the Second Punic War the authorities felt the need for recurring stimuli to keep up the morale of the plebs. Perhaps also the recent discovery of the oracles of Marcius, whose text was evidently published, made anything less seem lacking in impressiveness. One cannot tell also whether in this use of religious propaganda the Roman establishment was working in complete unanimity. In the assignment of military commands and the strategy of the war there were evident struggles between factions in the governing class, and it is possible that the variations in religious propaganda corresponded to personal feuds or rival uses of different expedients.

In 205 BC there was a revival of the use of the Delphic oracle in conjunction with the Sibylline books. After the victory of the Metaurus two years before, ambassadors had been sent to Delphi with a golden crown and silver figures as a gift from the spoils of Hasdrubal. When they returned, they carried a Pythian response promising the Romans a much greater victory. Their return was followed by a consultation of the Sibylline books occasioned by repeated rains of stones. The Sibyl declared that 'whenever an enemy from abroad had carried war into the land of Italy, he can be driven out and defeated if the Idaean Mother had been brought from Pessinus to Rome.' Evidently Livy here reproduces in Latin some phrases which were attributed to the Sibylline text. Probably, as in 207 BC, an oracle was published *in extenso*. Accordingly another embassy was sent to fetch the goddess from Phrygia and was instructed first to call at Delphi for Apollo's sanction. This was given in a response which recommended that their mission could be accomplished with the help of King Attalus. The goddess was successfully transported to Rome in the form of a black stone, and installed in a temple on the Palatine.[23]

Again one feels that behind the great parade of religious pageantry there was a background of intrigue. For instance, did the earlier embassy to Delphi discuss with the priesthood there the possibility of introducing some exciting form of foreign worship? Delphi was at the time in close touch with Attalus and might have provided the original suggestion of the *Magna Mater*. It is impossible to believe that Sibylline oracles of the sixth century BC would have contained any reference to such a goddess, unless in the form of Rhea in a theogony. But the paraphrase in Livy implies a text with specific reference to the cult in Pessinus. The second embassy to Delphi was a recognition of this co-operation and a means of bringing religious sanction for the combined actions of Attalus and the Roman state. The Senate may have got more than it had bargained for in the violent orgiastic practices of the *Magna Mater*. Romans were forbidden to castrate themselves so as to become *Galli*. But the new worship introduced with elaborate ceremonial may have fulfilled its intended purpose in providing a final boost to popular morale.

From the end of the Second Punic War with the easing of stress the need to call on the Sibylline books for more and more striking remedies ceased. But the Romans were suffering from a form of drug addiction and could not dispense with the opium of religion. Throughout the first third of the century when we still have the books of Livy, every few years some occasion for consulting the books is reported. Livy himself was conscious that this kind of activity and the recording of it in annals were quite out of keeping with the practice of his own times, the Augustan age. But he excuses his diligence in the subject as typical of the good old days. Of the many examples which he chronicles only a few show special features which are worth separate discussion.[24]

In 189 BC after the capitulation of Antiochus III, Cnaeus

Manlius Vulso had been engaged in taking over the ceded territory in Asia Minor. On his return to Rome he applied for leave to celebrate a triumph, but was bitterly opposed by the majority of the ten ambassadors responsible for concluding the Peace of Apamea. They alleged that Manlius had longed to cross the Taurus and had been restrained with difficulty from his wish 'to put to the test the disastrous defeat which the Sibylline oracles had foretold to those who crossed the boundaries ordained by fate'. This reference to the Sibyl in the body of the narrative has no obvious connection with the consultations recorded in the annalistic notices. The immediately previous occasion reported had been in 190 BC, just before the brothers Scipio set out against Antiochus. Then, after various unfavourable omens, the decemvirs had ordained a *supplicatio* to certain specified deities and had themselves made a sacrifice by night with suckling victims. But nothing is mentioned about the impending expedition or the limits on Roman arms. Actually it may seem premature before the battle of Magnesia to warn the Romans about the risks of crossing the Taurus. But of course we cannot be sure that the text as cited was explicit. Perhaps the ambassadors' warning was based on the interpretation of some deliberately vague warning. However, at least it seems to be implied that some of them believed they could convince the Senate that some such warning had been extracted from the Sibylline books. This suggests that the decemvirs in 190 BC may have included in their report a gratuitous reference to the impending war, perhaps deliberately phrased to try to put some constraint on the activities of the Scipios.[25]

Otherwise in the first half of the second century there are no signs of any but the usual type of ritual prescriptions extracted from the *Libri Sibyllini*. The more remarkable of these were a fast in honour of Ceres in 191, which became an annual ceremony; a statue of Hercules set up in his temple for some unspecified reason (189 BC) and the extension of the *Ludi Romani* to ten days (172 BC). One development was a tendency to involve the whole of Roman Italy in the ceremonies. In previous centuries the ritual requirements applied to Rome only, but in this period they could include 'all forums and market-places' (*omnia fora conciliabulaque*). Also sacrifices could be prescribed further and further from Rome: for instance, in 172 BC 'in Campania at the promontory of Minerva' (i.e. Cape Sorrento).[26]

One other feature worth noting is that sometimes the *haruspices* were called in about the same time as the decemvirs. In 191 when two oxen climbed the stairs to the roof of a building in the heart of Rome (the Carinae), the *haruspices* commanded that they should be burnt alive and their ashes cast into the Tiber. Various other prodigies reported immediately afterwards were referred to the decemvirs. Again, in 172 BC when a column decorated with ships' beaks was struck by lightning both forms of divination were invoked for the same prodigy. The *haruspices*, who were tradition-ally expert in this phenomenon, reported that it was to be taken as a good omen because the object damaged in the storm was spoil taken from an enemy. The decemvirs are not recorded as providing any interpretation, but they prescribed a complicated series of rituals to 'procure' the prodigy. Each religious body had concentrated on its own traditional function without obvious conflict, but perhaps there may underlie this double action a certain unspecified rivalry or the presence of two bodies in the Senate supporting different procedures. At least it is possibly significant that a few years later in 163, when the *haruspices* had been called in because of a sudden death at a consular election, and had declared the election invalid, Tiberius Gracchus, the presiding consul, delivered a bitter invective against them as Tuscan barbarians who had no power to explain the significance of a Roman election. Actually Tiberius later had to admit a technical error on his part, so that the *haruspices* were vindicated. It may all have been simply a matter of personal pique on the part of the consul, but the possibility of some underlying dissension on the validity of the *haruspices* cannot be ruled out. Actually they continued to be called in together with the decemvirs or independently through the remainder of the second century and the first half of the first.[27]

After 167 BC with the loss of the books of Livy our chief source of evidence vanishes. Obsequens' late work on prodigies, which was indirectly derived from this lost history, gives a few indications which suggest that to the end of the second century much the same reporting of prodigies and procuration in accordance with the Sibylline books may have continued. In 143 BC Obsequens records that, following on a defeat of the Romans by the Salassi, the decemvirs reported that they had found in the Sibylline books that, whenever they were to invade the country of the Gauls, the Romans ought to offer sacrifice on their frontier. The implication is that the defeated commander, Appius Claudius, had failed to fulfil this previously unknown requirement.

This retrospective explanation of a disaster was not attributed before to the Sibylline books, but it is easily to be explained as a development of earlier practices.[28]

A century after the *Ludi Saeculares* of 249 BC the festival was repeated, but later authorities disagreed over the precise year. An alleged celebration in 126 BC appears to be a fake, produced to provide an antecedent for Augustus' celebration of 17 BC.[29]

Besides the annalistic records of consultations a couple of special episodes are known from other authors. In 133 BC the violent death of the tribune Tiberius Gracchus was treated as a prodigy, and the Sibylline books were consulted. Accordingly an embassy of the decemvirs was sent as far as Sicily. So far our sources agree, but Diodorus, drawing on some Greek historian or local tradition, describes them as going through the whole of the island seeking altars consecrated to Zeus of Etna and fencing them off and making them inaccessible except to those who had an ancestral right to sacrifice there. Cicero, in a passage designed to enhance the picture of Verres' impiety, says that the Sibylline books had contained the instruction to placate the most ancient Ceres. So the decemvirs had gone, not to the goddess's temple in Rome, but to her shrine at Etna. If one is forced to choose between these two versions, that of Cicero is the more suspect, because of its obvious adaptation to the prosecutor's case. But perhaps one should accept both. Sibylline oracles earlier had often advised several different rituals at the same consultation. Cicero would obviously have selected the one to suit his purpose, while Diodorus, as a Sicilian, may have been especially interested in the strange interference with his native sanctuaries.[30]

Obsequens, under 114 BC, describes a peculiarly ghastly instance when a maiden daughter of a Roman knight was struck by lightning while riding. The reply (presumably of the *haruspices*) was that it portended dishonour to virgins and to the order of knights, since the horse's trappings were scattered. There followed the disclosure of the unchastity of three Vestal Virgins with three knights as their lovers. The Sibylline books were approached and for the first time for many years prescribed a new temple and cult-title — Venus Versicordia (she who turns the hearts). She was to be invoked to turn the hearts of maidens and matrons from lust to modesty. According to Plutarch the Sibylline books also authorised the repetition of the sacrifice of Gauls and Greeks, as on the previous occasions of Vestal unchastity.[31]

Venus Versicordia was the only instance of a new cult ordained by the Sibyl in this century, and also her temple was the last to be erected on these instructions. This was not because no new temples had been built in this period. In the second and first centuries generals vowed such dedications and erected them from their spoils to celebrate their victories. None of these had been supported by Sibylline oracles. The remaining references to the books are very peculiar. Obsequens records under 108 BC that in consequence of some prodigies thirty free-born Roman boys and as many maidens, whose parents were alive, went to the island of Cimolus to offer sacrifice. If this means the well-known island in the Cyclades, it seems extraordinary for a sacred mission to be sent so far and in such numbers of adolescents. It was one thing for the decemvirs as senior officials to go on an expedition to Sicily, which with its close geographical and cultural links with Rome was in a special relationship. But nothing like this pilgrimage to Cimolus is otherwise recorded; which may make one wonder whether the story stems from a misunderstanding. Again, in 100 BC, the colony of Eporedia among the Salassi was said by Pliny to have been founded on the orders of the Sibylline oracles. The foundation of Greek colonies normally had oracular authority, but it is unique for Rome.[32]

There is no evidence of consultation of the Sibylline books for the first dozen years of the first century BC, but in 87 BC one fragment indicates that they were used in the bitter party struggles of the time. Octavius the consul had driven out his colleague Cinna together with six tribunes. He defended his action to the people by openly reading a text from the books which was taken to mean that when Cinna and the six tribunes had been banished from the land there would be calm, peace and tranquillity. His action in reading this oracle on his own initiative instead of acting on behalf of the college of decemvirs is stigmatised.[33]

Any further use of the *Libri Sibyllini* in party politics elsewhere was soon precluded, for in 83 BC the burning of the temple of Juppiter Optimus Maximus on the Capitol destroyed them completely. The invasion of Sulla prevented any immediate action, and he himself as dictator did nothing to restore them. But this omission may merely have been due to greater preoccupations. Since he increased the numbers of the colleges of *pontifices* and augurs, it is usually believed that he also raised the membership of the decemvirs from ten to fifteen. The earliest evidence for the change is a casual reference in a letter of Caelius dated 51 BC. Seven years after the fire, in 76 BC, a senatorial commission was appointed to assemble a new collection of oracles. The work was accomplished with difficulty, but there is no sign that this second edition of the *Libri* was put to any immediate use. In 63 BC when Lentulus told the Allobrogian ambassadors that according to the Sibylline oracles three Cornelii would rule Rome, he may have been claiming some private information from the official books, but also he may have quoted from some Sibylline oracle of his own.[34]

The first well-documented consultation occurred at the beginning of 56 BC. The image of Juppiter on the Alban mount was hit by a thunderbolt — a prodigy which obviously could not be ignored. The *quindecimviri*, apart from any ritual of procuration, which our authorities ignore, produced instructions bearing on the chief political issue of the day. In the previous year Ptolemy Auletes had fled from Egypt and appealed to the Senate to restore him. It was generally believed that Pompey wished to be given the commission, which would then entitle him to raise an army and so strengthen his position in the triumvirate. Various senators wanted to frustrate this scheme. So, late in 57 BC, a *senatus consultum* had been passed on the proposal of Lentulus Spinther, that as the new governor of Cilicia he should undertake the task. It was then reported to the Senate that the Sibyl had declared: 'If the king of Egypt shall come begging help, do not refuse him friendship, but also do not assist him with any multitude, or else you will have toils and dangers.' This was evidently devised to spike Pompey's plan, even if he managed to secure the command. Rumours of the general meaning of the oracle had become common talk, 'as usually happens', Dio remarks. But Caius Cato, newly elected tribune, was afraid that the Senate would hush up the oracle and still transfer the command of restoring Ptolemy to Pompey. So he brought the whole subject before the plebs and summoned the quindecemvirs. In the presence of the gathering he compelled them to disclose the text of the oracle, though it was not permitted to reveal the contents of the Sibylline books without a decree of the Senate.[35]

In mid-January 56 Cicero wrote to Lentulus, who was on his way to his province, telling him that this warning against restoring Ptolemy with an army had been accepted by the Senate, but the *senatus consultum* in favour of Lentulus still stood, subject to this qualification. All sorts of rival proposals were made, but the

Senate failed then or later to agree on a clear line of policy, and Lentulus, in spite of Cicero's pressure, avoided taking any further action. A year later Gabinius, the proconsul of Syria and an old associate of Pompey, received a letter from him urging that he restore Ptolemy, which he proceeded to do by force of arms. This flagrant contempt for the Sibylline oracle and the rules governing the action of proconsuls led later to his prosecution.[36] Cicero raised the matter in the Senate and tried to compel the reading of the Sibylline oracle in full, in the belief that it would contain some penalty for the infringement. In 55 BC the consuls, Pompey and Crassus, resisted this motion, but in 54 BC it was carried. It produced no effective result, for it proved that there was no such proviso in the text. Also those who supported Gabinius replied with the counter-argument that the oracle had been misinterpreted, because it did not refer to this occasion or this Ptolemy. Gabinius was acquitted of treason with regard to the invasion of Egypt but later condemned for other offences. Towards the end of the year when C. Rabirius Postumus, Ptolemy's chief banker, was being defended by Cicero, he quotes casually from the Sibylline oracle in Latin translation the phrase that the king had been expelled 'by crafty plots'. It shows how he could assume that the jury was familiar with the words of the Sibylline books.[37]

The whole episode reminds one of the occasion a hundred and forty years before when Manlius Vulso had been prevented by a Sibylline oracle from crossing the Taurus. That was the earliest instance of such a use of the *Libri Sibyllini*, and it had apparently been treated seriously by all parties concerned, and the prohibition strictly observed. In the later instance the oracle had been completely ignored by Pompey and Gabinius, and was described by Cicero when writing to Lentulus as 'an assumed name of faked religious obligation'. No doubt he was right that the text had been heavily doctored. But it is worth noting the difference in this respect between the two occasions. No modern scholar is likely to suppose that the Sibylline oracles of the sixth century could have contained a reference to the Taurus. On the other hand the text available to the quindecimvirs in 56 BC, which had been collected some twenty years earlier, might easily have included a mention of the Ptolemies. Presumably these oracles might have resembled a pagan version of *Oracula Sibyllina*, Book 3, and so might well have alluded, under the guise of a prophecy, to such an event as when Popillius Laenas in 168 BC had rescued Egypt from the Seleucid invasion. The encounter with such an allusion in the text may have stimulated in the quindecimvirs the application of the Sibylline books to this contemporary issue. Also when fuller extracts of the oracle were at last disclosed to the Senate, the supporters of Gabinius may have been right in suggesting that the subject of the prophecy was not Ptolemy Auletes but some other Ptolemy. Of course both sides were acting not as philologists or religious thinkers but as politicians, but I simply suggest that at the basis of their controversy may have lain some actual document and not an entire fantasy.[38]

Still the Sibylline books continued also to be used in quite a traditional way without obvious political intent. Pliny records an instance of a prodigy just before the Civil War in 49 BC — a tree near Cumae sank into the ground leaving only a few branches emerging. The Sibylline books were found to contain a warning that this foretold human slaughter, the greater the nearer the prodigy was to the city of Rome. If a means of procuration was specified, Pliny fails to mention it.[39]

At the end of Caesar's dictatorship it was possibly intended to use the oracles again for a political purpose. For immediately after Caesar's death, if not before, the rumour was current that the Sibylline books contained a prophecy that only a king could succeed in war against the Parthians, and that accordingly Lucius Cotta, on behalf of the quindecimvirs, was to propose to the Senate on the Ides of March that the title should be conferred on Caesar to be borne outside Italy. Cicero appears to reject the story of Cotta's intended proposal, but treats the occurrence of the prophecy in the books as possible, while questioning its application to this situation. Actually, as was noted in connection with the alleged oracle about Ptolemy, it would have been quite possible that a recently collected prophecy might have alluded to the conquest of the Parthians by a king — perhaps originally a Seleucid. Since the consultation of the *Libri Sibyllini*, if it had taken place, was never reported officially to the Senate, the whole story remains subject to doubt, but it well demonstrates how there could be leaks in the security of the quindecimvirs, or at least how such leaks could readily be believed to have occurred.[40]

No more consultations of the Sibylline books are recorded under the Republic. Augustus soon after the establishment of the Principate made fresh arrangements for the storing of the books in the new temple of Apollo on the Palatine, and in 18 BC gave instructions for the oracles, which were alleged to have become damaged by age, to be copied out by the quindecimvirs themselves, so that no one else might have occasion to read them. What an educated Roman of the day imagined them to contain is illustrated by Tibullus in his poem in honour of the youthful Messalinus, newly appointed to the quindecemvirate (21 or 20 BC).

> [The Sibyls] told that a comet would be the evil signs of war, and how plenty of stones would rain down on the earth. They say that trumpets have been heard and weapons clashing in the sky, and that groves have prophesied defeat. The cloudy year has seen the sun himself fail in his light and yoke pale steeds, and the images of the gods shed warm tears and cattle acquire speech and warn of the fates.

The poet then invokes Apollo to avert such prodigies. He may have derived this picture of the contents of the *Libri Sibyllini* from those passages of Livy which we have just considered. For the *Histories* were being published exactly at this period and were a great success with the public.[41]

Augustus employed the books which had just been re-copied as his basic authority for the celebration of the *Ludi Saeculares* in the following year (17 BC), when the text of a lengthy oracle prescribing the festival was published. But there is no sign at all that he wished to revive their frequent consultation on the occasion of reported prodigies. In fact it would have been altogether against his principles in directing the state for an opportunity to have been given to priests and magistrates for raising uncontrolled proposals and manipulating the strings of religious propaganda outside the imperial system. So the official Sibyl remained silent; which may be one reason why instead we hear of various unofficial Sibylline oracles circulating among the people.[42]

Early in Tiberius' reign (AD 15) Asinius Gallus, a veteran quindecemvir, attempted to revive the former practice. The Tiber, swollen with unusual rains, had caused devastating floods in the lower parts of the city. So Asinius proposed that the books be consulted, but Tiberius vetoed the proposal, substituting for it practical measures to prevent future flooding. Only in AD 64 Nero used the books in the traditional way to 'procure' the Fire of Rome. It was a time of great agitation among the plebs, and the emperor authorised a negative statement about their contents so as to refute the authority of a popular version.[43]

In contrast it is perhaps significant that Claudius took measures to create a college of *haruspices*, while deploring the neglect of their science. This was what one might expect from his well-known study of Etruscan antiquities. Claudius also managed to find occasion to celebrate the *Ludi Saeculares* in his reign by reinterpreting the terms of the cycle which governed it. No doubt then and in the subsequent celebrations under Domitian and Septimius Severus the books were formally consulted as the authority. But other evidence for their consultation is quite dubious. The frequent references in the later lives of the *Historia Augusta* are probably fictitious decorations. The only plausible occasion in the late imperial period was when Julian enquired at the oracle-centres before his expedition against Persia. Ammianus, a contemporary, records that he sent commands from Antioch to Rome that the Sibylline books should be consulted, and received a written reply which openly stated that the emperor should not cross the boundaries of the empire that year.

On 17 March 363 while Julian was on his fatal invasion, the temple of Apollo on the Palatine was burnt down, but the Sibylline books were saved in time from the conflagration. However, they were not fated to survive for long. Some time in the first years of the fifth century AD, Stilicho, general of the Western Empire and a Christian, ordered their destruction. Shortly after, Prudentius, the Christian poet, would proudly boast that Sibylline books could no longer be used to utter the fates.[44]

If we look back cursorily over the history of the Sibylline books at Rome, a certain pattern of development in their use can perhaps be observed. In the earliest years they may have been strictly employed for the 'procuring' of prodigies or public disasters. In this function they resembled the books of purification (*katharmoi*) or initiations (*teletai*), which the Greeks associated with Orpheus or Epimenides, rather than the typical form of Sibylline oracles. But it may well have been true that the books of hexameter verse acquired under the last dynasty of kings had been of this kind, and were attributed to the great name of the Sibyl by the *chrēsmologos* who purveyed them. By the third century BC the decemvirs had evidently tended to be more and more lax in their use of the text, reading into it whatever they wanted. An advanced stage in this process came with the Hannibalic War, when it was recognised by the authorities that the Sibylline books and any other forms of religious propaganda must be manipulated to maintain the morale of the people. In the second century the intense stress on the interpretation of the books was relaxed, but they continued to be consulted frequently. At last in the period immediately before and after the destruction of the first collection and their replacement they were occasionally exploited merely for party political ends. This was followed by a strict clamp-down on their use under the principate. Though the quindecimvirs were still supposed, as one of their chief duties, to consult the books, in practice it was very rarely called for, but instead they were chiefly active as priests of Apollo and the *Magna Mater*.[45]

Notes

1. The Cumaean Sibyl and King Tarquin, *supra* pp. 76–8. The connection with Cumae, *supra* pp. 80–2 and *infra* pp. 201 (Phlegon, *F. Gr. Hist.* 257 f. 36, p. 481, 1.54). The Pisistratidae and Onomacritus, Appendix I, *supra* pp. 178–9.

2. Dion. Hal. 4.62.4–5 (M. Atilius). Dio fr. 10.8, Zonaras, 7, 11 (M. Acilius). Decemvirs, 367 BC, Livy, 7.37.12; 7.42.2.

3. *Novendiale Sacrum*, Livy, 1.31 (a legendary *aition*); 31.62.6, etc. Hermaphrodites, Livy, 37.11.4; 37.5; 31.12.8. Cf. *infra* pp. 200–1.

4. R.M. Ogilvie, *The Romans and their gods in the age of Augustus* (1969), 62, suggests that the oracles were written on loose leaves, and so could be drawn at random. This form of *liber* would be inconsistent with the picture conveyed by the legend of the Sibyl and King Tarquin. For the Sibyl writing on leaves at Cumae, cf. *supra* pp. 82–3. Claudian's belief that she wrote on linen (*Bell. Poll.* 232) is probably a confusion with Macer's *libri lintei*. Could the oracles have been written on thin sheets of wood stuck together, like the documents from Vindolanda (A.K. Bowman and J.D. Thomas, *Vindolanda; the Latin writing tablets* (1983), 32ff)?

5. From the fall of the kings to the end of the fifth century BC: out of seven consultations, two (Ceres, Liber and Libera, 496 BC and Apollo, 433 BC). The temple of Mercury, 495 BC, is not attributed to the Sibylline books in our sources. Fourth century: out of six consultations, only one (Juno Moneta, 346 BC). Third century: out of fourteen, four temples (Aesculapius, 293 BC, and at the end of the century, Venus Erycina and *Mens* in the same year, 217 BC, and *Magna Mater*, 205 BC). Second century: out of twenty-seven consultations only one (Venus Versicordia, 114 BC), though in the same period a number of temples were vowed and dedicated by generals. No dedications of temples in the first century BC are connected with the Sibylline books. I take the reference in Ovid, *Fasti* 3.209–13 to a temple of Hercules erected after a Sibylline oracle and bearing Sulla's name, to imply that it was restored by the dictator. If so,

the original date of dedication is uncertain. If it was the temple of Hercules at the Circus Maximus, it may have been in 189 BC (Livy 38.35.4).

6. *Ludi Saeculares*, 509 BC (Zonaras, 2.3.3); 504 BC (Plut. *Publ.* 21); 456 BC (Censorinus p. 36 (Sallmann)); 449 BC (Censorinus p. 36 (Sallmann)). The classic discussion in Nilsson, *RE* IA (1920), col. 1696ff.

7. 461 BC, Livy 3.10–14; Dion. Hal. 10.1–8. 460 BC, Livy 3.15–22; Dion. Hal. 10.9–19.

8. First *Lectisternium*, Livy 5.13.6: for discussion see R.M. Ogilvie, *A commentary on Livy Books 1–5* (1965), 655ff.

9. 365 BC, Livy 7.2. 348 BC, Livy 7.27.1 (Festus, p. 440 (Lindsay) dates *Ludi Saeculares* 99 years before 249 BC). 295 BC, Livy 10.31.6. 293 BC, Livy, 10.47.6; Val. Max. 1.8.2. Ovid, *Met.* 15.622 introduces, perhaps fictitiously, a consultation of the Delphic oracle (Parke and Wormell, *DO* II, no. 353). Livy, *Per.* 4, a brief description of Aesculapius' reception without mention of oracles. Strabo 12.5.3 cites as an analogy the fetching of the *Magna Mater*. For the fetching of Aesculapius to Athens in 420/19 BC, H.W. Parke, *Festivals of the Athenians* (1977), 135. 273 BC, Orosius, 4.5.6; August. *De Civ. D.* 4.17.

10. 433 BC, Livy, 3.25.1; 40.51.6. For a possible earlier shrine on the site, Livy 3.63.5 with Ogilvie's note. In 364 BC *ludi scaenici* (in an Etruscan form) were first established, but neither Livy (7.2.3) nor Orosius (3.4.5) make it clear that this was part of any Sibylline prescription of that year.

11. 238 BC *Floralia* (Pliny *HN* 18.69.286). Vellius (1.14.8) dates to 241 BC without mention of the *Libri*. 249 BC *Ludi Saeculares* (Censorinus p. 36 (Sallmann); Ps. Acro Sch. in Hor. *Carm. Saec.* 8). Underground altar, e.g. at Paestum, R. Stillwell (ed.), *The Princeton encyclopaedia of classical sites* (1976), 664. The Etruscan connections of the *Libri Sibyllini* are strongly argued by R. Block, *REL* 40 (1962), 118–20; W. Hoffmann, *Wandel und Herkunft der sibyllinischen Bücher in Rom* (diss. 1933), 26ff.

12. Plut. *Marc.* 3 (who connects it with the outbreak of the Insubrian War); Dio fr. 48, (who dates it to the consulship of Fabius Maximus Verrucosus, i.e. Cos. II, 228 BC); Zonaras 8.19; Orosius, 4.13.3. Dio fr. 49, if it refers to the same occasion, mentions as a prodigy the fall of a thunderbolt near the Apollonion. Plutarch's mention of a contemporary sacrifice each November, which suggests some kind of hero cult, is probably a sheer misunderstanding. For the dead occupying a land, Aesch. *Ag.* 453 with Fränkel's note.

13. Hoffman (*supra* n. 11) 26ff. He does not allow for the possibility that the Sibylline books might only have been supposed to contain the occupation of the city by Greeks and Gauls, and that the Roman authorities in 228 BC devised the ritual to counter the prophecy. Incidentally no oracle of Magna Graecia or Etruria in the late sixth century BC would have been likely to foresee the Gauls as invading enemies.

14. On *pharmakoi* in the Greek world, see W. Burkert, *Greek religion. Archaic and classical* (Engl. transl. 1985), 82–4.

15. Livy 21.62.1–5.

16. Livy 22.1.8–19 (where he writes as though the *Saturnalia* was a new

institution, but the innovation must have been this particular ritual).

17. Livy 22.9.7–10. Plut. *Fab.* 4.4. Is this the context for Macrob. *Sat.* 1.6.13 (an *aition* for the right of the sons of *libertini* to wear the *toga praetexta*)? Ovid, *Fasti* 6.241 (6 June) and in Cicero's imagined law (*Leg.* 2.19). *Ver sacrum*, Festus p. 519 (Lindsay).

18. On 'tithing', Parke and Wormell, *DO* I, 51ff.

19. Livy 22.26.6; 57.2–3. Fabius Pictor at Delphi, Parke and Wormell, *DO* I, 271–2; II, no. 354.

20. Livy 25.12.3–13; Zonaras 9.1; Macrob. *Sat.* 1.17.25.

21. 210 BC, Livy 27.4.11–15 (prodigies and procession without mention of the Sibylline books). 209 BC, Livy 27.11.1–6 (hermaphrodite at Sinuessa). 207 BC, Livy, 27.37 (hermaphrodite at Frusino).

22. Phlegon, *F. Gr. Hist.* 257 f.36(x). H. Diels, *Sibyllinische Blätter* (1890), 84ff. Cic. *Div.* 2.111 and cf. *supra* p. 139. References to the war, A.28–9 and B.67–70. Foundation of Cumae, B.53–6. Cf. Livy 8.22. Hera and Cumae, *supra* pp. 89–90. Romans at Cumae in 213 BC, Livy 32.12ff.

23. Livy 29.10.6; 11.5; 14.6ff. Diod. 34.33.21. Ovid, *Fasti* 4.253ff. Parke and Wormell, *DO* 1, 272 i II, nos. 355 and 356.

24. Polybius, 6.56.6, writing after the middle of the second century, saw this 'fear of the supernatural' (*deisidaimonia*) as peculiarly characteristic of the Romans and serving to hold together their state. Livy, 43.13.1ff. Consultations recorded in Livy but not discussed here: 200 BC: Livy 31.12.9; 6 (a hermaphrodite, with a reference back to 27.37.6, cf. *supra* p. 200); 193 BC: 34.55.1; 35.9.2; 188 BC: 38.36.4; 187 BC: 38.44.7; 179 BC: 40.45.4; 174 BC: 41.21.10; 173 BC: 42.2.3 (cf. Pliny, *HN* 11.40.105).

25. Livy 38.45.2. The previous consultation of 190 BC, 37.3.1. In 39.4.4 Livy reports that the plebs saw in the pitching of tents in the Forum the fulfilment of a forecast given by seers, but I assume that this was popular superstition, not an official reading of the Sibylline books.

26. 191 BC: Livy 36.37.1; 189 BC: 38.35.4; 172 BC: 42.20.1; 40.19.1 (*per totam Italiam*); 42.37 (*per omnia fora conciliabulaque*). The promontory of Minerva, 42.20.

27. 191 BC: Livy 36.37.2; 172 BC: 42.20.2; 163 BC: Cic. *De Nat. D.* 2.4.10–11; Granius Licinianus, p. 7.8 (Criniti). For later instances of calling in of *haruspices*: Obseq. 18 (152 BC); 22 (142 BC); 25 (136 BC); 28 (130 BC); 29 (126 BC); 44 (104 BC); 44 (102 BC); 56 (86 BC); 61 (63 BC). See also Cic. *Cat.* 3.8.19 (65 BC).

28. For typical instances from Obsequens e.g. 13 (165 BC); 22 (142 BC); 35 (118 BC); 143 BC, Obsequens 21 (cf. Dio fr. 74.1). 266 BC, August. *De Civ. D.* 3.17.

29. 149 BC: Livy, *Per.* 49; Censorinus, pp. 36–7 (Sallman) citing Valerius Antias and Varro; 146 BC: Censorinus, loc. cit., citing Piso, Cn. Gellius and Cassius Hemina. 126 BC: Censorinus, loc. cit., citing the *Commentarii* of the *quindecimviri* (i.e. Augustan period).

30. Diod. 34.10. Cic. *Verr.* 2.4.49. Val. Max. 1.1, echoing Cicero.

31. Obsequens. 37; Ovid, *Fasti* 4.157; Plut. *Mor.* 264D; Val. Max. 8.15.3; Pliny, *HN* 7.15.120. Pliny (*HN* 28.3.12) also stated that this ceremony applied 'to a Greek man and woman and numbers of other peoples with whom the state was involved'. Such instances are otherwise unrecorded.

32. 108 BC: Obsequens, 40. 100 BC: Pliny, *HN* 3.123 (other references to Eporedia's foundation without mention of the Sibylline books, Strabo 4.6.7; Velleius, 1.15.5. Alexandre connects it with the events of 143 BC, but this is improbable).

33. Granius Licinianus, p. 13 (Criniti). For the events of the period without reference to the Sibylline books, App. *B.Civ.* 1.64.5; Livy, *Per.* 79; Velleius 2.20.3.

34. The burning of the Capitol, *supra* p. 137. Sulla's increase in the number of the colleges, Victor, *De Vir. Ill.* 75; Livy, *Per.* 89. The earliest literary reference to *quindecimviri*, Caelius *ap.* Cic. *Fam.* 8.4.1. Lentulus Sura, *supra* p. 140.

35. Dio 39.15.1–16.2. Cic. *Fam.* 1.1.3 (Ides of January, 56 BC).

36. Cic. *Fam.* 1.1.3; 1.4.2 (two days later); 1.7.4 (end of June 56 BC). Dio 39.55.3; 56.6. App. *B.Civ.* 2.24. *Syr.* 5. Lucan 8.823.

37. Dio 39.59.3; 60.4; 61.4; 62.3; Cic. *Rab. Post.* 4.

38. Cf. *supra* pp. 202–3. Cic. *Fam.* 1.4.2 (Jan. 56 BC), *nomen inductum fictae religionis*. For references to the Ptolemies in the *Oracula Sibyllina*, e.g. 3.668ff.

39. Pliny, *HN* 17.38.243. Alexandre compares Dio 41.14.4, but I think that refers to popular Sibyllina.

40. Cic. *Div.* 2.116, written immediately after the Ides of March. Suet. *Caes.* 79.3; Plut. *Caes.* 60.2; App. *B. Civ.* 2.110; Dio 44.15.3. Some scholars have taken the reference to L. Cotta in Cic. *Att.* 13.44.1 (July 45 BC) to imply that the plan was already conceived and talked about. But the passage is so vague that it might bear any meaning, and to accept that implication makes nonsense of all our other evidence. For discussions, see Pease on Cic. *Div.* 2.116; S. Weinstock, *Divus Julius* (1971), 340 n.l.

41. For Apollo on the Palatine, *supra* p. 141. The recopying of the books, Dio 54.17.2. Tibullus, 2.5.71–80; on this poem cf. *supra* pp. 35–6.

42. The Sibylline Oracle on the *Ludi Saeculares*, Phlegon, *F. Gr. Hist.* 257 f. 37, pp. 1189–90; Diels (*supra* n. 22), 13ff.

43. AD 15: Tac. *Ann.* 1.76. R. Syme, *CQ* 35 (1985), 181–2. The previous serious flood of 27 BC (Dio 53.20.1) had been interpreted by *haruspices* as favourable to Augustus. AD 64: Tac. *Ann.* 15.44.1; Dio 52.18.4. Cf. *supra* p. 143.

44. Claudius, Tac. *Ann.* 11.15. SHA, *Hadr.* 2.8; *Gordiani*, 26.2; *Gallieni*, 5.51; *Aurelian*, 18.5–21.4; *Tacitus*, 11.6. Julian, Amm. Marc. 23.1.6. The Palatine fire, Amm. Marc. 23.3.3. Stilicho's destruction of the Sibylline books, Rut. Namat. 2.52. Prudent. *Apoth.* 4.39.

45. By the later Republic the decemvirs were regarded chiefly as priests of Apollo. Cf. Livy 10.8.2 (a speech put into the mouth of P. Decius Mus) or Plutarch's paraphrase for decemvir, Plut. *Cat. Min.* 4 (also the use of the dolphin and the tripod as their symbols on coins). Probably this was due in part to the acceptance of Apollo as the chief god worshipped *Graeco ritu*. Also the Sibyl became associated with Apollo as the god of prophecy, though I have argued above that this was not the original source of her inspiration. For the importance of the quindecimvirs in the cult of the *Magna Mater* under the empire, Lucan 1.599, Statius, *Silvae*, 1.2.176.

Appendix III
Ecstatic Prophecy in the Near East '

As a first example we may take the results of the excavations at Mari on the middle Euphrates. These have supplied plentiful records of a highly developed system of divination in the form of letters preserved in the royal archives of King Zimrilim. Men and women wrote to inform the king of revelations from a number of different gods and goddesses. Sometimes these had taken the form of dreams in which the deity had uttered the message. But in a few instances individuals had been seized with a sudden impulse to prophesy. Some of the persons mentioned were recognised as belonging to classes of religious officials, either 'seers' or 'answerers', but others were just members of the laity. Their messages again varied greatly from encouraging assurances to Zimrilim of the gods' goodwill and support, to instructions to avoid some particular course of action, and even in one instance a dire warning. Mostly the messages are brief, simple, and not in any particular literary form, but a few, particularly a prophecy against Babylon, have quite a Sibylline tone with the use of symbolic language. One might sum up the situation by saying that at Mari there was some spontaneous, inspired prophecy, uttered by laity apart from cult-centres and capable of threatening the government as well as foreign powers, but not in a fully literate and discursive form. This was a milieu in which a Sibylline prophetess might have arisen, but there is no evidence that such a development took place. Instead Zimrilim's more powerful neighbour, Hammurabi of Babylon, invaded and sacked Mari about 1757 BC.[1]

The phenomenon of divination in Mari ceased more than a thousand years before the appearance of Sibylline literature in Aeolis. So they are separated by a vast gap in time and space. To some extent this can be bridged by intervening examples in the Semitic cultures. The possibility of private individuals producing ecstatic utterances which affected state policy is evidenced for northern Phoenicia, 1085–1060 BC, by the report of Wenamun. The king of Byblos was influenced in his favour by a spontaneous prophecy of a young courtier, but this remains only an isolated instance.[2]

If we turn to the Old Testament, Balaam, the son of Beor, emerges as something of a Sibylline figure. Balak, king of Moab, sends for him from a district vaguely located in the direction of the Euphrates. He was to be hired to curse the people of Israel, but instead he uttered a series of blessings in the form of prophecies of Israel's victory and future prosperity and of disaster for Israel's neighbours. Balaam uses two forms of divination; when invited to accompany Balak's ambassadors, he requires them to stay the night so that he can consult God, evidently in a dream. Subsequently he goes apart to consult God before uttering his oracle in front of Balak. In it he speaks of his special relation with God, but never loses his own personality. He is a clairvoyant, not a medium. Also his oracles are fairly extensive and use the metaphorical style which is typical of poetic prophecy.[3]

All this biblical description of Balaam could be discounted as historic evidence on the supposition that it was fabricated so as to enhance the picture of Israel as God's chosen people triumphing over its enemies, with probable allusions to the period of the Davidic kingship. But a surprising recent discovery in inland Syria has shown that Balaam himself was not the fictitious creation of a Jewish romancer. In 1967 a Dutch expedition excavating an Iron Age temple at Deir'Allā found numerous fragments of an inscription written in ink on plaster. This inscription recorded oracles of Balaam, the son of Beor, described as a seer to whom the gods came by night. There can be no doubt that there we have a local tradition of the same prophet who appears in the Old Testament, but the two streams of tradition are quite independent. The passage in the Book of Numbers may date from early in the Jewish kingship and treats Balaam as a monotheistic follower of El or Yahweh. The inscription can be dated stylistically and linguistically two centuries later to the period 750–650 BC and belongs to a fully polytheistic culture. Balaam appears to be treated as a prophet native to the neighbourhood. The fact that his oracles were inscribed in a temple implies official acceptance. His date is left undefined, but he may have been recognised as belonging to a distant past, though his oracles were still valid.

The narrative starts with a warning vision to Balaam at night. When he is asked to explain why he weeps on the following day, he is led to deliver a long and elaborate prophecy of doom. This discursive oracle is full of symbolism and metaphorical language. The later developments are very obscure owing to the fragmentary condition of the inscription. Balaam appears to hold a dialogue with the people and to have referred to past examples as corroborative evidence. The original editor thought that there were signs of a happy ending to the oracle, but this has been doubted.[4]

The Balaam of Deir'Allā is much more like a Sibyl in his attitude to the people than the Balaam of the Old Testament. Also in date the inscription could fall only shortly before the original date of Sibylla of Marpessus. Moreover the evidence for a literary text in Aramaic of the Oracles of Balaam suggests a medium of communication which might have reached Greeks travelling in the Near East. The Hebrew of the Old Testament would not have been as likely to reach Greek travellers or to be intelligible to them. So the discovery at Deir'Allā goes much nearer to bridge the gap from Semitic to Hellenic prophecy than the Hebrew prophets, such as Amos and Isaiah, who already in the last quarter of the eighth century were producing warning prophecies in the name of Yahweh. (But a certain affinity between the prophets of Israel and Judah and the Sibyls of Greek Asia Minor would ultimately lead to the confluence of these two streams.)

There is abundant documentation on the religious practices of the Hittites. They had an elaborately organised system of divination by three methods: (1) augury; (2) the inspection of sacrificial entrails; and (3) the technique called the 'kin'. This last was practised by old women who hence have been rashly translated as Sibyls. But though the exact form of this divination is uncertain, the evidence points to some use of the lot. Dreams containing messages from the gods could be conveyed through anyone, whether private individuals or even the king himself. But formal incubation was not practised as a ritual, and ecstatic prophecy is not recorded. So there was no Sibylline element in the Hittite tradition which could plausibly have been taken over by their successors in Anatolia, the Phrygians and the Lydians.[5]

Modern scholars instead call attention to the evidence for inspirational prophecy among the Assyrians. Deities such as Ishtar of Arbela and Bel send messages to Esarhaddon (680–669 BC) or Ashurbanipal (668–633 BC). These oracles, however, are more like those of the Pythia than of the Sibyls. The priestess describes herself as a mouthpiece, and the god or goddess speaks through her in the first person. The messages are brief, encouraging and lacking in any ambiguity or picturesque symbolism. They would by themselves provide little or no basis for the development of a Sibylline oracle.[6]

In contrast there is one small group of oracles known from cuneiform tablets in the library of Ashurbanipal. These contain one discursive prophecy extant in several copies which is in the form of a pseudo-chronicle in the future tense. It is based on a pattern of successive reigns of kings, each marked off from the next with a horizontal line. The scheme is very formulaic: 'A prince shall arise and shall exercise sovereignty for x years', followed by a brief description in general terms of his reign. The tone is reminiscent of the Old Testament Book of Chronicles; kings who do good in the eyes of the Lord are universally successful, the rest are the reverse. There is generally a lack of specific facts; the kings are never named and only a few place-names are scattered about. No prefatory matter is extant to explain the oracle and it ends incomplete. So it is impossible to tell who was supposed to utter it and in what circumstances. Also there is no indication of date. Attempts by scholars to fit the lengths of the different reigns to some known sequence of kings are unsuccessful. Hence the real purpose behind the oracle remains quite uncertain. Grayson and Lambert have suggested that it was produced by an author who wishes to prove his close connection with his god by this impressive document, and then to use it to back up other prophecies. This would be a motive very appropriate to the forecasts of past events inserted into Sibylline oracles, but Sibylla at least took care to make her prophecy of the Trojan War unmistakable, while the Assyrian forecasts do not evidently relate to any known reigns. Also the rigid pattern into which events are fitted is quite unlike the picture of the earlier Sibylline oracles which we get from all our evidence. Only the late books of the *Oracula Sibyllina* with their descriptions of the reigns of Roman emperors show some superficial resemblance to the Assyrian scheme.[7]

The conclusion to be drawn is that though ecstatic prophecy in the Near East exhibits some interesting features which can be compared with the Sibylline oracles, there is no overall likeness at any period or place which would impel a belief in the Sibyl's derivation from the Orient.

Notes

1. F. Ellermeier, *Prophetie in Mari und Israel* (1968). On the history of the period, *CAH* vol. 1.1 (3rd edn, 1970), 210–11.

2. For the Report of Wenamun, see *CAH* vol. 2.2 (3rd edn, 1975), 511–20; 642–3. There is an almost complete translation of the Report in A. Gardiner, *Egypt of the Pharaohs* (1961), 306–13.

3. Numbers 22–4. There is also a hostile tradition in which Balaam is treated as an enemy of Israel: Numbers 31: 8, 16; Deuteronomy 23: 4–6; Joshua 13: 22; Nehemiah 13: 2.

4. J. Hoftijzer, *Aramaic texts from Deir'Allā*, trans. van der Kooij (1976); H.-P. Müller, *Zeitschrift des deutschen Palästina-Verein* 94 (1978), 56ff.

5. O.R. Gurney, *Annals of Archaeology and Anthropology* 27 (1940), 27; 89.

6. J.B. Pritchard, *Ancient Near Eastern texts relating to the Old Testament* (2nd edn, 1955), 449–51.

7. Pritchard (*supra* n. 6), 451–2. A.K. Grayson and W.G. Lambert, *Journal of Cuneiform Studies* 18 (1964), 7–30.

Bibliography

Alexander, P.J. (1967) *The oracle of Baalbek: the Tiburtine Sibyl in Greek dress*, Washington.

L'antre corycien I (1981) *Bulletin de Correspondence Hellénique*, Suppl. VII.

L'antre corycien II (1984) *Bulletin de Correspondence Hellénique*, Suppl. IX.

Arnim, J. von (1905) *Stoicorum Veterum Fragmenta* 3 vols, Leipzig.

Barnes, T.D. (1981) *Constantine and Eusebius*, Cambridge Mass.

Bartlett, J.R. (1985) *Jews in the Hellenistic world*, Cambridge.

Bevan, E. (1928) *Sibyls and seers*, London.

Bloch, R., (1965) 'L'origine des livres sibyllins à Rome, méthode de recherche et critique du récit des annalistes anciens' in Welskopf, E.C. (ed.), *Neue Beiträge zur Geschichte der alten Welt* II, Berlin, 281.

Bousset, W. (1906) 'Sibyllen und sibyllinische Bücher', *Real-Encyclopedie der protestantischen Theologie und Kirche* 18, 265.

Brandt, S. (1891) 'Über die Quellen von Lactanz' Schrift *de opificio dei*', *Wiener Studien* 13, 255.

Burkert, W. (1983) 'Itinerant diviners and magicians. A neglected element in cultural contacts' in Hägg, R. (ed.), *The Greek Renaissance of the eighth century B.C.: Tradition and innovation, proceedings of the Second International Symposium at the Swedish Institute in Athens, 1–5 June, 1981*, Stockholm, 115.

—— (1985) *Greek religion archaic and classical* (Engl. trans. Oxford, 1985).

Burstein, S.M. (1978) *The Babyloniaka of Berossus*, Malibu.

Cairns, F. (1979) *Tibullus: a Hellenistic poet at Rome*, Cambridge.

Cardauns, B. (1961) 'Zu den Sibyllen bei Tibull 2,5', *Hermes* 89, 357.

—— (1976) *M. Terentius Varro. Antiquitates rerum divinarum*, 2 parts, Wiesbaden.

Clark, R.J. (1977) 'Vergil, Aeneid 6.40ff. and the Cumaean Sibyl's Cave', *Latomus* 36, 482.

—— (1978) *Catabasis: Vergil and the wisdom-tradition*, Amsterdam.

Collins, J.J. (1974) *The sibylline oracles of Egyptian Judaism*, Missoula, Montana.

—— (1983) 'Sibylline oracles' in Charlesworth, J.H. (ed.), *The Old Testament pseudepigrapha*, I Garden City.

—— (1987) 'The development of the sibylline tradition', *Aufstieg und Niedergang der römischen Welt* 20. 1, 421.

Cook, J.M. (1973) *The Troad: an archaeological and topographical study*, Oxford.

Diels, H. (1890) *Sibyllinische Blätter*, Berlin.

Doria, L. (1983) *Oracoli Sibillini. Tra rituali e propaganda (studi su Flegonte di Tralles)*, Naples.

Dunbabin, T.J. (1951) 'The oracle of Hera Akraia at Perachora', *Annual of the British School at Athens* 46, 61.

Eddy, S.K. (1961) *The King is dead. Studies in the Near Eastern resistance to Hellenism 334–331 BC*. Lincoln, Nebraska.

Ellermeier, F. (1968) *Prophetie in Mari und Israel*, Herzberg.

Fontenrose, J. (1978) *The Delphic Oracle*, Berkeley.

Frederiksen, M. (1984) *Campania*, London.

Fuchs, H. (1964) *Der geistige Widerstand gegen Rom in der antiken Welt*, ed. 2 Berlin.

Gatz, B. (1967) *Weltalter, goldene Zeit und sinnverwandte Vorstellungen*, Hildesheim.

Geffcken, J. (1902) *Komposition und Entstehungszeit der Oracula Sibyllina*, Leipzig.

Grayson, A.K., and Lambert, W.G. (1964) 'Akkadian prophecies', *Journal of Cuneiform Studies* 18, 7.

Guarducci, M. (1946–8) 'Un antichissimo responso dell'oracolo di Cuma', *Bulletino della Commissione Archeologica Communale di Roma* 72, 129.

Gurney, O.R. (1940) 'Hittite prayers of Mursili II', *Annals of Archaeology and Anthropology* 27, 1.

Hardie, C. (1969) 'The great antrum at Baiae', *Papers of the British School at Rome* 37, 14.

Harnack, A. (1893–1904) *Geschichte der altchristlichen Literatur bis Eusebius*, 3 vols, Leipzig.

Hoffman,W. (1933) *Wandel und Herkunft der sibyllinischen Bücher in Rom*, diss. Leipzig, 1933.

Hoftijzer, J. and Kooij, G. van der (1976) *Aramaic texts from Deir 'Allā*, Leiden.

Horsfall, N. (1979) 'Some problems in the Aeneas legend', *Classical Quarterly* 29, 372.

Huxley, G.L. (1966) *The early Ionians*, London.

Jeanmaire, H. (1939) *La sibylle et le retour de l'age d'or*, Paris.

Josifovic, S. (1968) 'Lykophron', *RE* Suppl. 11, col. 925.

Kranz, W. (1961) 'Sphragis. Ichform und Namensiegel als Eingangs — und Schluss-motiv antiker Dichtung', *Rheinisches Museum für Philologie* 104, 3.

Kurfess, A. (1948) 'Die Sibyllen bei Tibull (II, 5)', *Würzburger Jahrbücher für die Altertumswissenschaft* 3, 402.

—— (1951) *Sibyllinische Weissagungen*, Berlin.

—— (1954) 'Virgils vierte Ekloge und die Oracula Sibyllina', *Historisches Jahrbuch der Gorres Gesellschaft* 73, 120.

Lewy, H. (1978) *Chaldaean oracles and theurgy*, ed. 2, Paris.

Maass, E. (1879) *De sibyllarum indicibus*, Berlin.

Maiuri, A.G. (1958) *The Phlegraean Fields*, Engl. trans. Rome.

McKay, A.G. (1972) *Ancient Campania* I. *Cumae and the Phlegraean Fields*, Hamilton, Ontario.

Momigliano, A. (1975) *Alien wisdom. The limits of hellenization*, Cambridge.

Müller, H.-P. (1978) 'Einige alttestamentliche Probleme zur aramaischen Inschriften von Dēr 'Allā', *Zeitschrift des deutschen Palästina-Verein* 94, 56.

Nikiprowetzky, V. (1970) *La troisième sibylle*, Paris.

—— (1987) 'La sibylle juive et le 'troisième livre' des 'pseudo-oracles sibyllins' depuis Charles Alexandre', *Aufstieg und Niedergang der römischen Welt* 20.1, 460.

Nilsson, M.P. (1967, 1961) *Geschichte der griechische Religion*, 2 vols, 1 ed. 3, Munich, 1967; 2 ed. 2 Munich, 1961.

Nisbet, R.G.M. (1978) 'Vergil's Fourth Eclogue: easterners and westerners', *Bulletin of the Institute of Classical Studies* 25, 59.

Ogilvie, R.M. (1978) *The library of Lactantius*, Oxford.

Paget, R.F. (1967) *In the footsteps of Orpheus*, London.

—— (1967) 'The antrum of initiation at Baiae', *Papers of the British School at Rome* 35, 102.

—— (1967) 'The great antrum at Baiae', *Vergilius* 13, 42.

—— (1968) 'The ancient ports of Cumae', *Journal of Roman Studies* 58, 152.

Parke, H.W. (1935) 'Pausanias' description of the Temple of Delphi', *Hermathena* 49, 102.

—— (1967) *Greek oracles*, London.

—— (1967) *The oracles of Zeus*, Oxford.

—— (1978) 'Castalia', *Bulletin de Correspondence Hellénique* 102, 200.

—— (1981) 'Apollo and the Muses, or prophecy in Greek verse', *Hermathena* 130/1, 99.

—— (1985) *The oracles of Apollo in Asia Minor*, London.

Parke, H.W., and Wormell, D.E.W. (1956) *The Delphic Oracle*, 2 vols, Oxford.

Payne, H.G.G. (1940) *Perachora: the sanctuaries of Hera Akraia and Limenia*, Oxford.

Pichon, R. (1901) *Lactance. Étude sur le mouvement philosophique et religieux sous le règne de Constantin*, Paris.

Potter, D.S. (1984) *An historical commentary to the thirteenth sibylline oracle*, diss. Oxford.

Robert, L. (1954) *Les fouilles de Claros*, Limoges.

Rohde, E. (1898) *Psyche: Seelencult und Unsterblichkeitsglaube der Griechen*, ed. 2, Freiburg.

Rzach, A. (1891) *Oracula sibyllina*, Leipzig.

—— (1923) 'Sibyllinische Orakel', *RE* 2 A, col. 2073.

Salmon, J. (1972) 'The Heraeum at Perachora and the early history of Corinth and Megara', *Annual of the British School at Athens* 67, 159.

Schnabel, P. (1923) *Berossos und die babylonisch-hellenistische Literatur*, Leipzig.

Schürer, E. (1986) *The history of the Jewish people in the age of Jesus Christ (175 BC–AD 135)*, revised and edited by G. Vermes, F. Millar, M. Goodman, vol. III pt 1, Edinburgh.

Thompson, B. (1952) 'Patristic use of sibylline oracles', *The Review of Religion* 6, 115.

Vogt, E. (1967) 'Das Akrostichon in der griechischen Literatur', *Antike und Abendland* 13, 80.

Wehrli, F. (1969) *Herakleides Pontikos, Die Schule des Aristoteles* vol. 7, ed. 2, Basel.

West, S. (1983) 'Notes on the text of Lycophron', *Classical Quarterly* 33, 114.

Will, E. (1953) 'Sur la nature de la mantique pratiquée à l'héraion de Pérachora', *Revue de l'Histoire des Religions* 143, 145.

Windisch, H. (1929) *Die Orakel des Hystaspes*, Amsterdam.

Wolff, M.J. (1934) 'Sibyllen und Sibyllinen', *Archiv für Kulturgeschichte* 24, 312.
Ziegler, K. (1927) 'Lykophron', *RE* 13, col. 2316.

Index

Abaris 21n24
Academy 24
Acilius, C. 72
Acilius, M. (or Atilius) 191
Acropolis, Athens 77, 179, 190
Acrostics 138, 139, 149n7, 165, 169, 200
Actium, battle of 141
Adeimantus 106, 122n10
Aeantis, tribe 181, 189n24
Aegira, Achaea 90, 93, 99n41
Aegispotami, battle of 100, 105–6, 179
Aelian 45, 187n7
Aemilius, M. (pr. 213BC) 199
Aemilius Lepidus, M. (cos. I, 46BC) 142
Aeneas 24, 52, 56, 74, 75, 82, 143, 148, 150n11
  and Aeneid 77, 79–80;
  and Sibyl's prophecy 33, 36, 48n29, 57, 72
Aeolic dialect 30, 38, 47n17
Aeolis 54, 60, 62, 64, 102, 216
Aeschylus 20n13, 20n19, 57, 68n13, 95n5
Aesculapius 194–5, 212n5, 213n9
Agesilaus 129
Ahaz 169
Aidoneus, river 38, 51, 52, 136
Ajax 56
Akkadian 55
Alba Longa 75, 76
Albula, near Tibur 36, 49n30
Albunea, Tiburtine Sibyl 31, 36, 49n30
Alcibiades 122n10
Alcmaeon 143
Aletes (Bacis) 183
Alexander, of Epirus 94n2
Alexander, Polyhistor 42, 144, 150n17
Alexander, the Great 30, 32–3, 41, 48n21, 107, 125
Alexandra, of Lycophron 16–17,

22n36, 47n14, 71–2, 75, 78, 99n41, 108, 127
Alexandria 6, 13, 16, 22n36, 140, 174
Alexandria, Troas 37, 40, 117
Allobroges 140, 207
Alyattes 62, 68n22
Amalthea, Cumaean Sibyl 31, 36, 77, 78
Amazons 119–20
Ammianus 211
Ammon 121n5
Amos 218
Amphiaraus 60–1
Amphictyony 114
Amphilytus 189n28
Amphion 184, 185, 189n32
Anacreon 99n39
Anaxilas, of Rhegium 98n33
Anchises 76
Anio, river 9, 31, 36
Anna Perenna 147
Annaeus Seneca, L. (cos. AD55/6) 135n16
Annales Maximi 137, 192
Anthedon 96n18
Anticlares, of Eleon 181–2, 189n26
Antimachus, of Colophon 27
Antinous 158
Antioch 140, 167–8, 211
Antiochus I 43, 126
Antiochus III 202–3
Antiope 185
Antiphanes, of Argos 100–1
Antoninus Pius 133, 135n18, 158
Antonius, M. (cos. 44BC) 144
Apamea, Peace of 203
Aphrodite 56
Apollo 18, 19n6, 40, 55, 62, 66, 67, 71, 76, 79, 80, 94, 102, 135n12, 166, 177, 179, 186, 198, 199, 210
  and Cassandra, 20–1n19, 56–8, 62n12; and Sibyls 7, 9, 12, 26–7, 38, 39, 49n35, 57, 58, 111-12, 114; at Abae 135; at Chalcedon 127; at Claros 10, 85, 93, 113,

127; at Cumae 37, 71–2, 74, 81, 87 96n21, 162; at Didyma 62, 85, 93, 125, 166; at Gergis 107–8, 122n13; at Hylla 69n31; at Rome 76, 95n15, 193–4, 212n5, 215n45; Smintheus 37, 40, 117; temple at Delphi destroyed 112–13; temple on Palatine 141, 149–50n11, 209, 211, 215n41

Apollodorus, of Erythrae 28, 31, 44, 47n13, 109–10

Appian 131–2

Apuleius, *Golden Ass* 154, 170–1n3

Aramaic 55

Aratus, *Phaenomena* 139, 157

Archytas 44

Ardea 197

Arginusae, battle of 106

Argonauts 118

Argos 66, 70n32, 100–1, 186, 188n12

Aricia 86, 99n42

Arisbe 122n14

Aristeas 21n24

Aristobulus 6

Aristocrates 122n15

Aristodemus, of Cumae 86–9, 92, 93, 94, 97n31, 98n33

Aristophanes 16, 17, 18, 23, 27, 46n1, 105, 179, 180, 183, 188n22
and Sibyls 102–4; *Birds* 16, 103, 104; *Knights* 16, 103, 104; *Peace* 103, 180–1

Aristotle 175, 180

Artemis 10, 12, 26, 71, 111–13, 194
Delphic Sibyl 26–7, 38, 39, 49n35, 111–12

Artemisium, battle of 102, 121n4, 182, 183, 189n27

Artemius 166

Ascanius 76

Asclepius 158

Ascra 189n25

Ashurbanipal 54–5, 219

Asinius Gallus (*XVvir*) 210

Asius, epic poet 65, 69n29

Asopus 120, 182

Assyria 54–5, 219

Athenagoras 158

Athenais, prophetess 28, 47n13, 107, 125, 134n1

Athenion 136

Athenodorus, of Eretria 188n12

Athens 21n19, 65, 174, 176, 177, 178–9, 180, 182, 183, 187n3, 188nn10,19, 194, 213n9
and Sibylline oracles 102–7, 136

Athos, Mt. 14, 121n4

Attalus I 122n13, 126, 132, 134n3, 202

Attus Navius (*augur*) 91

Augustine 169–70, 171n5

Augustus 81, 84, 91, 96n20, 142, 205, 215n43
and *Libri Sibyllini* 141–2, 143, 158 192, 209–10

Aulai 69n31

Aurelius Cotta, L. (*cos.* 65BC) 149n10, 209, 215n40

Avernus, lake 73, 80, 92, 93, 95n5, 148

Baalbek 14

Babel, Tower of 7, 20n12, 43, 144, 150n16, 161

Babylon 8, 10, 33, 42, 43, 110, 216

Babylonian Sibyl 10, 42–3, 128, 134n8, 168

Bacis 9, 18, 44n1, 58, 62, 120, 121n4 124n35, 128, 178, 179, 180–7, 188nn20,21, 189n27–8
and Aristophanes 103–4; and Philetas of Ephesus 27, 189n25; and Thucydides 102–3

Baiae, Great Antrum, 73–4, 92, 97n31
Temple of Apollo 97n31; Temple of Zeus 97n31

Balaam, son of Beor 54, 217–18, 220n3

Balak, king of Moab 217

Baris 133, 135n19

Batcia 108, 122n14

Bel 32–3, 219

Berosus 33, 41, 42, 43, 50n40, 144, 150n16

Blasta 176

Bocchus 110

Bocotia 180, 181, 183

Boethius 128, 134n9

Briareus 118

Buthrotum, in Epirus 76
Bura 112
Byblos 217

Caelius Rufus, M. (*pr.* 48BC) 207
Caere 91, 94, 99nn44,48
Caicus, river 122n13
Calchas 127, 134n7
Callimachus 178
Callisthenes 28, 107, 109
Camarina 4, 19n6
Campania 72, 73, 79, 81, 86–7, 94,
    96n20, 201, 203
Caninius Gallus (*XVvir*) 143
Cannae, battle of 20n13, 198, 199,
    201
Canopus 25
Caphye 183
Capitol, Rome 4, 31, 34, 77, 137, 141,
    149n9, 193, 206, 215n24
Capua 86
Caria 54, 65, 69n31, 132
Carmenta, prophetess 79, 90, 99n42
Cassandra 16, 20n13, 68nn11,13, 75,
    76, 79, 127
    and Apollo 20–1n19, 56–8, 62n12
Castalia 85
Cataonia 133
Catilinarian Conspiracy 140–1
Catullus 148
Celaeno, the harpy 76, 95n12
Celsus 155, 171nn4,5
Censorinus 214n29
Cephale, of Gergis 20n16
Cephisus, river 119, 185
Ceres 203, 205, 212n5
Chaeronea, battle of 14, 21n30,
    119–20, 189n27
Chalcedon 127
Chalcis 95n18
Chaldaean, history 42–3, 144
    oracles 160; priests 32–3
Chaldaean Sibyl 35, 42, 50n39,
    150n16, 167, 168
Champions, battle of 100–2
Chaones 126–7, 134n2
Charon, of Lampsacus 187n5
Chios 110, 123n18
Chrēsmologoi 17–18, 23, 77, 78, 104,
    121n6, 176, 178, 180, 181, 183,
    187, 190, 211
Christ 164, 166, 167
Christian, Fathers 4, 6, 35, 46, 152,
    154, 156, 160, 162, 165, 168
    interpolation in *Or. Sib.* 155, 156,
    162, 166, 167, 169, 171n5
Christianity 133, 136, 158, 159, 163,
    164, 166
Christians 155, 157, 159, 160, 167
Chronicles, Book of 219
Chrysippus, the Stoic 30, 33, 48n22,
    118, 123n23
Church, the 153–4, 155–6, 159, 160,
    162, 171n6
Cilicia 54, 133, 207
Cimmerian Sibyl 30, 33, 35, 72–4, 80,
    93
Cimmerians 60, 72, 73, 74, 92,
    99nn45,46
Cimolus 206
Circe 42, 43, 44
Circus Maximus 213n5
Cissotas 122n15
Cithaeron, Mt. 90, 181
Civil Wars 138, 141, 209
Claros 40, 58, 83, 84, 85, 99n47, 113,
    127
Claudian 212n4
Claudius 211
Claudius Pulcher, Ap. (*cos.* 54BC),
    147, 151n24, 204
Clement, of Alexandria 12, 25–7, 46,
    111–12, 127–8, 156–7, 160–1,
    171n6
Cleomenes 179
Cleon 183
Cleromancy 93
Cohortatio ad Graecos 41, 42, 84, 85,
    162–3, 167, 170n2
Colophon 58
Colophonian Sibyl 40, 46, 127, 128
Colossus, of Rhodes 135n18
Commodus 158, 159
Conon 44
Constantinople 3, 14, 168
Coretas 78, 96n16
Corinth 54, 118–19
Cornelius Cinna, L. (*cos.* I, 87BC)
    140, 149n9, 206, 207

Cornelius Lentulus Spinther, P. (*cos.* 57BC) 207–8
Cornelius Lentulus Sura, P. (*cos.* 71BC) 140, 159n9, 207, 215n34
Cornelius Sulla, L. (*cos.* I, 88BC) 137, 138, 140, 144, 149n9, 206, 207, 212n5, 215n34
Cornelius Tacitus, P. (*cos.* AD97) 84, 142, 150n14
Coronea, battle of 183
Corycus 122n15
Creation, the 11, 21n33, 43, 161
Crete 174, 175, 176, 177, 187n3, 188n12
Crinagoras 122n15
Croesus 25, 54, 60–3, 68n22, 68n23, 101
Cronus 158
Cruxifixion, the 2
Ctesias 158
Cumae, and Dikaiarchia 87–9, 92, 93, 98n33, 116, 123n27
Cumae, disc 88–9, 93
Cumaean Sibyl 2, 3, 7, 28–9, 31, 32, 46, 47n14, 48n25, 57, 67, 67n6, 71, 72, 75, 77, 78, 79, 88, 90, 97n23, 134n8, 134n11, 138, 141, 147–8, 150n13, 152, 154, 170, 201
    and Aelian 45; and Apollo 49n35; and Isidore, 35; and Pausanias 40–1; and Samos 87–9; and *sortes* 88–9, 91, 93; and the Tarquin 31, 33–4, 48n25, 76–8, 81, 88, 91, 129, 139, 140, 190, 212n1, 212n4; cave of 80, 82, 83–5, 89–92, 97n29; named Amalthea 31, 36, 77, 78; named Deiphobe 35, 76, 79, 80, 96n18; named Demophile 31, 40, 42, 77, 81; named Herophile 31, 36, 38, 77, 89, 109, 122–3n17; origin of 75–9
Cydas 183
Cylon 174
Cyme, in Aeolis 54, 67n6, 88, 98n35, 145, 189n25
Cynoscephalae, battle of 130–1, 132
Cynosura 182
Cypria, the 54, 56, 57
Cyprus 54, 133, 167–8

Cyrus 25, 27, 31, 34, 60–3, 64, 101

Daedalus 74, 95n7
Daniel, Book of 8, 11
Daphne 113, 165
    Delphic Sibyl 49n34
Dardanus 108, 122n14
Datis 135n12
David, king 217
Dawn Goddess 57–8
De Mirabilibus Auscultationibus 78, 94–5n2
De Origine Gentis Romanae 72
Decemviri 137, 192, 194, 195, 197–8, 199, 200, 201, 203, 204, 205, 206, 211, 215n45
Deiphobe, Cumaean Sibyl 35, 76, 79, 80, 96n18
Deir'Allā 217–18
Delos 40, 70n33, 128, 134n12
Delphic Sibyl 10, 12, 25–6, 28, 30, 33, 38–9, 40, 46, 51, 67n6, 72, 110–13, 113–17, 118, 119, 127
    and Apollo, 26–7, 38, 39; named Daphne 49n34; named Herophile 10, 37, 38–9
Demeter 69n30
Demetrius, of Magnesia 176
    of Phalerum 94n2; of Scepsis 67n1; of Syria 126, 133, 135n18; the Chronographer 6
Demo, Cumaean Sibyl 28, 40, 42, 81
Demophile, Cumaean Sibyl 31, 40, 42, 77, 81
Dercyllidas 107
Diana 80, 193–4
Dictys, of Crete 9
Didyma 58, 85, 97n28, 98n36, 99n47, 125, 134n1
Dikaiarchia 87–9, 92, 93, 98n33, 116, 123n27
Dio Cassius 143
Dio Chrysostom 4, 118
Diocletian 160, 162, 163, 166
Diodorus Siculus 81, 110, 113–14, 205
Diogenes Laertius 24, 174
Diomedes 199
Dionysius, of Halicarnassus 75, 193
Dionysus 25

Dis 195
Divine Child, Emmanuel 146,
    151n22
Dodona 7, 25, 75, 76, 95n10, 121n5,
    126, 127, 134n6
Domitian 211
Doricus 181, 182
Duris, of Samos 119–20
Duumviri 191, 193

Earth Goddess 111, 113
Egeria 91, 99n42
Egypt 11, 13, 14, 21n27, 149n10,
    207–8
Egyptian Sibyl 41, 45, 46, 128, 134n8
Eira 184, 189n31
Ekpyrosis 11, 172n8
El 217
Elagabalus 22n32
Eleon 181, 189n25
Eleusis 106, 179, 180
Elissa (Sibyl) 134n8
Elpenor 72, 95n4
Empedocles 11
Epaminondas 183, 184
Ephesus 61, 64, 65, 71
Ephorus 73–4, 92
Ephyre 118
Epic Cycle 55–9
Epidaurus 194
Epigoni 113
Epigoni 113
Epimenides 9, 11, 12, 137, 148n2,
    174–8, 186, 187nn7,8,12,20, 211
Epirus 126–7
Eporedia 206, 215n32
Er, myth of 116
Eratosthenes 29, 31, 64–6,
    69nn28,30, 88, 107, 109
Eretria 22n36
Erichthonius 108
Erymanthe 41, 43, 50n43
Erymanthian boar 41, 50n38, 87,
    98n33
Erythrae 42, 43, 64, 78, 79, 88, 89,
    91, 98n35, 123n18, 138
Erythraean Sibyl 3, 10, 19n3, 21n20,
    25–6, 27, 28, 29, 31, 35, 38, 45, 46,
    50nn40,45, 69n25, 70n33, 72, 88,
    110, 115–16, 123n18, 125, 139,

164–5, 169–70, 172n25, 173n33
    named Herophile 24, 25, 26, 35,
    36, 38, 40, 49n34, 59, 64, 65–6,
    77, 108, 109, 122n17, 126;
    named Symmachia 48n27; rival
    with Marpessus 24, 51–3, 59,
    107–9, 117, 122n15, 140
Esarhaddon 219
Etruria 54, 86, 87, 94, 149n9, 195,
    196, 200, 211, 213nn10,11
Euboea 54, 182
Euclus, of Cyprus 180, 188n21
Eudoxus, of Cnidua 186
Euhemerism 11, 13, 21n23
Euphrates, river 216, 217
Euripides 23, 30, 32, 38, 46n1, 49n33,
    124n32
    and Sibyls 104–6; *Busiris* 104–5,
    114, 121–2n9
Eusebius 29, 69n30, 159, 160, 164
Eustathius 135n20
Evander 47n17, 76, 91
Exodus 6, 7, 20n12
Extispicy 68n8
Ezekiel 6

Fabianus 169
Fabius Maximus Verrucosus, Q.
    (*cos.* I, 233BC) 197, 213n12
Fabius Pictor, Q. (*leg.* 216BC).
    198–9, 214n19
Falerii 91, 99n44
Faunus 49n30
Favorinus 118
Flood, the 43, 50n42, 144, 150n13,
    158, 164, 165
Flora 195, 213n11

Gabinius, A. (*cos.* 58BC) 208, 209
Galli 141, 202
Gallienus 168
Gauls 126–7, 195–6, 204, 205,
    212n13
Gē, sanctuary of 90
Gehenna 157
Gematria 16
Genesis 11, 21n23
Gergis 25, 31, 51–2, 53, 67n4, 107,
    117, 122n13
Glanis, brother of Bacis 103

Glaucus 79, 96n18
Glisas 120
Gnosticism 133
Gnostos 42, 43, 44
God 152–6, 159, 161, 164, 167, 169,
170, 217
Golden Age 13, 21n28, 145–6, 147,
150n20, 151n21
Gordius, king of Phrygia 54
Gyges 62, 68n22

Hadrian 137, 200
Haimon 119–20
Hammurabi 216
Hannibal 197, 201, 211
Haruspices 54, 140, 149n9, 200, 203–4,
205, 211, 214n27, 215n43
Hasdrubal 201
Hebrew Sibyl 41–5, 128, 134n8,
150n16, 168
Hecabe 40
Hector 56
Hegesianax, of Alexandria 20n16
Helen, of Troy 8, 38, 55, 109, 110
Helena, St. 167
Helenus 56, 68n11, 76, 82
Helice 112
Helicon 26, 113, 114
Heliopelis 14
Helius 118, 124n32
Hellanicus 58
Hellespont 121n4, 126, 178
Hellespontine Sibyl 25, 28, 31, 34, 36
Hera 66, 69–70n32, 70n35, 71, 88–9,
91, 93, 98n38, 98–9n39, 138, 141,
148n4, 201
Heraclea, Minoa 181
Pontica 24
Heracles 17, 158, 193–4, 203,
212–13n5
Heraclides, of Pontus 24–7, 28, 29,
31, 39, 46, 53, 60, 65, 67n1, 109,
110–13, 122n17
Heraclitus 12, 17, 20n15, 23, 46n1,
58, 63–4
Herculaneum 123n27
Herdonius, Ap. 193
Hermaphrodites 137, 191, 200,
212n3, 214nn21,24

Hermas 152–6, 163, 168, 170nn1,2,
171n3
Hermes 169
Hermesianax 21n21
Hermippus 122n15
Hermodorus 64
Herod 150n17
Herodotus 17, 37, 53, 54, 60, 61, 62,
67n7, 101, 102, 120, 134n12, 175,
178–9, 180, 181, 182, 185
Herophile 10, 24, 27, 36, 49n29, 61,
65, 66, 69n30
Cumaean Sibyl 31, 36, 38, 77, 89,
109, 122–3n17; Delphic Sibyl
24, 25, 26, 35, 36, 38, 40, 49n34,
59, 64, 65–6, 77, 108, 109,
122n17, 126; Marpessian Sibyl
122–3n17, 128; Samian Sibyl 24,
69n30, 123n17
Hesiod 10, 11, 12, 114, 127, 145, 177,
181, 186
Hexameter verse 6, 20n10, 51, 65, 77,
129, 133, 143, 211
Hezekiah 169
Hierocles, of Oreus 121n6, 180–1
Hieroglyphs 97n23
Hipparchus 178
Hippias 9, 178, 179, 188n15
Hippocrates 20n13
Hippotensis 48n27
Historia Augusta 211
Hittites 218
Homer 4–5, 13, 19n7, 28, 31, 40, 44,
45, 49n34, 50n44, 55, 56, 58, 59,
68n9, 73, 74, 99n46, 109–10, 113,
167, 168, 171n6, 180
Iliad 55, 56, 68n11; *Odyssey* 56, 72,
73, 92
Homeric Hymns 40, 44, 52, 55–8
Horace 148, 150–1n20
Horus 44
Human sacrifice, at Rome 195–6,
198, 205, 213n12
Hydales 122n15
Hyperochus, of Cumae 28, 40, 81,
97n31
Hystaspes 156–7, 158, 171n7

Iamblichus 85
Iapetus 158

Ida, Mt. 38, 51, 75
Idaean Mother, 202
Iliou Persis 56
Incarnation, the 2, 145
Initiations 137
Ionia 60, 62, 64, 66, 71, 102
Irenaeus 171n5
Isaiah 13, 146, 151n22, 218
Ishtar, of Arbela 219
Isidore 35
Israel 13, 217
Isthmian Games 118, 124n32

Jerome, St. 29
Jerusalem 14, 168
Jewish Sibyl 10–11, 35, 45
Johannes Lydus 35, 167–8
Josephus 160
Jesus 155, 156, 165
Judaea 154, 156, 161, 163, 169
Judah 13
Julian 166, 211
Julius Caesar, C. (*cos.* I, 59BC) 29,
    144, 209
Juno 93, 99n44, 141, 197, 200, 201,
    212n5
Juppiter 34, 137, 141, 190, 198, 207
Justin 131, 157–8
Juvenal 91, 148

Lactantius 2–3, 19n3, 21n23, 25, 28,
    29–35, 36, 41, 47n16, 47–8n20,
    69n30, 78, 110, 163–4, 170, 171n5,
    172n25
Laius 181–2
Lame Kingship, oracle 129, 134n10
Lamia 23, 26, 30, 37–8, 39, 49n35,
    104–5, 114, 118, 121–2n9, 123n23,
    124n32
Lampusa 127
Laodicea 15, 22n32
Last Judgement, the 11
Lasus, of Hermione 9, 178
Latium 74, 75, 76, 87, 90, 91
Lavinium 36, 49n30, 75
Lebadeia 37, 90
Lectisternium 105, 193–4, 197, 198,
    213nn8,9
Lesbos 59
Leto 9, 115, 193–4

Leucanians 78–9, 95n2
Lex Terentilia 193
Liber, Libera 212n5
Libri Fatales 91
Libri Fatidici 142
Libri Sibyllini 4, 19n2, 34, 75, 81–2,
    95n15, 96n20, 129–30, 137–43,
    148n2, 149nn9,10, 213n11
    and temples 192–3, 195, 198,
        212–13n5; in Regal period
        190–1; in Republic 191–209; in
        Principate 141–3, 209–11
Libyan Sibyl 23, 30, 32, 33, 37–8, 39,
    51, 72, 104, 105, 114, 122n9,
    124n32, 139
Licinius Crassus, M. (*cos.* I, 70BC)
    208
Livius Andronicus, L. 200
Livius, T. 20n13, 77, 79, 141,
    151n24, 193–204, 210
Lobon 21n24
Lucan 141, 147
Lucanian Sibyl 134n8
Lucius Verus 109
Lucretius 148, 151n21
Ludi, Apollinares 20n13, 199–200
    Romani 203; *Saeculares* 192, 195,
        205, 211, 213nn6,11, 215n42;
        Scaenici 213n10
Lycia 132
Lycomidae 179
Lycophron, *Alexandra* 16–17, 22n36,
    47n14, 71–2, 75, 78, 94n2, 99n41,
    108, 127
Lycus of Rhegium 29, 72, 78, 82,
    94n2
Lycus, river 22n32
Lydia 54, 59, 60, 62, 99n48, 101
Lysander 105–6

Macedonian Sibyl 46, 128, 134n8
Macedonian War, Second 129, 130,
    131–2
Maenad 26
Magna Mater 202, 212, 212n5, 213n9,
    215n45
Magnesia, battle of 203
Magnesia, on the Maeander 69n31
Magus 24, 43
Malians 39, 49n35, 114

Manlius Vulso, Cn. (*cos.* 189BC)
203, 208
Manto 49n34, 113, 134n8
Marathon, battle of 102
Marcius, prophecies of 20n13, 83,
97n23, 199–200, 201
Marcus Aurelius 158, 159, 160,
171n5
Mari 216
Marpessian Sibyl 8, 21n20, 25–6, 30,
31, 35, 36, 40, 48n29, 60, 75, 76,
95n10, 110, 122–3n17, 128,
134n11, 139, 159, 176, 181, 218
named Herophile 12–13n17, 128;
rival with Erythrae 24, 51–3, 59,
107–9, 117, 122n15, 140
Marpessus 37, 38, 64, 67n1, 89, 110,
136
Mars 198
Martial 148
Martianus Capella 35
Maximilla 159
Maximus, of Tyre 177
Megara 120
Melampus 56, 68n12, 186
Melancraera 78
Meles 54, 67n7
Melos 121n5
Menelaus 175
Mens 198, 212n5
Mercurey 193–4, 212n5
Messala Corvinus, M. 91
Messene 183, 184
Messenian War, Second 180, 184,
188n20
Metaurus, battle of 201
Michelangelo 170
Midas, of Phrygia 54, 58
Miletus 54, 58, 125, 144
Miltiades 45
Minerva 203
Minos 74, 175, 178
Mithridates, VI Eupator 136–7, 144
Molossi 126
Montanists 159–60
Moon, the 115, 116, 180, 187n7,
188n19
Mopsus 127
Moses 6, 26, 167, 171n6
Moso 150n16

Munichia 176, 178, 182, 187n6
Musaeus 9, 11, 18, 100, 106, 122n11,
137, 148n2, 178–80, 186, 187,
187n7, 188n19
Muses, the 10, 12, 18, 26, 114,
123n24, 177, 179
Museum, Alexandria 16, 22n36, 29,
174
Mytilene 59–60

Naevius, Cn. 30, 33, 72–4, 79, 93
Nais 108
Nekyomanteion 69n32, 74, 95n5,
99nn39,46, 151n24
Neon 185
Nero 143, 168, 210–11
Neso 108, 122n14
Nestor 147
Nicander 10, 21n21
Nicanor 30, 32–3, 38, 41, 125
Nicias 177, 188n10
Nicolaus, of Damascus 12, 25, 60–1,
64, 67n7
Nicomedia 163
Noah 7, 20n12, 42, 43, 144, 150n16
Novendiale Sacrum 191, 197, 212n3
Numa 9, 20n16, 69n30, 91
Nymphs 58, 68n17, 70n35, 76, 102,
176–7, 179, 181, 184, 186

Obsequens 204–6, 214n28
Oceanus 118
Octavius, Cn. (*cos.* 87BC) 206
Odysseus 72, 73, 74, 95n5
Old Testament 167, 216, 217, 218,
219
Olympia 25
Omphalos, at Delphi 177, 178,
188n10
Onomacritus 9, 178–80, 190, 212n1
Oresteia 57
Orestes 143
Origen 155, 160, 171n5
Orops 44
Orpheus 9, 11, 26, 106, 113, 156, 162,
179, 180, 187, 188n19, 211
Ovid 57, 58, 147–8

Pacuvius Taurus, S. 91

Palatine 4, 91, 141, 149–50n11, 202, 209, 211, 215n44
Pandia 188n19
Paris 16, 17, 40, 56, 57
Parthia 149n10, 209
Paul, St. 12, 156–7, 177
Pausanias 4, 10, 25, 26–7, 28, 36–45, 51, 52, 55, 65, 81, 89, 100–2, 105–6, 109–10, 114, 118, 120, 121n1, 124n32, 126–7, 128, 131–3, 140, 171n6, 179, 180, 181, 184, 185, 186
Pax Deorum 191, 197
Peloponnesian War 14, 21n30, 102–3, 105, 106, 107, 179, 183
Perachora 66, 89, 99n39
Pergamum 132
Periander 45
Persephone 195
Persian Sibyl 30, 32–3, 35, 37–8, 41–2, 45, 50n39, 51, 72, 125, 167
Persian Wars 62, 120, 175, 176, 178, 180, 187n6, 189n27
Pessinus 202
Petronius 20n15, 41, 81
Petrou kerygma 156–7, 161, 171n6
Phaennis 126–7, 134n4
Pharmakoi 199, 213n14
Philetas, of Ephesus 27–8, 45, 183, 189n25
Philip, II of Macedon 119–20, 132
  V of Macedon 21n30, 129, 130–1, 132, 134n10
Philo 167
Philodamus 188n19
Phlegon 107, 115–16, 117, 118, 137–8, 139, 140, 200
Phocis 112, 184–5, 186, 189n33
Phocus 184–5, 189n33
Phoenicia 54, 55, 129, 130
Phrygia 27, 54, 59, 113, 114, 159–60, 202
Phrygian Sibyl 31, 32, 34, 134n8
Phyto 35, 46, 134n8, 183
Pindar 40
Pisistratus 17, 77, 178–9, 180, 182, 188nn15,22, 190, 212n1
Piso, *Annals* 30, 72
Pittacus 59

Pius, Bishop of Rome 152
Plataea, battle of 102, 120, 121n4, 178, 181, 182, 183, 188n14, 189n27
Plato 24, 27, 35, 46n1, 116, 158, 162, 180, 189n28
Plinius Caccilius Secundus, C. (*cos.* AD100) 85, 91, 206, 209,
Plutarch 4, 17, 26, 39, 46, 63, 113–17, 119–20, 123n27, 124n29, 128–31, 134n11, 181, 205
Pollio 150n17
Polycrates, of Samos 65, 66–7, 70nn33,34, 87–8, 97n32, 98n34
Pompeii 123n27
Pompeius Magnus, Cn. (*cos.* I, 70BC) 144, 207, 208
Pontifex Maximus 142, 191
Pontifices 192, 194, 197, 200, 206
Popillius Laenas, C. (*cos.* I, 172BC) 208
Porcius Cato, C. (*tr. pl.* 56BC) 207
Porcius Cato, M. (*cos.* 195BC) 47n17, 86
Porta Capena 91, 99n42
Poseidon 26, 37, 39, 104, 114, 118, 122n9, 124n32, 194
Poseidonius 131, 135n16, 136
Priam 16, 56, 57
Priene 65
Priscilla 159
Prochyta 72
Proclus 27, 56
Propertius 44, 147
Prophets, Hebrew 8, 13, 14, 20n14, 46, 146, 156, 158, 161, 170, 218
Prudentius 211
Ptolemies, the 2, 6, 208, 215n38
Ptolemy, II Philadelphus 17
  VI Philometor 6, 14, 21n30;
    XII Auletes 207–8, 209
Punic War, First 198
  Second 91, 131, 138, 195, 197–202, 211
Purifications 137, 175
Puteoli 87, 123n27
Pyramus, river 4, 19n6, 133
Pyrrhus 17
Pythagoras 24, 98n32
Pythia 6, 7, 9, 33, 63, 65, 78, 79, 84,

85, 90, 99n41, 104, 111, 113, 118, 119, 121nn7,8, 123n20, 129, 130, 147, 159, 162, 165, 175, 219

Quinctius, K. 193
Quinctius Flaminius, T. (*cos.* 198BC) 131
Quindecimviri 2, 19n2, 29, 34, 75, 130, 139, 143, 150n11, 207, 208, 209, 212, 214n29, 215nn34,45
Quintilianus (*tr. pl.* AD32) 142–3

Rabirius Postumus, C. 208
Rhea 202
Rhodes 132–3, 135nn18,19
Rhodian Sibyl 128, 134n8
Rome 78, 129, 130, 131, 132, 134n11, 136, 140, 142, 144, 148, 150n13, 158, 160, 168, 201, 214n24
Romulus 75, 169
Rufus 50n47

Sabbe 41, 42, 43
Sacred War, Third 112, 123n21
Salamis, battle of 102, 121n4, 178, 182, 183, 188n14, 189n27
in Cyprus 180
Salassi 204, 206
Sallustius Crispus, C. (*pr.* 46BC) 149n9
Sambas 50n39
Sambethe 32, 42, 43, 45, 46, 50n39
Samian Sibyl 29, 31, 34, 40, 45, 46, 64–7, 72, 77, 88, 107, 108, 109, 134n8, 139
named Herophile 24, 69n30, 123n17; named Phyto 35, 183
Samos 24, 40, 64–7, 69n31, 70nn33,35, 71, 87, 98n32, 99n39, 107, 128, 139
Samothrace 108
Sarapion 114–17, 118, 129–30, 131, 134n10
Sardian Sibyl 27, 45, 68n19
Sardis 27, 64, 101
Saturnalia 197, 213n16
Scepis 107
Scribonius Curio, C. (*cos.* 76BC) 138
Selene 180
Semele 188n19

Semiramis 158
Semonides, of Amorgos 55, 68n9
Sempronius Gracchus, Tib. (*cos.* 163BC) 204
(*tr. pl.* 133BC) 205
Senate of Rome 130, 131, 138, 139, 140, 141, 143, 148n9, 191, 197, 199, 201, 202, 203, 207, 208
Septimius Severus 211
Septuaginta 146
Servius 79, 97n23, 146–7, 150nn13,17
Shipton, Ursula 53, 67n3
Sibyl 2–4, 7, 10, 13, 28, 31, 46, 58, 115–17, 152–6
primeval origin and great age 7–9, 11, 20n15, 55, 57, 58, 63, 69n25, 108, 115, 116, 147–8, 154, 177; shrinks away 41, 79, 81, 108, 117
Sibylla, as name 18, 23, 24, 30, 33, 37–8, 42–3, 46n1, 49n33, 53, 109
Sibylline leaves 82–3, 138, 148n4, 212n4
Sibylline Oracles
ambiguity and obscurity 15–17; gloom 12–13, 17, 18, 63, 112, 119; low literary quality, 18, 162–3; popular circulation 16, 17, 62, 141, 143, 149n10, 163, 167, 168; subject matter 10–14, 114–17, 128, 132–3, 137
Sibyllistae 155
Sicilian Sibyl 134n8
Sicily 82, 103, 105, 117, 121n5, 134n8, 139, 175, 181, 205, 206
Sicyon 132–3, 135n18
Sidon 135n16
Silius Italicus 151n24
Simonides, of Cos 68n9
Sistine Chapel 170
Solinus 35, 59, 110
Solon 25, 31, 34, 60
Sophocles 92, 179
Sors, sortes 88–9, 91, 97n23, 98n36, 191
Sozomenus 166–7, 168
Sparta 65, 100–1, 109, 129, 184, 186, 188n12
Spartacus 129–30, 135n16
Speusippus 24

Sphinx 16, 107
Sphragitid nymphs 90, 99n41, 181
Spiliani cave, Samos 70n35
Statius 147, 151n25
Stoics 11, 117–18
Stesichorus 57
Stilicho 211, 215n44
Strabo 4, 66, 109, 133, 135n20
Stratonicaea 135n18
Suda, the 27, 39, 114, 127, 128, 134n8, 174
Suetonius 143, 149n11
Supplicatio 197, 198, 203

Tanagra 120, 181
Taraxandra 46, 134n8
Tatian 16, 171n6
Taurus, Mts. 203, 208
Telmessus 54, 67n7
Telos 135n18
Terentius Varro, M. (*pr.* c. 75BC) 2, 3, 25, 29–35, 36, 37, 38, 41, 44, 45, 48n20, 69n30, 72, 77, 78, 79, 81, 82, 84, 88, 89, 97n23, 109, 121n9, 125, 134n11, 138, 140, 144, 163, 167, 171n6
Tertullian 158–9
Teucri 53
Teucros 108
Thalassocracy list 59, 68n18
Thebes 113, 184, 185, 186, 189n30
Theodorus 44, 108, 122n15
Theophilus, of Antioch 19n3, 21n23, 161, 163
Theopompus 176, 186
Theoxonia 193
Thera 130, 131, 132, 135n13
Therasia 130
Thermodon, river 119–20, 182
Theseus 104, 121n7
Thespesius 116
Thesprotia 127
Thesprotian Sibyl 46, 127
Thessalian Sibyl 46, 134n8
Thessaly 120, 185
Theurgy 160
Thrace 106, 179, 188n19
Thucydides 102–3, 121n5, 135n12
Thyestean feast 20n13
Thyrea 100, 101

Tiber, river 49n30, 76, 79, 150n14, 194, 204, 210
Tiberius 142–3, 150n14, 158, 210–11
Tibullus 35–6, 48–9n29, 49n30, 75–6, 150n11, 210
Tibur 31, 49n30
Tiburtine Sibyl 3, 9, 14, 31, 32, 36, 49n30
Timacus 29, 72, 95n2
Tiresias 49n34, 113, 134n8
Tiryns 85, 86
Tithonus 57–9, 68n15
Tithorea 184–5, 186
Titus 117, 123n28
Trasimene, battle of 197
Trebia, battle of 197
Tria Fata 91, 99n43
Triumvirate 145, 147
Trivia 80, 150n11
Troad 24, 37, 40, 51, 52, 53, 55, 58, 59, 64, 66, 74, 88, 108, 181
Trojan War 4, 7, 15, 17, 19n7, 33, 38, 40, 45, 49n34, 50n44, 51, 55, 74, 88, 109–10, 171n6, 173n33, 175, 219
Trophonius 37, 49n31, 90, 99n41
Troy(Ilion) 16, 17, 22n38, 25, 28, 31, 36, 38, 40, 44, 48n29, 52, 56, 57, 68n11, 72, 74, 75, 76, 108, 109, 129, 130, 199
Tübingen Theosophy 35
Tullius Cicero, M. (*cos.* 65BC) 33, 139, 140–1, 147, 148n9, 165, 172n25, 200–1, 205, 207–8, 209
Tydeus 106
Tyrtaeus 65, 69n28
Tzetzes 135n20

Valerius Maximus 64–5, 151n24
Valerius Messala Messalinus, M. (*XVvir.* 21/20BC) 35, 50n11, 210
Venus, of Eryx 198, 212n5
   Versicordia 205–6, 212n5
Ver Sacrum 198, 214n17
Vergil 20n15, 73, 74, 76, 79–80, 82, 83, 84, 85, 93, 97n23, 138, 150nn13,17,20, 151n21, 152, 166
   Aeneid 7, 36, 75, 76, 79–80, 82, 147–8, 150n11, 166; 4th *Eclogue* 13–14, 35, 144–7, 150n18,

151n20, 165, 172n26
Verres, C. (*pr.* 74BC) 205
Vestal Virgins 149n9, 196, 198, 205
Vesuvius, Mt. 116, 123n27
Via Domitia 147
Vindolanda 212n4
Vulcan 143
Vulcatius 72

Wenamun, report of 217, 220n2

Xanthus, the Lydian 25, 60–1, 64,
  65, 69n30

Xenocrates 24
Xerxes 102, 121n4, 178, 182, 185

Yahweh 11, 13, 217, 218

Zephaniah 8, 13
Zethus 184, 185, 189n32
Zeus 25, 26, 37–8, 39, 57, 60, 61, 75,
  77, 98n33, 99n39, 105, 106, 112,
  113, 122n9, 123n20, 125, 127,
  135n12, 176, 188n19, 205
Zimrilim 216
Zosimus 126–7